Contested Identities in Costa Rica:
Constructions of the *Tico* in Literature and Film

Contemporary Hispanic and Lusophone Cultures

This series aims to provide a forum for new research on modern and contemporary hispanic and lusophone cultures and writing. The volumes published in Contemporary Hispanic and Lusophone Cultures reflect a wide variety of critical practices and theoretical approaches, in harmony with the intellectual, cultural and social developments that have taken place over the past few decades. All manifestations of contemporary hispanic and lusophone culture and expression are considered, including literature, cinema, popular culture, theory. The volumes in the series will participate in the wider debate on key aspects of contemporary culture.

Contested Identities in Costa Rica

Constructions of the *Tico* in Literature and Film

LIZ HARVEY-KATTOU

LIVERPOOL UNIVERSITY PRESS

First published 2019 by
Liverpool University Press
4 Cambridge Street
Liverpool
L69 7ZU

This paperback edition published 2022

British Library Cataloguing-in-Publication data
A British Library CIP record is available

ISBN 978-1-78962-005-4 cased
ISBN 978-1-80207-003-3 paperback

Typeset in Borges by
Carnegie Book Production, Lancaster
Printed and bound by CPI Group (UK) Ltd, Croydon CR0 4YY

Contents

Figures

Acknowledgements

I went to Costa Rica for the first time in 2006 and I got to know it as a beautiful country filled with warm, kind, interesting people. The longer I spent there the more I began to delve into the nation's history, its literature, its culture, and its newly burgeoning film scene. It was then that I discovered that academic discussions of Latin America could – and should – be had outside the usual borders. Six years after visiting Costa Rica for the first time – and after many subsequent trips – this research project began.

There are many people to whom I am hugely indebted for their help and support over the course of this project. First and foremost, I am extremely grateful to Professor Stephen Hart who has been a great source of supervisory and pastoral support for many years. Without his contributions and encouragement I would not have been able to start – let alone finish – this project. I would also like to thank Dr Debbie Martin and Dr Claire Lindsey from UCL, Professor Chris Harris from the University of Hull, and Dr Atef Alshaer from the University of Westminster for their feedback and valuable support at different stages of this process. I am also indebted to the Arts and Humanities Research Council whose financial support allowed me to undertake this research project.

I am extremely grateful to all those in Costa Rica who agreed to be interviewed as a part of this project, and my special thanks go to: Quince Duncan, María Lourdes Cortés, Claudia Mandel Katz, Raysher Morgan Foster, Jimena Cascante Matamoros, and the other *ticos* who allowed me to film their interviews. Special thanks must also go to film directors Paz Fábrega, Jurgen Ureña, and Esteban Ramírez for their time during interviews, email conversations, and for allowing me to use stills from their films as part of this book.

I am also eternally indebted to several people in Costa Rica for their continued friendship and presence. In particular I would like to thank Dianna Durán Castro – my filming companion – in addition to Laura

Castro Vargas, Vale Durán Castro, Albert Durán Abarca, and the extended Durán-Castro family.

Finally, I would not have been able to complete this process without the unwavering support and encouragement of Stephen Kattou, Anne, Peter and Sarah Harvey, Joan and Don Bryars, Laura Sarkis, Ellie Lloyd, and the PhD community of Amanda, Christiane, Mathelinda, Magali, Gabriella, Niall, and Agnes. Thank you all for always being optimistic and keeping me sane.

Introduction

This book arose from of a series of observations made while living, working, researching, and sharing conversations with people in Costa Rica. The first of these was that Costa Rica is a nation visibly proud of its shared identity, beautiful scenery, and title as the world's happiest country (Happy Planet Index, 2015). Secondly, in spite of this rhetoric of inclusion, it is possible to see that several groups and communities have been actively excluded from the nation through the use of government policy or because of their nonconformity with wider nationalist ideology, and their existence has been rendered invisible as a result. The third observation was that the nation is also home to a rich body of literature and film which has been largely ignored abroad – and often even within national borders – despite the poignant and challenging cultural and social critiques offered by up authors and film-makers.

National identity is a broad and multifaceted topic, especially in the increasingly globalized world of the twenty-first century, and while marginalization on the basis of skin colour, geographic provenance, gender, or sexuality exists across multiple nation-states, the way it interacts with pre-existing ideas of the nation is often perceived to be specific to each country's history, culture, and ideological rhetoric. While this book therefore discusses ideas of what constitutes the concept of a national identity, how this is (falsely) constructed, and the ways in which it becomes a weapon of exclusion, it also seeks to underline the falsehood of constructing national identity as something rigid and immutable. With a focus on this process of constructed meaning in the Central American nation of Costa Rica and the ways in which nationalist ideals have been bound up in one word – *tico* – this book also aims to prove the actual fluid, constantly shifting, and plural nature of identity itself.

The Real Academia Española defines the term *tico* as 'adj. coloq. costarricense (de *-ico*, por la abundancia de diminutivos con esta terminación en Costa Rica)'. According to this interpretation, *tico* is merely the linguistic equivalent to the term *costarricense*, an appellation that refers to any member of the Costa Rican population. Anecdotal evidence surrounding the first use of the term abounds, with most Costa Ricans believing that a Honduran or Nicaraguan soldier invented it when fighting alongside the Costa Rican army against William Walker in the Central American war of 1857 (Láscaris, 1975, 107). The soldier noticed the Costa Ricans' tendency to use the diminutive suffix -*tico* and as a gesture of camaraderie began to call the Costa Rican soldiers *ticos*. The nickname has become widespread and popular, to the point where many Costa Ricans merely use *tico* as a noun or adjective to refer to their or others' nationality, rather than repeat the word *costarricense*. Indeed, it has also been coined as a term to describe the country itself – *tiquicia* – and can be seen in the branding of much Costa Rican daily life, such as in the naming of the national television station, *Teletica*, or the English-language newspaper, *The Tico Times*, or in the unofficial national song which glorifies the country and its citizens and hangs on the much-repeated line 'soy tico'.

The *Tico*

Despite these uses of *tico* as an adjective to identify country of origin, however, the term is loaded, and carries with it far more associations than merely a nationality printed in a passport. In fact, the concept of the *tico* equates with Costa Rican identity and has been used to create and foster a culture of exceptionalism over the course of the nation's history. Moreover, the *tico* refers to an idealized, and fallible, version of the nation and national stereotypes, and contains ethnic, gendered, sexual, religious, and geographic implications; the *ticos* have long prided themselves on their white, patriarchal, Catholic society, with the country's Central Valley region an exemplary representative of this myth. The documentary, *Retratico* (Harvey-Kattou, 2015), which was made as part of the research for this project, documents both the normative associations and the exclusionary power of the term among Costa Rican citizens. When asked what the term *tico* means, many interviewees describe the happiness of Costa Rican citizens, the natural beauty of the nation, the sustainable ways of promoting its ecological systems, and the attraction tourists feel to the country. Some participants consider the term to be more complex, however, and Jorge Zúñiga states: 'pienso que el tico es patriotista hacia su Costa Rica, que es el mejor país del mundo, el más feliz … siempre nos gusta ser "Costa Rica, el más feliz del mundo"' (Harvey-Kattou, 2015). The idea that the *tico* is a weapon of nationalist rhetoric is also mentioned by Jimena Cascante, who asserts that the *tico* is defined in opposition to the rest of Central America;

'la identidad tica se ha construido desde un lugar de "somos mejores que ...'", thus demonstrating the perceived exceptionalism existent within the national imaginary.

Within this paradigm of exceptionalism, then, the true provenance of the term *tico* is rarely questioned while its widely accepted creation story becomes of paramount importance. As the North American, William Walker, and his men did battle for Central America in the nineteenth century, these newly formed, poor nations with few resources fought back. They clinched victory, cemented the region's independence, and protected geographic country frontiers in the process. The courageous act of war which is said to have won the final battle against Walker was instigated by a young Costa Rican boy, the first hero of the nation. According to the legend, Juan Santamaría, a drummer, was the only soldier brave enough to creep up on Walker's stronghold in Nicaragua and set fire to it, winning the battle against the USA and getting killed in the process. Having sacrificed his life for the sake of his country, he has been posthumously rewarded with two statues and several high-profile namesakes, including the international airport in Alajuela. While many *ticos* appear unsure of the veracity of this story-cum-legend, it has long been used in Costa Rica to build an account of heroism, unity, and peace (Museo de Juan Santamaría, 2015) – values which have been lauded as national attributes ever since.

The term *tico* therefore encompasses these values, just as it denotes patriotism and a love of Costa Rica which goes far beyond geography or a sense of national belonging. It also glorifies a certain type of Costa Rican: anyone can self-define as *tico* if they hold a Costa Rican passport, but the image of the traditional *tico* is far more specific and indicates a certain type of social value. Mavis Biesanz et al.'s 1999 social studies work, *The Ticos: Culture and Social Change in Costa Rica*, delves into the psyche of the country in an attempt to explore who or what is *tico*. Although the authors do not question the significance of the term itself, they do offer two definitions of it. First, in adherence to the dictionary definition, Costa Ricans and *ticos* are referred to interchangeably, with one explanation stating: 'Ticos – as Costa Ricans call themselves' (1). In the second instance, the authors claim that 'when we refer to "Ticos" or "most Ticos," we generally have in mind the politically and culturally dominant ... majority' (6). This latter assertion clearly demonstrates that not only is there an imagined centre and periphery in existence within Costa Rica, but that the cultural agenda for the rest of the country is set by a mainstream power. This notion of a dominant culture can be seen most clearly through the existence of the Costa Rican common ancestral myth which states that when the Europeans arrived, finding no indigenous people in the country, they became the first Costa Ricans and formed classless, peaceful, agrarian societies. This myth has created and perpetuated the defining traits of Costa Rican national identity, and its role in the nation has been investigated by several scholars from varying disciplines.

In Meg Tyler Mitchell and Scott Pentzer's area studies guide, *Costa Rica: A Global Studies Handbook*, the authors state that, although the image the nation portrays does change over time, 'Costa Rica generally thinks of itself as an inherently democratic, peaceful, and ethnically homogeneous society ... this is, then, an image of Costa Rica as *exceptional*, not at all like its Central American neighbours' (2008, 227). Giselle Chang Vargas and Fernando González Vásquez's 1981 *Cultura popular tradicional: fundamento de la identidad cultural* explores this contention in terms of the anthropological contribution of folklore to the national myth of homogeneity, arguing that much cultural production is valorized precisely because it supports this myth. Furthermore, Rafael Cuevas Molina uses his historical 2003 work, *Tendencias de la dinámica cultural en Costa Rica en el siglo XX*, to argue that although cultural differences within the country do exist, 'hay, sin embargo, una cultura hegemónica, es decir, que es aceptada como la cultura "de todos"' (2). In the only work to consider the national, *tico*, identity in terms of literature, Carlos Cortés states in his 2003 collection of essays, *La invención de Costa Rica*, that Costa Rica is much more about a symbolic idea of nationhood than a real, lived-out version of the nation. In other words, the entire identity of the nation is based on myth (15–16). Indeed, he goes on to describe these founding myths before exploding them, concluding that Costa Rica has represented itself internally as:

> un paraíso de campesinos pobres, aislados, sin conflictos, sin clases sociales, étnicamente blanqueados y que, como resultado de su propia pobreza e igualdad de condiciones materiales y sociales, opta por la democracia. Este es, más o menos, el texto del mito. (Carlos Cortés, 2003, 27)

As all these scholars point out, within the Costa Rican national context there exists the concept of a rigid, homogeneous ideal which is, nonetheless, not borne out by the nation's history.

Internal 'Others'

This constructed idea of an exclusive and exceptional national identity is highly problematic, as it inherently places itself at the centre of the nation's imaginary while creating and pushing out 'Others' who do not fit the idealized stereotype of the *tico*. Indeed, Carlos Sandoval García notes the existence of what he classes as external and internal 'Others' within the framework of Costa Rica. He states that 'Costa Rican national identity has been historically represented through the accentuation of differences in relation to external "others" (neighbour nations) and internal "others" (indigenous, peasants and blacks)' (2000, 2), thus demonstrating that the nation's sense of exceptionalism is not solely concerned with national borders. While he asserts that the Nicaraguan-next-door is the ultimate external 'Other' (2000, 1), he also contends that Costa Rican nationhood connotes a white, male, middle-class society which actively 'misrecognises' the presence of internal 'Others' which oppose or undermine this view (2000, 11). Michelle Christian expands on this theme as she considers the ethnic disparity between Costa Rica's tourist image and the national reality with reference to Afro-Costa Ricans, concluding that racism and the wilful exclusion of Afro-Costa Ricans, is apparent within Costa Rica's dominant tourist literature. Gisella Díaz-Azofeifa also explores the place of the ethnic internal 'Other'. She relates the prevalent rhetoric of multiculturalism to the 'invisibilization' of the indigenous population in the country. As can be seen from these examples, then, the internal 'Other' has been constructed as the binary opposite of the *tico* ideal. Indeed, if the *tico* is Eurocentric, Catholic, middle-class, and patriarchal, then this image opposes people of colour, women, and LGBTQ+ individuals, despite the fact that identity is not, as will be seen in the following chapters, a matter of dichotomies or a single, rigid construct.

Another facet of Costa Rican identity which lends itself to the rhetoric of Central American exceptionalism is its close relationship with the USA. Often referred to – especially in tourist literature (Christian, 2013, 1600) – as the Switzerland of Central America, Costa Rica's peaceful reputation stems from having abolished its national army after the revolution of 1948. Not only did this curtail future uprisings against the new government but it also produced the need for a strategic ally with a strong military presence. Although there is no official military agreement in place between the USA and Costa Rica, anecdotally many *ticos* assume that if the country were attacked – an unlikely scenario in many people's eyes – the US army would step in to protect them. This supposition is based on the level of political, ecological, trade, and diplomatic ties between the two: the US–Costa Rica Counter-Narcotics Cooperation Agreement was signed in 1999, the Central American Free Trade Agreement (CAFTA) was signed by Costa Rica in 2006, and the 2011 census found that over 15,000 US citizens were resident in the Central American country (Censo, 2011). In order to ensure the continued harmony of this relationship and to increase tourism and trade revenue,

Costa Rica has sought actively to pursue a highly branded tourist image which has become its primary mode of visibility internationally. Much of the advertising surrounding this image, however, concentrates on the promotion of a homogeneous, Eurocentric national identity.

The creation of Costa Rica as a tourist brand began in the 1950s and enjoyed its heyday in the 1990s and twenty-first century. It has been inextricably linked to nature, eco-tourism, and peace, and ever since the *Instituto Costarricense de Turismo* (ICT) was founded in 1955, it has worked hard to market itself to the outside world as a paradisiacal haven. Its first ever tourist slogan – 'The Garden of the Americas' – reflects this. Until the 1980s, however, tourism was just one of many economic activities within the country, with the export of agricultural goods – mainly bananas and coffee – core to the country's economy. Biesanz et al. argue (1999, 53) that since tourism became Costa Rica's largest source of income in 1994 there has been an increasing concern for the country's image abroad (1999, 89). Indeed, an interviewee in the documentary *Retratico* contends that treating tourists politely and showing them the best of Costa Rica are values taught to all *ticos* which they are expected to uphold for the good of the country (Harvey-Kattou, 2015). This fits the ICT's tourist campaigns which have focused on peace, nature, and ecotourism, and yet despite the adherence to the image of a peaceful, biodiverse haven these ideas stand at odds with the figure of the *tico* as a Central Valley, city-dweller. In other respects, however, the national stereotype has been adhered to and enhanced to make the *ticos* palatable for a global – mainly US – audience. Michelle Christian notes that whiteness, stability, and peace are constantly promoted as positive traits to entice tourists to visit (2013, 1601–6). This leads to a distorted view of Costa Rica both from within and externally, as these two complementary images have been dominant in twentieth-century narratives despite their geographic disparities which suggest that the coastal provinces of the nation exist for tourists, while 'real life' occurs for the *ticos* in the Central Valley.

Normative Identity: Constructions and Challenges

This book explores who and what constitute the *tico* norm and how this national identity has been constructed within the nation, before laying out the ways in which citizens who do not fit this mould have been excluded from the imagined community of Costa Rica, thus demonstrating the fallacy of the myth of a rigid and static national identity. It then pinpoints and analyses two key cultural revolutions which have sought to challenge previously accepted norms. The first is the sociological revolution of the

1970s whereby the Central American crisis – which saw civil wars raging across the region – touched many citizens, while the power of US civil rights movements of the 1960s also filtered through to Costa Rica. At the same time, that decade saw several protests against war, oppression, and corruption explode in the nation, while cultural protests in the form of artistic and academic endeavours also flourished, with a literary publishing boom that remains unequalled. The second revolution of national identity is the digital revolution which began in the early years of the twenty-first century as new technologies, internet penetration, and then social media took hold of the nation, allowing citizens to communicate and share events and ideologies at the touch of a button. This also resulted in another creative boom, this time in the field of film-making, as more productions were made in the ten years between 2001 and 2011 than in the entirety of the twentieth century (M. L. Cortés, 2011, 4).

This book uses as a premise that a dominant and exclusive *tico* identity exists within the national imaginary in order to interrogate the endurance of the national myths and stereotypes prevalent within Costa Rican society and demonstrate that there cannot, in fact, be one fixed identity. Taking this as a point of departure, the presence and history of the internal 'Others' within the nation are examined while the theory and practice of 'Othering' is highlighted. Chapter 1 begins by considering the history of Costa Rican national identity before attempting to arrive at a definition of the concept of national identity for the Costa Rican context. In accordance with the work of Benedict Anderson (2006, 5), it posits that nations are invented, imaginary communities while states constitute the administrative and institutional elements which maintain the illusion of a cohesive national identity. It then discusses the physical and symbolic nation-building project which began in Costa Rica after its 1821 independence and which has carried on until the twenty-first century, exploring the foundations of the sociological revolution of the 1970s and the digital revolution of the early twenty-first century. This chapter then goes on to demonstrate that the link between the imagined and the real power structures at work within Costa Rican society over the course of its history strongly resembles the colonial power formations exposed by scholars such as Edward Said, Homi Bhabha, Frantz Fanon, and Gayatri Spivak in their work on postcolonial societies. As Walter Mignolo argues, Latin America as an idea would not exist without colonialism, and, as demonstrated through the history of the *tico* identity, Costa Rica's ideals certainly stem from the Eurocentrism present within the nation. This chapter suggests that the image of Costa Rica has been colonized and therefore constantly subjects its citizens to an exclusive and exclusionary rhetoric. The characteristics of colonized internal 'Others' are expanded upon in terms of their history, culture, and identity, and theories of 'subalternity', 'race', ethnicity, gender, and sexuality are then discussed in order to approximate a theoretical framework for the analysis of the counterhegemonic texts which are dealt with in Chapters 2 and 3.

Chapter 2 focuses in on the sociological revolution of 1970s Costa Rica and the ways in which protest literature inserted itself in this movement. As already discussed, the 1970s was not only a time of protest but also a fecund period of literary production in the country, and it has been pointed out that several authors chose to attempt to redefine Costa Rican identity in their works in this 'boom' decade (Quesada Soto, 2008; C. Cortés, 2007, 45–51). As such, this chapter explores the concept of counterhegemonic authorship in the 1970s, whereby authors have attempted to harness the soft power of literature to encourage a change in habitus and attitude towards the internal 'Other' in society. As Doris Sommer notes (1991, 10), the literature of Latin America has, historically, influenced national identities because it has 'the capacity to intervene in history, to help construct it'. While this chapter demonstrates the studied authors' intention to attempt to alter the written history of Costa Rican identity and lived experience, it is also interested in the reciprocal relationship between the text and national identity. To explore this facet of these works fully, the chapter considers the place of the idealized *tico* in the shaping of the literary works studied, as well as analysing exactly how the challenge to this dominant identity has been constructed. It suggests that many works are written from the platform of identity politics, and that depending on the social issue they wish to expose, the authors under consideration must veil their criticism in a variety of ways including through the use of allegory, subtext, and code. This chapter includes close readings of the novel *Los cuatro espejos* by Quince Duncan, the short stories 'Simbiosis del encuentro' and 'A los payasos todos los quieren' by Carmen Naranjo, and 'El hilo del viento' and 'La lluvia. El silencio. La música.' by Alfonso Chase. These writers have all been cited as key authors of protest literature during the Costa Rican 'boom' of the 1970s (C. Cortés, 2007, 54), and these works deal with ethnic, gendered, and sexual exclusion and discrimination respectively. While these authors have been studied to varying extents, these works have not been considered in relation to their interaction with the notion of *tico* identity before. This chapter attempts to redress this balance while offering new literary interpretations of certain textual nuances within these works.

Chapter 3 moves on to consider the digital revolution of the early years of the twenty-first century. It considers the surge in film-making which took place from 2001 onwards, and the ways in which creative practitioners have used their productions to consider – and often re-evaluate – the notion of what it is to be *tico*. When academics such as Mavis Biesanz et al. and Rafael Cuevas Mclina penned their summations of Costa Rican identity, they were yet to encounter the full effect of the digital turn on the country, its imagined borders, and its identity. Indeed, Cuevas Molina ends his work by asking (2003, 38) what the *tico* will look like in the twenty-first century, perhaps assuming that changes in perception from within the nation were in store. This chapter therefore examines the new spaces of 'Otherness' which have been opened up in an age of digitalization and globalization, while also considering the place of traditional conceptions of 'Otherness' surrounding ethnic, geographic, gendered, and sexual belonging in this era. This chapter also explores the growth of the tourist image and the ways in which it aligns with, and escapes from, traditional concepts of identity. It demonstrates the consequences of the fight for cultural supremacy that has taken over the nation, largely fought between US hegemony in terms of media and tourism and the powerful rhetoric of the traditional *tico*. It posits that while the nation has become increasingly urban, it has created several divisions. First, the divide between the centre – or Central Valley – and the rural and coastal periphery has widened, while, secondly, the gap between the idyllic, eco-paradise of the tourist image and the lived experience of many within the Central Valley has created a chasm. As such, Carlos Cortés' statement (2007, 25) that 'el Valle Central es, en el imaginario nacional, Costa Rica' will be examined in terms of the privileging of San José and other cities in the Central Valley within Costa Rican creative media. It also explores existing spaces of 'Otherness' and the counterhegemonic productions which seek to revalorize internal 'Others' within the nation's visual repository of national film. It has been stated that without cinema, a country is invisible (M. L. Cortés, 2002, 9), and as such this chapter seeks to analyse reflections of national identity from a filmic perspective. It offers a close analysis of the films *Gestación* (2009) by Esteban Ramírez, *Agua fría de mar* (2009) by Paz Fábrega, *Dos aguas* (2014) by Patricia Velázquez, and *Abrázame como antes* (2016) by Jurgen Ureña. Academic studies of Costa Rican film are conducted by very few scholars, and little attention has been paid to it outside the country's borders – and even less attention has been paid to the specific motifs found within it. As such, this chapter considers the ways in which geographic disparities and tropes of ethnic and gendered 'Otherness' are constructed within their narratives and aesthetics.

I conclude by offering some answers to the questions pertinent to this book, namely who or what counts as *tico* and how creative production is used both to construct and to challenge normative ideas of identity in the country. The broad, theoretical ideas around national identity creation and its harmful legacy found in Chapter 1 are designed to be used for the exploration of any nation-state. While a 'one-size-fits-all' approach is impossible when considering the complex structures that make up different nation-states, there are certainly issues such as racism, sexism, homophobia, and other social exclusions that are common across borders. Moreover, the idea that national identity is fixed and immutable and the reality that it is necessarily fluid, plural, and constantly shifting is pertinent the world over. Chapter 1 therefore details how national exclusion is perpetuated in one nation – Costa Rica – and this analysis, alongside Chapters 2 and 3, are models for the discussion of the soft power of creative protest globally.

CHAPTER ONE

The Creation of *Tiquicidad* and Theories of National Identity

The Creation of *Tiquicidad*

Biesanz et al. assert (1999, 6) that the *ticos* 'share a sense of national identity. They believe they have a unique way of life and a distinctive national character'. This belief is deeply rooted in the historical narratives which have been disseminated in Costa Rica about the foundations of the modern-day nation. Leonard Bird claims (1984, 11) that the indigenous peoples inhabiting the land which now constitutes Costa Rica were largely driven out by the Spanish conquerors. Thus, he argues (1984, 11), the colonizers who eventually settled there permanently were exclusively European farmers and smallholders who lived in egalitarian communities. John Bell also states (1996, 5) that Costa Rica's land was run as an agrarian democracy under colonial rule. Indeed, because of this lack of large-scale agriculture, Bird asserts that during the colonial period, 'Costa Rica had been the poorest and most backward province in the "Kingdom" of Guatemala' (1984, 32). This has led Biesanz et al. to insist that this 'official' version of Costa Rica's history 'has ... long served as the unifying myth of the nation and is still taught in schools and repeated in patriotic speeches' (1999, 13). Vargas Chang and González Vásquez also contend that 'dentro del marco de la identidad cultural la población muestra tener conciencia de un pasado de determinados ancestros y devenir histórico "común"' (1981, 12–13). This narrative of a common, European, ancestry, which both Bird's and Bell's works have assumed as a historical truth – and which has been disseminated and perpetuated throughout the history of the nation – is, however, far more complex and contested than these readings denote. As Vargas Chang and González Vásquez point out: 'al costarricense se le ha impuesto una *falsa* conciencia basada en una supuesta ascendencia española relativamente pura que niega los verdaderos antepasados (esto se nota por ejemplo en cierta propaganda turística sobre el país)' (1981, 12–13; emphasis my own). It is these true roots which are often hidden in modern-day Costa Rica in favour of the homogeneous ideal.

Despite the falsehood of Costa Rica's repetition of this ancestral myth, then, it became the foundation for the unified nation in the 1870s when Costa Rica's post-independence nation-building project got under way (Cuevas Molina, 1999 and Biesanz et al., 1999). Although independence from Spain was achieved in 1821, it was with the election of President Tomás Guardia in 1870 and Rafael Yglesias in 1894 that democratic government and liberal ideals were ushered in and the national identity building project began: the *tico* was, in effect, invented during this later period (Cuevas Molina, 1999, 3). These governments sought to consolidate disparate factions within the country – still largely held together by a mutual hatred of William Walker – by constructing monuments and creating national administrative bodies (Biesanz et al., 1999, 25–6). Indeed, the 1880s saw the founding of *El Archivo Nacional*, *La Biblioteca Nacional*, and *El Museo Nacional* (Cuevas Molina, 1999, 5) as a means of recording the history which this generation wished to create for its country. The ideals that this identity was built around were rooted in Eurocentric thought whereby high culture was prized. This trend can be seen in the building of the *Palacio Nacional* in 1851–6, the ornate, European-style *Teatro Nacional* in 1897, and the bourgeois San José residential community of Barrio Amón in the 1890s (Cuevas Molina, 1999, 6). It has even been noted that the statues and monuments celebrating the history of the nation, such as the *Monumento Nacional* (1895) and the statue of Juan Santamaría (1891), were constructed in a style perpetuating the idea that the European aesthetic was to be more highly valued than indigenous or even creole traditions (Cuevas Molina, 1999, 6–8).

It was not just the erecting of monuments and administrative bodies which formed a part of this nation-building project, however, but the governments of the late nineteenth and early twentieth centuries also actively encouraged a spirit of patriotism. As Cuevas Molina notes, at this time 'ser ciudadano era amar, respetar y compartir los símbolos de la Patria antes que los de la pequeña comunidad' (1999, 5), denoting the importance placed on the nation over individualism. Moreover, the virtues of education, hard work, and peace were all propagated within family, personal, and national life (5). The liberals also promoted a 'vallecentrista' culture (9), whereby the cities and towns of the Central Valley – San José, Heredia, Cartago, and Alajuela – connoted these positive attributes, while attempting to reconcile this urban-centric perspective with the founding myth that suggested that the nation was descended from humble farmers (9). This attempt was not entirely successful, however, and it was through the burgeoning literary scene of the early twentieth century that the significance of the forgotten *campesino* was once again promoted. In order to counterbalance the exaltation of the Central Valley elite, characters were created which were attributed 'algunas características que "los ticos" consideraron que les diferenciaban de "otros": pacíficos, democráticos, blancos, cultos' (9). These values were seemingly being forcibly placed at the centre of national life in the late nineteenth and early twentieth centuries, then, and the ingraining of peace, democracy, and whiteness, as well as the highlighting of the ancestral myth, can be seen in the words of the Costa Rican national anthem. Written in 1903, by M. T. Zeledón, it declares:

> Noble patria tu hermosa bandera
> Expresión de tu vida nos da;
> Bajo el límpido azul de tu cielo
> ¡Blanca y pura descansa la paz!
>
> En la lucha tenaz de fecunda labor
> Que enrojece del hombre la faz;
> Conquistaron tus hijos
> Labriegos sencillos
> Eterno prestigio, estima y honor[.]

These first two stanzas underline the widely accepted notion that the ancestors of the nation were of humble origins: they are praised as simple labourers who achieved eternal prestige, admiration, and honour through their hard work and patriotism. The vigorous last line of the first stanza further cements these values by proclaiming '¡vivan siempre el trabajo y la paz!' Also noteworthy in the first stanza are the adjectives used to describe peace: 'blanca y pura descansa la paz'. This demonstrates the extolling of whiteness and purity in the country – Eurocentric and Catholic colonial values which are still held in high esteem. The typical *tico*, then, is described as white, Catholic, living in the Central Valley (while praising the humble *campesino*), and adhering to patriarchal social rules. Indeed, this is most apparent when considering the *leyenda blanca* that envelopes the country, with the vast majority of Costa Ricans ethnically identifying as white (Biesanz et al., 1999, 5) and ignoring the other cultures making up their backgrounds (Chang Vargas and González Vásquez, 1981, 13). These myths continue to pervade national stereotypes, and at the end of the twentieth century Biesanz et al. maintain that the *tico* has long believed itself to be a 'traditionally egalitarian people of European descent' (1999, 6), despite the fact that geneticists have demonstrated that almost all Costa Ricans are *mestizo*, or have a mixture of European, indigenous, and African genes (98).

Although these founding myths include the lauding of a peaceful existence, in 1948 the Costa Rican state – and its national identity – found itself the subject of a violent challenge. After the global economic crisis of the 1930s, President Rafael Ángel Calderón Guardia, in alliance with the Catholic Church, attempted to dispel the economic and cultural concerns of opposition parties which comprised the socialists, led by the *Partido Vanguardia Popular*, and a powerful group of intellectuals. It was this group of academics that formed the *Centro para los Estudios de los Problemas Nacionales* (CEPN) in 1940 in order to lobby for social democracy to take over from what they saw as the ever-repressive rhetoric of liberalism (Cuevas Molina, 1999, 18–19). Despite holding an election in 1948, accusations of fraud were levelled at President Calderón Guardia, and the head of the armed forces soon led an uprising supported by the CEPN. The civil war which ensued lasted just 44 days and ended in April 1948 with the harmonious transition of power to the new President, José Figueres Ferrer, who had led the army to victory (Bird, 1984, 12). The initial days of Figueres' *Segunda República* saw many social guarantees passed while also underlining the continued importance of the traditional and idealized *tico* in unifying the nation. The emphasis on the importance of democracy and education was cemented by the new constitution, and free education and healthcare were extended to all citizens (Biesanz et al., 1999, 32). The exaltation of peace as a national quality was also furthered as, despite having led a military coup which overthrew the government, President Figueres abolished the army in December 1948, a decision that has not been overturned since. Following the nationalization of banks, insurance, and all amenities, state employment also rose rapidly, meaning that the dominant classes were now bureaucrats – who remained firmly rooted in the urban centres of the Central Valley – rather than landowners (Cuevas Molina, 1999, 23; Mitchell and Pentzer, 2008, 228). As such, Biesanz et al. note that the 'myth of classlessness gradually gave way to the myth that Costa Ricans were all middle class' (1999, 102) in this era.

Despite the social and political upheaval of the state in 1948, then, the imagined nation – or the *tico* ideal which had been created in the nineteenth century – remained largely unchanged. Indeed, it was not until the 1970s that the nation's internal image and norms were first actively challenged. This was a decade of change as civil wars were fought in other Central American countries, wars of independence continued throughout the colonized world, and the consequences of the US civil rights movements came to be felt. The existing idea of Costa Rica's exceptionalism, especially in relation to its Central American neighbours, was cemented in the nation's imaginary at this time, and, according to film-maker Paz Fábrega, 'Costa Rica se ha desarrollado a su propia manera y encerrado a sí mismo' (2015). At the same time, however, the 1970s also saw a cultural boom in Costa

Rica, and the *Ministerio de Cultura, Juventud y Deporte* was created alongside other initiatives which served to promote national culture (Cuevas Molina, 1999, 28). In large part due to both this socio-political environment and the emphasis placed on cultural endeavour, this decade also came to be seen as a defining period for anti-hegemonic cultural creation in Costa Rica, primarily in the form of literature and documentary.[1] While the 'boom' authors began to take hold of the discipline of 'Latin American literature', Costa Rica saw the emergence of a very different writing style. The authors who began to publish in the late 1960s and the 1970s – the 'generation of the 70s' – penned literature which challenged the *tico* norm often from a platform of identity politics.

These turbulent years – which also saw anti-government demonstrations in San José – led to a neo-liberal refashioning of Costa Rica's economic and cultural policies in the 1980s. This in turn led to the swelling of the Central Valley and an increase in immigration. While Cuevas Molina points out that Costa Rica's social ills were generally blamed on the Nicaraguan 'Other' (1999, 32–3), Chang Vargas and González Vásquez contend (1981, 70) that prejudice against the internal cultural 'Others' of indigenous and African descent also increased at this time as there was a sharp uplift in the migration of individuals from these groups from rural to urban areas. Despite the protests against national stereotypes in the 1970s, then, cultural, economic, and political power remained more highly concentrated than ever in the Central Valley in the decades that followed. This trend has continued into the twenty-first century, as the centralized government acts out of San José and the majority of wealth and employment is found there (Anon., 2012b, 4). This has aided the creation of a physical centre and periphery, where the Central Valley – the provinces of San José, Heredia, Cartago, and Alajuela – has power and wealth, and the lowlands – Puntarenas, Guanacaste, and Limón – are less-developed and fiscally poorer. The founding myths of the nation have persisted, however, leading

1 The Costa Rican government felt that its national audiovisual production rate was falling behind that of other Latin American nations in the 1970s and as such designated funds to the Ministry for Youth, Culture, and Sport to encourage documentary filmmaking. Ironically, although hundreds of documentaries were consequently made through official programmes, their content was not policed, resulting in embarrassing results, as prostitution, alcoholism, poor worker conditions, and corruption were often highlighted. This culminated in the release of *Costa Rica: Banana Republic* by Igno Niehaus in 1976, which was so negative in its portrayal of the nation's image that the government threatened to censor it. This led to the resignation of the country's Minister for Culture, Carmen Naranjo, who herself was a protest author of 'the generation of the 70s'.

Biesanz et al. to claim (1999, 12) that, despite all the changes that had occurred in the country, many of the cultural observations made about the values of the *tico* in the 1850s remained unchanged in the year before the new millennium.

These highly valued myths and 'typical' *tico* traits could not have been maintained and perpetuated for over a century without their continual promotion, and it has been observed that the Costa Rican government has traditionally fostered national unity in turbulent times by harking back to the myth of the idealized *tico*. Biesanz et al. state that:

> most Ticos are probably unaware that they are subject to a continual 'ideological bombardment' that assures them they live in the best of all countries – that there is no other as democratic, peaceful, and beautiful or any as concerned with its citizens' welfare. Presidential speeches, campaign oratory, editorials, school lessons, and celebrations all stress these themes, as they have since the late nineteenth century. (Biesanz et al., 1999, 79)

With such a focus on education, and state education controlling the sector, the extolling of the *tico* norm and ideal has been ingrained since childhood. Indeed, children must learn the national symbols, emblems, and heroes by heart, as well as the entire national anthem in order to sing it every Monday morning, and the Lord's Prayer in order to recite it each day before class. Quince Duncan, a Costa Rican author, claims that this bombardment of idealism from a young age has caused citizens to have a very distorted view of the country:

> Tenemos como un mito. El mito costarricense, del país más feliz del mundo. Entonces, nosotros no podemos ver nada malo de Costa Rica. Sobre todo cuando nos aproximamos a un extranjero, no, todo lo nuestro es perfecto. Lo peor que le puede pasar es oír a un tico fuera del país hablando de Costa Rica. Yo me quiero esconder ... porque a mí me da vergüenza. (Q Duncan, 2013)

Evidence from the 2015 documentary *Retratico* concurs with this idea of the Costa Rican nation embodying ideals of peace and happiness; as one interviewee states, 'Pura vida es una de las cosas más importantes que nos caracterizan ... es una manera ... de definir el país ... siempre viéndolo como algo muy positivo, como algo bonito ... Es algo muy tico' (Harvey-Kattou, 2015). Her assertion demonstrates that the *tico* is bound up with positive attributes, with the country's catchphrase – *pura vida* – consistently used to perpetuate this affective bond between citizens.

While Biesanz et al. are clear that the ingraining of these types of ideals and their continual promotion in the country's psyche has been purposely managed by the state, the decades that followed the sociological revolution of the 1970s saw US mass culture gain power in Costa Rica and begin to influence the way the country viewed itself. Indeed, Carlos Cortés points out (2007, 138–9) that the Costa Rican literary 'boom' of the 1970s and the associated trend of social challenge visible in these works actually came to be replaced by popular culture – such as film and television – in future decades. This has led Chang Vargas and González Vásquez to note (1981, 73) that the surge in foreign products, companies, and media also resulted in the importation of US-centric lifestyle models, thus replacing the Eurocentric colonial model with a US-centric neo-colonial one. Cuevas Molina demonstrates this as he notes that in Costa Rica, 'Hollywood es no solamente el centro de uno de los más grandes emporios económicos sino, también, el generador de valores que se distribuyen a través de cines y aparatos de televisión por todos rincones del orbe' (1999, 37). Despite this new set of aspirations being screened to citizens in their homes and in cinemas, the traditional *tico* values have, in some ways, been boosted by this focus on material culture, with many people favourably comparing Costa Rican ways of life with US consumerism. This even led the ICT to focus their 2014 tourist campaign on this very juxtaposition; 'Save the Americans' plays with conservationist rhetoric showing how Costa Rica's eco credentials can save Americans from long hours in offices and downtime in urban jungles.

This contrast between the traditional image of the *tico* and the globalized, consumer society being promoted by North American influences has ushered in a new phase of identity challenge: the digital revolution. Despite the influx of information about protests, wars, and civil rights movements over the 1960s and 1970s, Chang Vargas and González Vásquez argue that Costa Rican mass culture – which valorizes an essentialized past and an idealized national stereotype – actively worked to curtail any support for these. Instead, it acted to socialize citizens into further adopting and cementing the notion of an unchanging, homogeneous national culture into the national imaginary, attempting to unify individuals through the promotion of normative social values (1981, 74). As a result, there has only really been one, core change to Costa Rican identity in the national imaginary: the idealization of two opposing figures of the urban bureaucrat and the rural *campesino*. By the twenty-first century, the city-dwelling office worker is seen as the modern *tico*, while the humble farmer represents an antiquated version of an idealized ancestral past (74). The modern *tico*, however, is still described as living in a 'Catholic and entirely middle-class society' (Mitchell and Pentzer, 2008, 227) which maintains the majority of traditional traits that it believes make it special and unique, such as the use of certain words and phrases,[2] the lack of army, free education, and folkloric traditions (228). Indeed, evidence from the documentary *Retratico* points towards the longevity of this national ideology. When asked what being *tico* means, the majority of interviewees' responses include mentions of being an exceptional country in terms of happiness or nature. *Ticos* are described as 'las personas más amigables del mundo', characterized 'por cuidar la naturaleza', and as 'gente muy linda'; while another interviewee states that 'ser tico significa amar a Costa Rica, creer que todavía se puede tener un país verde y definitivamente disfrutar de cada centímetro del país' (Harvey-Kattou, 2015). It is clear from these responses that the *tico* ideology remains strong for many in the twenty-first century.

Despite the challenges to national identity in the sociological revolution of the 1970s, then, the conception of what it is to be *tico* has remained largely unchanged into the new century. Protest against normative stances since the year 2000, however, have seen creative media used as a means of challenge in the digital era just as in the 1970s. These protests have become steadily more visible and the reason for their increased presence is owed in large part to globalization, the popularity of the liberal global rhetoric of multi- and pluri-culturalism, and the digital revolution. It is this latter point which has perhaps had the biggest influence on Costa Rican identity since the year 2000, with social and mass media allowing protest to be shared and galvanized quickly and easily. The results of many of these movements have been radical when compared with the rigid sense of identity promoted in the country. In 2014, Article One of the constitution was changed, declaring for the first time that the Republic of Costa Rica was 'multiétnica y pluricultural' (Sequeira, 2014). In this same year, the incumbent Partido de Acción Ciudadana, led by President Luis Guillermo Solís, also passed a law stating that family social security could now be used by same-sex couples (Á. Murillo, 2014). These fundamental tenets of whiteness and Catholic views on morality have, it would appear, gradually begun to be challenged by government.

Despite these strides forward in the recognition of some groups traditionally excluded from the *tico* imaginary, however, Costa Rica has still been described as an intolerant society (Mitchell and Pentzer, 2008, 235). Indeed, Mitchell and Pentzer state that a 2006 survey showed that 60 per cent of people in the country were opposed to homosexual rights, while they

---

2 Examples abound, but notably *ticos* frequently use the diminutive suffixes -ico and -ito, the formal 'usted', and occasionally the more informal 'vos', and the catchall 'pura vida' in conversation.

note that there is very little acknowledgement of regions outside the Central Valley in much of everyday life (236 and 247). This attitude is highlighted in interviews contained within *Retratico*; one interviewee notes that 'la gente de la costa es muy distinta', while others speak about the different lifestyles and values that exist between people living in urban and rural areas (Harvey-Kattou, 2015). Moreover, Gisella Díaz-Azofeifa contends that:

> Costa Rica has introduced an important number of international standards and norms on human rights, racial discrimination and ethnic diversity. Despite this apparent shift towards multiculturalism, it has officially remained a monocultural (a white and Europeanized mestizo culture), monolinguistic (Spanish) and Catholic state. Because of the double standard, multicultural policies promoted by the state over the last decades have not only been insufficient but also contradictory. (Díaz-Azofeifa, 2012, 137)

It would appear, then, that the Costa Rican government has been forced to adopt a rhetoric of inclusion in order to be outwardly seen as a progressive and liberal state by the outside world. At the same time, despite law changes and shifts in government rhetoric, the firm grip of the imagined community which has been built around nationalism has led to a failure on behalf of much of the population to embrace these new, non-traditional values. It has even been said that the term *tico* as used to describe a plethora of national characteristics has become even more popular, as noted in an article for *La Nación* written by José Ricardo Chaves: 'el paso creciente de costarricenses a ticos no es algo inocente, sin consecuencias, y revela mucho más que un mero giro lingüístico' (Chaves, 2017). Twenty-first-century Costa Rica in many ways therefore demonstrates that the official stance is yet to impact fully the rights and participation of internal 'Others' in the tico norm.

What Defines Us? Theories of National Identity

As demonstrated by the history of Costa Rican identity since independence, it is clear that the idea of a shared national past has been created and perpetuated in the country. This apparently unique ancestry has then been used to shape a national and cultural identity, maintaining Costa Rica as distinct from the rest of Central America and the wider world. The term 'nation-state' – often used interchangeably with 'nation' – is defined by the *Oxford English Dictionary* as 'an independent political state formed from a people who share a common national identity (historically, culturally, or ethnically); (more generally) any independent political state' (*OED*, 2015).

This definition is problematic when considering the Costa Rican context, however, as not all its inhabitants actually do share a common history, culture, and ethnicity. In fact, these terms themselves and their associations are contested. Moreover, when considering any nations or national identities, it is clear that – given the differences between individuals – an entire body of people cannot share one, absolute, identity. Rather than a naturally occurring concept, then, Benedict Anderson contends (2006, 4) that nations and nationalisms, as we conceive of these today, are man-made constructs which first emerged in the eighteenth century to forge social cohesion and territorial unity. Anderson goes on to state that these nationalisms then merged across social groups and communities, eventually taking on political and ideological power (4). He therefore terms the notion of what is commonly said to constitute the nation-state as 'incoherent', noting that there exists within these arbitrary geographic boundaries a multiplicity of cultural traits with which different inhabitants will identify (5).

Indeed, Anderson asserts that the nation itself is 'an imagined political community – and imagined as both inherently limited and sovereign' (6). Gayatri Spivak also affirms this position as she contends that 'nationalism is the product of a collective imagination constructed through rememoration' (2010, 40), adding that nationalism is also a 'deceptive category' (46). Further unpacking the definition of a nation-state, Anderson's and Spivak's contention that the nation as a concept only exists in the imaginary also leads to the assertion that the nation and the state are separate entities: the nation as the imagined community and the state as the administrative and legal framework that holds this in place. Judith Butler and Gayatri Spivak, in their co-authored work *Who Sings the Nation-State*, suggest that within this distinction the state is defined as signifying 'the legal and institutional structures that delimit a certain territory ... the state is supposed to service the matrix for the obligations and prerogatives of citizenship' (2007, 3). This matrix, then, serves to remind the citizens of the presence of the nation, as though it were a distinct and observable entity. Homi Bhabha also argues that nations 'lose their origins in the myths of time and only fully realize their horizons in the mind's eye' and that, from this, 'the nation emerges as a powerful historical idea ... whose cultural compulsion lies in the impossible unity of the nation as a symbolic force' (1990, 1). This idea of the nation as a symbolic force, maintained and perpetuated by the state's administrative framework, appears true of Costa Rica. Indeed, the building of monuments, the writing of a constitution, and the promotion of certain 'national' values and traits in the late 1800s – as described earlier in this chapter – aided social cohesion, and in the country it is the state that has used education and propaganda to work in tandem with the imagined nation in order to maintain social unity and a spirit of patriotism.

The purpose of the state is not only to include citizens on the basis of patriotism and national identity, however, but also to work with the imagined nation to exclude 'Others'. Michael Hardt and Antonio Negri contend (2000, 138 and 395–99) that the idea of the nation is based upon the awarding of citizenship to certain inhabitants, thus creating a strong identity among those considered to fit the qualities the state wishes it to include. Butler and Spivak also contend (2007, 4–5) that the state is charged with maintaining the physical delineation of nationhood as well as choosing who the citizens of the nation will be. As such, they argue that the binary of citizen versus foreigner is often reinforced. This desire to create a national rhetoric which holds people together under the banner of patriotism – or the nation – therefore necessarily finds its opposition in the exclusion of all others. This demonstrates that the state can also 'signify the source of non-belonging as a quasi-permanent state' (4). Although the ideals of the nation may have been built in the imaginary, then, its power is tangible and substantial.

As well as the state choosing its citizenry, Butler and Spivak also maintain that holding a national passport does not necessarily preclude the possibility of living in the 'domain of disenfranchisement', which they contend the nation tries to push out (2007, 15). The issue with the creation of a rigid national identity such as the *tico*, then, becomes problematic for those who do not fit this ideal. The removal of such citizens from the nation's imaginary has widespread effects, and it has been noted that those 'failing the tests of social intelligibility required for minimal recognition include those whose age, gender, race, nationality, and labor status not only disqualify them for citizenship but actively "qualify" them for statelessness' (15). These qualifications are tied up in the notion of the *tico*, where the white, Central Valley-dwelling, Catholic citizen is upheld as both the norm and the ideal.

Although the idea of statelessness can be literal and physical, it can also be an intangible space; when one stops qualifying as a necessary and legitimate part of the nation, it is implied that the state will no longer work for you, but against you. Even when an individual is still included as a part of the state on paper, it may be inferior or accorded less value than other members, with Eurocentric and patriarchal views of society given preference. As Butler and Spivak argue, the 'monied and masculine subjects of dominant nationality are entitled to exercise its [the nation-state's] prerogatives' (2007, 27). Furthering this notion of a negative marginality, Bhabha argues (1991, 4) that existing at the margins is neither celebratory nor is it self-imposed; rather, it is forced upon all those who oppose modernism's drive towards homogeneity – which can include many, or even most, national citizens. Within the Costa Rican context, then, a national identity has been created so that those not adhering to the implicit rules of the *tico* are forced to either join the ranks of 'Otherness' or seek life in exile, both instances pointing towards living in a permanent state of non-belonging either within or outside the physical borders of the country.

The objective of the nation-state, then, is to preserve its sovereignty and power – or the illusion of both. In order to achieve this, a clear cause or goal is created to bind citizens together: a national identity. As Butler and Spivak point out, to exist, this identity must include some and forcibly exclude others; it must value some citizens, and ignore others, just as the *tico* praises some and reviles others. They sum up this binary when they state that 'the problem is not just one of inclusion into an already existing idea of the nation, but one of equality' (2007, 60). It is this notion of equality which sits hand in hand with human rights, and the dismissal of the equality of all people is what leads nation-states to discriminate. The right to rights is not a manifest law, but it belongs to the 'nature of equality', which is, in turn, a social condition (65). Where the public sphere is meant to be the very grounds for a plural nation, then, these national modes of belonging and the social categorization of people actually exist to delegitimize someone's presence (25). The very existence of internal 'Others' within Costa Rica but outside the *tico* norm demonstrates that both the physical and imagined nation-state is not a singular, harmonious body of people. Rather, it is made up of several groups who express differences of identity. As Thomas Docherty asserts, 'official identity operates at a remove from actuality' (2013, 22), thus demonstrating the very real gap between perceptions of national identity and the multiplicity of all national societies. I would suggest that the way in which power and identity is structured, then, can be envisaged as a circle within a wider sphere whereby the inner circle or core asserts control over the remainder – just as Costa Rica's Central Valley asserts control over its geographic periphery.

In framing the nation as a powerful, binding centre with a weaker periphery, a consideration of Antonio Gramsci's concepts of hegemony and civil society are relevant to the discussion (Moreiras, 2001). In the notebooks he kept while a political prisoner, Gramsci explored the location of national power while arguing against the enduring nature of national borders and the very idea of the nation-state (Hoare and Nowell Smith, 1971, 12). He termed the governing body found at the heart of the nation-state the hegemonic power; it is a person or political party which wields control over the nation's inhabitants (12). Gramsci's concept of hegemony divides society into different – and unequal – parts. In the centre there lies the state, or political society, which is the sum of all the parts and consists of people who are used to govern, order, and control civil society. Civil society is defined by Gramsci as the mass of citizens which is constituted by their relationship with the State whereby they attempt to negotiate with, and seek representation through, the hegemonic force but do not form part of the powerful elite. At the outer limits of this two-part social relationship lie the 'subaltern', or a marginalized people with no social voice who have been excluded from both the state and civil society (12). Gramsci defines 'hegemony' as a state which holds power over civil society and controls it through the propagation of its ideals, using intellectuals and government officials as its spokespeople – the 'deputies' of the state (12). As has been discussed, the promotion of the idealized *tico* through education and political propaganda has been used subliminally to persuade society into accepting 'traditional' values as the highest form of aspiration. This therefore certainly suggests that a hegemonic centre and an inferior periphery exist within the imagined national community of Costa Rica, whereby internal 'Others' are pushed to the margins.

The *Tico* 'Other' as a Postcolonial Power Formation

This power structure whereby a superior–inferior dichotomy has been created within Costa Rica mirrors the formation of colonial hierarchies. While colonization is generally thought of as the process by which one nation actively and forcibly takes over another, the colonizer–colonized relationship is also reproduced within societies such that members of the same nation are involved in a type of master–subordinate relationship when it comes to matters of power, identity, and recognition. The norms and accepted tropes of the *tico* identity discussed are based entirely on colonial concepts of culture, power, and superiority. They are Eurocentric (favouring white over black), patriarchal (valuing man over woman), Catholic ('invisibilizing' the LGBTQ+ community and those with opposing cultural or religious beliefs), and patriotic (praising nationalism while excluding the foreigner). The colonizer within Costa Rica is an internal set of cultural norms rather than an external force. This type of supremacist notion is not unique to Costa Rica, however, as it pervades every corner of the modern world due to the persistent philosophies of colonial legacy.

According to Enrico Santí, the whole of Latin America is at the bottom of a hierarchical relationship with the West. He states that 'Latinamericanism ... is never far from the collective notion that identifies Europe, and by extension the United States, as a superior culture in comparison with all other non-European peoples and cultures' (1992, 90). The very designation Latin

America is a colonized, European denomination (91) as is the name Costa Rica – termed the Rich Coast because of the invaders' mistaken supposition that they would find gold there. Latin America – and Costa Rica more specifically – clearly adheres to the imagined, implicit power structures which are a legacy of Spanish colonialism. Within this framework, many contemporary and historical social norms are seen to reflect colonial power formations whereby citizens who do not conform to the Eurocentric, *tico* ideal take the position of the colonized subject. These groups and individuals are constantly fed an idealized image of society, nationality, and culture which they are encouraged to conform to and strive for even when this is unattainable. Writing following several wars of independence, in 1963, Frantz Fanon asserts that decolonization does not change the notion that the 'natural' order of things maintains that the colonial power and all that it represents is superior, leaving the colonized people to defer to it or be shunned. Even when colonial governments were deposed, he argued (1963, 7–9), this power dynamic was merely reproduced by new national governments. Costa Rica's nation-building exercise of the 1870s onwards is testament to this assertion.

Moreover, the very concept of a cultural or national identity is a Western construct as implied by Benedict Anderson's reasoning (2006, 4) that nations as imagined communities were formed as part of the Enlightenment period of the eighteenth century. Nicholas Dirks further points out that culture is itself a 'colonial formation' (2006, 58), thus demonstrating the enforcement of Eurocentric values on the colonized world – including Latin America. Other than economic, territorial, and political factors, colonialism was also used as a means of imposing one culture upon another, and Butler and Spivak have pointed out that in contemporary society today's marginalized groups are treated as colonized peoples and thus are judged by strict rules which favour Eurocentricity above all else (2007). It is this notion which is of interest when considering Costa Rica, as it too judges and rules its own society according to Eurocentric patterns which promote the white, Catholic, male. These values are often so ingrained in cultural study that the elevation of them goes unnoticed. Within this context then, the idealized *tico* becomes the centre, the norm, the mainstream, and any person or trait which does not conform to this standard becomes the periphery, the 'Other', the abject.

This colonial formation of identity acts as a binary force, and the notion of dichotomies of difference as intimately linked with how mankind identifies and relates to others has been developed by several postcolonial scholars. Edward Said's *Orientalism* demonstrates that (1995, 207), over the course of centuries, the West has created a Foucauldian discourse of an East–West binary, which, he argues, also incorporates gender roles according to which the East is female, and the West is male. In this construction, the Orient – or the non-conformist Costa Rican – is lazy, untrustworthy, and extraordinary; the West – the typical *tico* – is hard-working, truthful, progressive, and democratic – the very definition of 'normal' (38–41). Said also asserts that the labels forced onto the Orient by the Occident are actually the elements of its own society that it views as transgressive due to their ability to undermine the superior, national project being undertaken (3). In this way the norm remains idealized, while the 'Other' is vilified and blamed. Santí uses this formation to develop his theory of Latinamericanism, which, he argues (1992, 90–1), acts in the same way as Orientalism where the West (Europe and the USA) invented the concept of Latin America. While Said's primary concern was one of racial and ethnic heritage – the Occident promoting a colour-hierarchy with 'white' at the top and 'black' at the bottom – Hélène Cixous also conflates the position of woman with 'black' in the postcolonial, patriarchal world stating that both are seen as 'dark and dangerous' by their oppressors (1976, 878). Clearly, in these paradigms, then, women of colour fall to the bottom of the social hierarchy.

Within this same power play Jean-Paul Sartre notes in his preface to Frantz Fanon's *The Wretched of the Earth* that the mainstream will do all it can to force the 'Other' to conform to its ways, while giving them no power or social prestige in return (Fanon, 1963, 13). The possible motivation for the 'Other' – the periphery – to continue to seek integration with the centre when it cannot possibly gain from it has been considered by Louis Althusser. Althusser's theory of interpellated ideas – or the unconscious set of assumptions by which all individuals are socially conditioned – demonstrates that dominant suppositions or notions of identity and normality are so widely disseminated that they become unconsciously absorbed and accepted by all, and their validity is therefore rarely questioned (1971, 174–81). He contends that all ideologies work to interpellate their ideals in the same way: first, by interpellating individuals as subjects, then by subjecting them to the ideal and forcing a mutual recognition of each other, before reproducing the 'absolute guarantee that everything really is so, and that on condition that the subjects recognize what they are and behave accordingly, everything will be all right' (181). Indeed, Robert Dale Parker has termed interpellation as 'the process of being passively, unconsciously drawn into dominant social assumptions' (2012, 201), and this process and its results are certainly seen through the propagation of ideals within education and government in Costa Rica.

This notion of the interpellation of ideals is very similar to Pierre Bourdieu's concept of habitus – or a set of assumptions which maintain the status quo. Bourdieu describes habitus as 'the source of ... [a] series of moves which are objectively organized as strategies without being the product of a genuine strategic intention' (1977, 73) and as the 'principle of regulated improvisations' (78). The theory of social habitus, then, demonstrates that individuals act out social situations according to strict rules of which each individual is unconscious. These social interactions are structured around mutually understood underlying systems of social assumptions which are present only quasi-consciously and which result in the success of the interaction (76–8). Each individual therefore becomes 'wittingly or unwittingly ... a producer and reproducer of objective meaning' (79). Thus, Bourdieu argues, a 'commonsense world' is produced which allows all individuals to understand and participate in the world and experiences around them (80). In relation to the *tico* identity, habitus and the interpellation of ideals have worked to inculcate a sense of identity upon the nation, one which promotes certain values, cultures, and ethnicities over others through implicit social assumption and the perpetuation of norms and stereotypes in everyday life. Indeed, Carlos Cortés contends that, in Costa Rica, 'el consenso simbólico es tan importante como el consenso real y no se logra por medio de la represión, ha estado sustentada por una serie de mitos históricos que, entre otras cosas, han legitimado la reproducción del orden social' (2007, 15). This assertion that a symbolic consensus has been reached in the country through the reproduction of habit in terms of social order demonstrates the importance of breaking with habit in order to oppose stereotypes and discriminatory prevailing systems of power.

It is these unconscious acts of habitus which have contributed to the perpetuation of norms within Costa Rica. Michael Chanan argues that 'Fanon maintained that a nation's sense of itself can be colonized, as well as its territory' (2006, 39), and it is clear when considering postcolonial formations of power in Costa Rica that it is the imagined nation which has been most recently subject to colonization through normative behaviour and habitus. Through history lessons, educational books, and cultural programmes, the 'typical' *tico* and his values have been ingrained in, and internalized by, Costa Ricans (Q. Duncan, 2013), resulting in the creation of an inferiority complex among those not attaining this social and cultural ideal. Fanon discusses the notion of the internalization of norms – no matter how much these work against the individual – as creating this divide between the colonial power and the internally colonized. In his work *Black Skin, White Masks* (1986), he demonstrates how an inferiority complex has been forced on those with dark skins, asserting that because society states that there exist superior and inferior cultures, colonized man internalizes this notion and acts accordingly. Indeed, in refusing to internalize the inferiority complex himself, he was able to see that the consequence of his non-conformity was that 'I was hated, despised, detested ... by an entire race' (Fanon, 1986, 118). He goes on to contend that:

> every colonized people – in other words – every people in whose soul an inferiority complex has been created by the death and burial of its local cultural originality – finds itself face to face with the language of the civilizing nation; that is, with the culture of the mother country. The colonized is elevated above his jungle status in proportion to his adoption of the mother country's cultural standards. (Fanon, 1986, 18)

Perhaps the use of the diminutive suffix '-tico' to describe and name Costa Rica is just another result of the internalization of the colonial myth of the inferiority of this nation in comparison with its European counterparts.

Resisting the internalization of social norms is not narrated as a simple task by Fanon, however, and it is this internal relationship between the colonizer and the colonized which Homi Bhabha also considers. Using Jacques Lacan's politics of the gaze, he concludes that the colonized will often mimic their colonizers through language, education, and government models, even after the de-colonial moment (Bhabha, 1994, 121–2). While both Fanon and Bhabha assert that this mimicry is a negative consequence of colonization, Bhabha states that it does have the power to unsettle the colonizer and question their superiority (123). The colonizing culture wants its 'Other' to assimilate to its ideals without giving it equality, but the very existence of mimicry actually serves to undermine the East–West, inferior–superior dichotomy, which is exposed as an artificial construction perpetuated by those in power in order to maintain that power. While the colonial power in the Costa Rican context is not a foreign nation, then, the *tico* social norms are considered to be superior and are imposed upon the internal 'Others'. It is these roles of both the enforced and internalized inferiority complexes and the consequences of the mimicry of social norms that are analysed within literary and filmic narratives in Chapters 2 and 3.

Despite the clear existence of the idea of dominant and subordinate cultural groups, then, it is widely accepted that the very fixity of such binaries is a part of the problem of culture itself. Bhabha, for example, criticizes the nature of the dichotomy of power as a rigid construct which denies variation, change, and history (1994, 94–5). Stuart Hall has also championed this standpoint, and his theory of identity is founded on the concepts of plurality and liminality. He states that:

> cultural identities come from somewhere, have histories. But like everything which is historical, they undergo constant transformation.

> Far from being eternally fixed in some essentialized past, they are subject to the continuous 'play' of history, culture and power. (Hall, 1994, 394)

This statement demonstrates that historical notions of a culture, nation, or a certain group are based on false premises, and must move from a place of immutability where they are seen as a fixed set of characteristics and instead be seen as fluid, and potentially even redundant, concepts. Where the dominant identity is forced upon an individual, group, or society, a politics of resistance must therefore be implemented in order to question the mainstream and usher in the recognition of more multiply placed identities. Although I agree with Bhabha and Hall that the employment of essentialisms as rigid categories is harmful when it comes to questions of identity, the existence and acceptance of such reifications within the Costa Rican imaginary renders their articulation and exploration a necessary stage of this project.

While recognizing the harmful effect of the imposition of (false) binaries, then, it has been suggested that resistance – as termed by Fanon and Bhabha – or counterhegemonic production – as termed by Hall and Spivak – is a means of overcoming the inferiority complex forced upon certain groups. Bhabha defines resistance as 'the effect of an ambivalence produced within the rules of recognition of dominating discourses as they articulate the signs of cultural difference and replicate them within the deferential relations of colonial power – hierarchy, normalization, marginalization, and so forth' (2006b, 41). Adherence to social norms occurs as a result of interpellation and the perpetuation of habitus, but Bhabha posits that ambivalence towards them and the questioning of these unwritten laws which govern society and behaviour leads to resistance. Within this rhetoric of resistance, Bhabha proposes (1994, 19) the notion of hybridity – meaning cultural multiplicity or existence at a crossroads – as a means of articulating the culturally plural nature of the postcolonial world. He states that 'hybridity is the revaluation of the assumption of colonial identity through the repetition of discriminatory identity effects' and that hybridization occurs when 'the colonial discourse has reached that point when, faced with the hybridity of its objects, the *presence* of power is revealed as something other than what its rules of recognition assert' (159). In this context, the colonial – or in this case the *tico* – is the dominating, mainstream force, and hybridity is the questioning of this identity as something natural or inherent to these internal 'Others': hybridity is a destabilizing force. Rather than reinforcing the dominant/subordinate roles required to maintain the accepted norm, hybridity inverts them, demonstrating that projected identities can change.

There are several modes of resistance open to those subjects wishing to expose the arbitrary nature of backwards-looking hierarchies, and it is the use of the soft power of creative, mass productions which are considered as hybrid tools of resistance in Chapters 2 and 3.

Costa Rica's Internal 'Others'

The existence of the idealized *tico* and the power of this concept is, according to its colonial formation, at once exclusive and exclusionary, creating the cultural binary of the *tico* and its 'Other'. The idea that those adhering to the image of the colonial elite are the elite within society is a part of Latin America's cultural formation, and while this dominant discourse has created a myth which very few citizens can actually live up to, the notion of an ethnically and culturally homogeneous nation is also historically flawed within Costa Rica. Rozana Hidalgo notes this when she asserts that a new perspective is needed for the redefinition of the nation:

> a la luz de la ponderación del papel de la otredad: lo pobre, lo étnico, la feminidad, lanzados al terreno de lo oculto por efecto de la 'distorsión semántica' que nos define homogéneos, blancos, iguales ... la presencia de esa otredad plantea a la pureza de la nación inventada. (Hidalgo, 2004, 7)

While using this image to appeal to North American and European tourists, it is also an image which has been promoted internally. In light of this, 'official' Costa Rican identity has remained relatively fixed since independence, and as such it has created and perpetuated a wide range of inclusive/exclusive binaries. This is described by one interviewee in the documentary *Retratico* as 'una cultura de pura vida irreal' (Harvey-Kattou, 2015). While these myths are numerous, the most frequently occurring to be dealt with within literature, film, and academic texts are those that centre on ethnicity, geography, gender, and sexuality. The internal 'Others' in this case are all those who do not fit the ideal model of the white, Central Valley-dwelling, heterosexual (and *machista*) male, so a revalorization of the history and existence of these 'Others' is central to a discussion of Costa Rican identity.

Although it is claimed that Costa Rica is an entirely 'white' nation, directly descended from Spanish ancestors, this supposition is inaccurate. The 2011 census demonstrates that while nearly 90 per cent of the population self-define as 'white' or 'mestizo', 7.8 per cent of the population describe themselves as Afro-Costa Rican, 2.4 per cent as indigenous, and 0.2 per cent as Chinese. The main indigenous groups still living in the country are the

Maleku and the Bribri, and – despite their exclusion from the Costa Rican history books – they have formed part of the nation since pre-colonial times. Still living in small communities in rural areas today, their presence is often played down by the *ticos*. The most famous incidence of this occurred when President Calderón declared, on a visit to Spain, that there were 'no Indians' in Costa Rica when the Spaniards arrived (Biesanz et al., 1999, 113). The largest minority ethnic group – Afro-Costa Ricans – have had a much more recent, and more complex, path to citizenship, however. In contrast to the majority of Afro-Latin Americans brought to the region as slaves, the Afro-Caribbean community of Costa Rica only dates back to the late nineteenth century, and is largely associated with the former British Caribbean islands – mainly Jamaica, Barbados, and St Kitts – and, within Costa Rica, with the province of Limón (Chomsky, 1995, 840).

In 1872, President Guardia undertook a project to build the country's first ever railroad that would be used to transport coffee from plantations in the Central Valley to Puerto Limón in order to be distributed to Europe (Perry and Sawyers, 1995, 216). A shortage of labour left the North American overseer of the project, Minor Keith, to look in the Caribbean islands for workers, where he offered attractive salaries and a free passage home when the job was completed. As a result of these promises, and due to a prolonged period of bad weather which negatively affected the sugar cane harvests across the Caribbean, more than 10,000 Caribbean workers entered Costa Rica from 1881 to 1891 in order to work on the railroad (Duncan and Meléndez, 1972, 64). It has been noted that these labourers' 'primary concern' was 'to make some money and then return to their home islands', in accordance with Keith's advertisement (Perry and Sawyers, 1995, 216). After they had gone without pay – some for up to nine months – while hundreds of others died after contracting tropical diseases, however, it became clear that the project was neither physically nor financially viable. This prompted Keith to merge the local banana plantations – owned by Costa Rican smallholders from the Central Valley – with the Boston Fruit Company to form the conglomerate, the United Fruit Company (UFC), which would then hire these out-of-work railroad workers on banana plantations in Limón (217).

This new, booming banana industry attracted a further 20,000 Caribbean labourers who entered the province between 1900 and 1913, and these waves of migration distinguished the area from the rest of the country, as 'the society which developed in Limón was an English-speaking enclave of white North American managers and black Jamaican workers, with a culture and history quite distinct from the rest of Costa Rica' (Chomsky, 1995, 837). A lack of economic stability also meant that for the workers 'return to the islands was little more than a dream' (Perry and Sawyers, 1995, 217). As Duncan asserts, although their stay in the country had become 'involuntariamente permanente', integration with the rest of Costa Rican society at this time was impossible (Duncan and Meléndez, 1972, 8). Indeed, discrimination was rife, and Harpelle notes that 'Costa Rica distinguished itself from its neighbours as a "white settler" society' that had no room for other ethnicities (2002, xvi and viii). This meant that before the 1948 revolution discrimination based on ethnic, cultural, and linguistic background was commonplace (Bell, 1996, 24–5).

As the banana harvests witnessed a sharp decline in the Caribbean region in the 1930s, however, production began along the Pacific coast. This led to the legal affirmation of ethnic prejudice as, in 1934, the Costa Rican government passed a law stating that 'queda prohibido en la zona del Pacífico ocupar gente de color en dichos trabajos [de producción y exportación bananero]' (Q. Duncan, 2001, xi). As Afro-Costa Rican workers and Caribbean migrants lost their jobs on one side of the country, this law forbade them from seeking work on the other. Within the same decree, any Afro-Costa Rican or Caribbean worker who had entered the country in Limón was prohibited from passing a certain point in Turrialba – about 50 km from the coast – into the rest of the country. The Afro-Caribbean population was in this way legally forbidden from moving freely outside Limón, thereby practically imprisoning them in the province (xi). This meant that second- and third-generation Afro-Costa Ricans who were of Caribbean descent but born in Costa Rica were not recognized as citizens by any country, which has led them to be termed a generation of 'nowhereans' (Perry and Sawyers, 1995, 218). After the 1948 revolution, however, Figueres' government abolished these laws and gave all descendants of the Caribbean population full citizenship, thus allowing them to travel freely throughout the country and to share in the newly nationalized Costa Rican education and healthcare systems (Chacón, 2004). This prompted some internal migration, with Afro-Costa Ricans learning Spanish for the first time and leaving Limón to study or work in San José (Bourgois, 1998, 123).

Following their sudden inclusion in the nation – and in national rhetoric – from 1948 onwards, second-, third-, and fourth-generation Afro-Costa Ricans became citizens almost overnight without being able truly to identify with the country of their citizenship (Duncan and Meléndez, 1972, 136). Moreover, simply because the law had now changed did not mean that integrating into 'mainstream' Costa Rican life would be easy: the *ticos'* pride in Costa Rica's white myth had lingered on since the days of colonization and concepts such as 'blanqueamiento' – the positive notion of the whitening of the bloodline over six generations – were still prevalent in both *mestizo* and Afro-Caribbean society, carried over from colonial rhetoric of the Caribbean islands (Q. Duncan, 2001, 124–6). Although Dorothy Mosby's 2003 statement that although 'Afro-Costa Ricans are not foreigners, they are perceived as an ethnic and cultural Other' (2003, 29) does still largely hold true in post-1948 Costa Rican society, a new generation of 'bicultural' third- and fourth-generation Afro-Costa Ricans began vocally to demand full political inclusion and rights in the sociological revolutionary period of the 1970s (Perry and Sawyers, 1995, 221). They spoke English and Spanish, were well versed in the cultures of Limón and the rest of Costa Rica, and were, all at once, West Indian, Costa Rican, African, Latino, and Afro-Hispanic (Mosby, 2003, x).

Although this period of change for the Afro-Costa Rican population also reflects the wider social changes occurring within the nation which were sparked in this decade, even in the twenty-first century, ideological and economic barriers exist between Afro-Costa Rican and normative *tico* society. Speaking in the documentary *Retratico*, an Afro-Costa Rican student discusses the idea that 'los ciudadanos costarricenses nunca aceptaron la idea de que unos inmigrantes … podían constituir una ciudad en su país', adding that Limón is 'una ciudad discriminada', which has seen economic and social barriers to wealth creation implemented by the government (Harvey-Kattou, 2015). He goes on to note that despite some migration from Limón to the Central Valley, 'todavía existe mucha discriminación … los mestizos siempre con esa creencia, esa idea de superioridad', which demonstrates the ideological and ethnic segregation that continues today. Two interviewees in this documentary also note that being Afro-Costa Rican necessarily precludes their inclusion – as well as their desired inclusion – into the imagined community of the *tico*. One interviewee is clear on this point as he asserts that:

> No me considero como tico, pero sí sé que soy costarricense …. la diferencia que a mí me enseñaron es que el tico tradicional es de San José, Cartago, Alajuela, Heredia … y tiene ciertos estereotipos que los marca. (Harvey-Kattou, 2015)

Moreover, Quince Duncan, who as an academic and author is certainly part of the lettered elite of the country, also notes of the ideology of the *tico* that 'yo me autodefino como afrocostarricense … hay diferencias. Hay una diferencia cultural y hay una diferencia que tiene que ver con la actitud del país o de la cultura occidental frente a uno' (Harvey-Kattou, 2015). From these contentions is it therefore clear to see that Afro-Costa Ricans and those living outside the Central Valley provinces feel themselves excluded from the perception of Costa Rican national – *tico* – identity.

Considering this idea of geographic exclusion, it is clear that while Afro-Costa Ricans suffer ethnic as well as geographic discrimination, they are not the only ones to experience the latter, as one study claims that that social mobility is impossible for 25 per cent of all Costa Ricans because of the underdevelopment or lack of opportunities in the province in which they live (Biesanz et al., 1999, 102). The nation's wealth and power remain clustered in the Central Valley, and the rural classes are looked down upon by those living in this centre who often refer to them, insultingly, as *polos*. This term is defined by Miguel Ángel Quesada Pacheco in the *Nuevo Diccionario de Costarriqueñismos* as '1. Campesino.// 2. Por extensión, mal educado, de mal gusto, rústico, que gusta vestirse con ropa de colores chillones' (2007, 322). The popularity of the term *polo* used in an offensive manner is widespread, as one Costa Rican blogger demonstrates when he states that the word is:

> un adjetivo descalificativo que incluye a todo aquel que va contra las normas minimas [*sic*] del 'glamour' y educación que impone la sociedad costarricense. No es sinónimo de pobre ... Los 'polos' abundan entre las personas con menos educación, ya que de alguna forma entre menor grado academico [*sic*] tiene una persona, hay más posibilidades que pueda ser encuadrada dentro de lo que llamamos 'POLO'. (Anon., 2009)

This abrasive statement gives the definition of a word which abounds in Costa Rica, and which, as stated above, does not refer to someone's wealth, but rather their educational status. It is frequently used in everyday conversation to describe someone living outside the Central Valley who may be seen as uncultured or unworldly, as well as being used as an insult among friends when someone commits a social or cultural faux pas.

The idea of those living outside the cities of the Central Valley as being uncultured or uneducated is, therefore, pervasive, and yet when considering the all-encompassing myth of the *tico* as a descendant of the humble farmer and the emphasis placed on the nation as a hub of biodiversity, this becomes problematic. On one hand, the exaltation of the countryside and the desire to commit to eco-tourism and sustainability remains a core focus within the nation. Interviewees in the documentary *Retratico* frequently mention the countryside and nature as positive attributes belonging to the country, and one states: 'Dios hizo la naturaleza, si cuidas el medioambiente, estás feliz', proselytizing the romanticized view of the countryside often propagated by the government (Harvey-Kattou, 2015). However, among Central Valley-dwellers there is also the idea that 'el Valle Central es otro mundo' as its surrounding countryside and coasts exist to be visited rather than as forming part of the nation (Harvey-Kattou, 2015). This notion is furthered as another interviewee states that 'la parte rural definitivamente es para el turismo ... toda la parte rural se ha dedicado al turismo – agriturismo, turismo sostenible. Es una prioridad para Costa Rica' (Harvey-Kattou, 2015). This idea that the rural, coastal provinces do not really form a part of the nation is also made clear by Quince Duncan as he describes attending a poetry reading in which the nation was described as 'bendecida por Dios, encerrada entre montañas', to which he responds, 'entonces eso te da la idea de que el asunto es gallo pinto, y que el rice and beans de Limón ... no entra ... es decir, el Valle Central es Costa Rica' (Harvey-Kattou, 2015). Despite both the exotic and romantic connotations many city-dwellers hold about the rural areas of the country, then, it would appear that it is often considered to lie outside the conception of the contemporary nation.

It is not just these ethnic and geographic ideals which have been promoted as part of the *tico* identity and the imagined, national community, as these internal 'Others' also include citizens who refuse to conform to gender and sexual stereotypes. Indeed, it has been said that 'para la gente lo que significa ser tico o ser tica tiene que ver con una cultura patriarcal' (Harvey-Kattou, 2015). Moreover, Biesanz et al. note that the national acceptance of gender-based differences where the female is inferior and the male is superior harks back to colonial times where 'men were seen as naturally superior in anything political, economic, or intellectual; women, in morality and spirituality as well as home life. This contrast justified male power and privilege as well as female weakness and self-sacrifice' (1999, 168). Hidalgo also points out (2004, 18) that the myth of the homogeneous Costa Rican society – which is still relevant in the twenty-first century – prescribes social inequality as the rule of law. In this imagined community created immediately after independence, God, the Catholic Church, national heroes, politicians, and stable families were upheld as the male foundations of the country (22). Just as the Central Valley with its white, peaceful, and hardworking inhabitants was idealized, the 'Other' was marginalized: 'asimismo, los pobres y las mujeres, por su cercanía con las pasiones del cuerpo, la naturaleza externa y el desorden social, son ubicados en este mismo lugar de la otredad excluida, marginada y silenciada' (22). This demonstrates the deliberate, exclusionary tactics employed by the post-independence governments in Costa Rica to maintain the subjugation of half the population for fear of social instability.

Moreover, as Hidalgo signposts, since the beginnings of the Costa Rican nation:

la 'madre patria', organizada a partir de las imágenes de los campesinos que labran las 'pacíficas montañas' del Valle Central, constituye una metáfora primordial sobre la cual surgirá la imagen de la nación costarricense, masculinizada y personificada en la imagen de la 'casa paterna'. (Hidalgo, 2004, 22)

Hidalgo clearly points towards a time in the late nineteenth century when a national identity and imaginary were being created, one where women had their place within the home and as bodies for procreation, whereas men inhabited and ruled the public and political spheres. Even in the early twentieth century, this disparity is carried forward and remains well documented. Grace Prada Ortiz contends (2005, 23) that the coffee oligarchy, who ruled the country at this time, did not agree with the idea of educating women. Moreover, she contends that the government of the day was shocked by the petition for women's rights and suffrage when, in 1923, the Liga Feminista was founded by Ángela Acuña (Prada Ortiz, 2005, 25). Although women eventually won these rights, and went on to win other legal equalities in the post-revolutionary Costa Rica of the late 1940s and 1950s, it has been noted that freedom has been, for many women across the social spectrum, an unachievable goal. This subjugation to patriarchy can also be seen in Costa Rica's long history of accepting – and in some cases encouraging – domestic violence. Hidalgo contends (2004, 60) that even after the 1948 revolution discrimination, exclusion, and violence have all been levelled at women within the country. Even nearing the end of the twentieth century, historian Ilse Abshagen Leitinger noted that 'in a society that is famous for its love of peace and tranquility, the perturbing record of violence against women is becoming painfully visible' (1997, xiii).

Although more and more women began to join the workforce in the 1960s and 1970s, their function in society was still primarily seen as that of housewife and mother (Araya, 2003, 198), and it has been noted that in any other public space – be it in politics or culture – women continued to be excluded from the history books (Prada Ortiz, 2005, 35). Author Carmen Naranjo has even stated that:

Se atribuyen muchas virtudes a las mujeres por su contribución a la economía familiar y social, por sus virtudes de claudicación individual en aras de su grupo cercano y el mantenimiento de una ética cínicamente utilitaria, para ensalzar lo que las mantiene virilmente esclavizadas. Se le ha permitido como un pasatiempo inofensivo dedicarse a algunas actividades creativas como bordar, tejer, pintar, leer, escribir poesía o cuentos ingeniosos y rítmicos que generalmente son bienvenidos alrededor de las cunas. Pero ¿pensar? Eso no, las mujeres no piensan, no tienen esa capacidad de los hombres para indagar problemas y sacar conclusiones. Ellas se limitan a guiarse por las indicaciones, instrucciones y consejos de las voces masculinas. Si osan dar una opinión, pues a callar porque no deben invadir un campo que les es ajeno. (Prada Ortiz, 2005, 18)

This brutal overview of the national opinion of women and their place in Costa Rican society is consequential of the culture of *machismo* prevalent in the country which promotes the existence of gender differences and propagates social inequalities. This attitude extends to the workplace, as although women increasingly make up a large proportion of the paid workforce – 41 per cent in 2005 – they are paid on average 14 per cent less than their male counterparts, and rarely hold positions of management (Flórez-Estrada, 2007). Indeed, Leitinger states (1997, xiv) that women have traditionally been disadvantaged in Costa Rican society when it comes to accessing resources, jobs, and power.

The *machista* culture also continues to ignore domestic violence and femicide; Biesanz et al. point out that:

> many Costa Ricans now acknowledge that their self-image as a peaceful people does not apply to domestic relations. Ombudsman Rodrigo Carazo Zeledón estimated in 1994 that physical, sexual, and psychological violence against women and children is common in 40 percent of households. (Biesanz et al., 1999, 190)

By 2004, that number had risen to 58 per cent, according to the first national survey explicitly to measure violence against women, while on average two cases of femicide occurred each month in the country (INAMU). While this has been noted as a pan-Latin American issue, with the UN Human Rights Commission in Mexico publishing a report stating that, in the region, 'los derechos humanos propios de la mujer son muy pocos' (O'Donnell, 2012), it would appear that in this instance Costa Rica cannot distinguish itself from its neighbours. It is interesting to note that interviewees in the documentary *Retratico* generally agreed that women's liberation and rights had been big wins for feminism over the course of the twentieth century, with one interviewee stating that 'la mujer tiene más oportunidades hoy en día' (Harvey-Kattou, 2015). At the same time, however, Jimena Cascante asserts (Harvey-Kattou, 2015) that many in twenty-first-century *tico* society believe that as women have some formal rights, contemporary feminism goes too far in asking for ideological equality and reproductive rights. As Esteban Ramírez states: 'somos un país muy abrazado con una fe muy católica ... todavía no somos muy abiertos con la religión' (Harvey-Kattou, 2015). While a secular state appeared to be on the cards after Luis Guillermo

Solis' presidential win in 2014, it would seem that this issue, which is at the centre of many feminist and LGBTQ+ rights movements, has since been pushed under the carpet.

It is, of course, not only women who suffer from gendered stereotypes, however, and the culture of *machismo* is seen negatively to affect men too. Richard Basham sees *machismo* to be a negative syndrome of 'hyper- or traditional masculinity' (1976, 126). The cult of the male, according to Basham, connotes sexual prowess, daring, confidence, strength, and, above all, the conquest of women (127). This dominant notion of how men and masculinity should act – as the virile heterosexual – is especially prevalent in Latin America and also creates a harmful image for *ticos* to live up to. Indeed, those living outside the construction of the rigid, traditional social norms of their gender or sexuality suffer discrimination, and the stigma surrounding lesbian, gay, bisexual, trans, and any other queer (LGBTQ+) communities is perhaps most visible through the relative silence surrounding this group throughout Costa Rica's history. An anonymous author stated in *Gente 10* – Costa Rica's only LGBTQ+ publication – in 1998, that there is so little published in the history books or elsewhere about queer history in Costa Rica that it would be easy to believe that they simply do not exist (*Gente 10*, 2012). As Alexander Obando notes, despite the progressive – and surprising – decision to decriminalize homosexuality as early as 1871, society has continued to identify LGBTQ+ people and their relationships as an offence to the nation's dignity ever since. He writes that 'la situación se mantuvo así durante casi cien años: la gente GLBT era invisibilizada, igual que los aborígenes, los negros, los chinos y cualquier otro grupo o etnia que no le diese a Costa Rica las condiciones de un país "blanco", eurodescendiente y totalmente paradisíaco' (Obando, 2008, xv).

The pro-gay rights movements of the 1960s and 1970s in Europe and the USA did not resonate with the Costa Rican public either, and the repression of LGBTQ+ people has been a core part of *tico* life over the course of the nineteenth and twentieth centuries as they have been associated with social disorder, disease, and even death (Alvarenga Venutolo, 2012). Aldo Facio contends that 'el tema del lesbianismo en nuestro país hasta ahora ha sido tratado prácticamente de manera clandestina' (Prada Ortiz, 2005, 211) – because of dual discrimination – while 'la historia nacional y, particularmente, la historia del pensamiento se ha escrito a medias' (245). This half-written, half-silenced history goes some way to explaining the exclusion of LGBTQ+ voices – and even their very existence – from the national history books. Indeed, until Alfonso Chase published his collection of short stories, *Mirar con inocencia*, in 1975, it has been argued that there had been no mention of LGBTQ+ peoples in the public sphere (Ulloa, 2011).

Chase, however, did not feel he could do more than implicitly allude to the possibility of homosexuality in his works until the late 1990s for fear of censorship and discrimination (Ulloa, 2011).

Since the explosion of social media in Costa Rica in the twenty-first century, however, the presence of the LGBTQ+ community has finally begun to surface more publicly. Faced with the possibility of joining virtual groups and forums full of like-minded people – especially transnational ones – the movement to promote the existence of, and counteract discrimination against, LGBTQ+ communities in Costa Rica has commenced, and with it debates about rights and prejudice have been opened. As previously discussed, using social media has meant the uniting of communities and individuals who wish to fight for civil and political rights and there are several examples of social actions which have had both a political and social impact within the nation. The group *Beso Diverso*, for example, began as an anti-homophobic campaign when a girl was asked to leave a restaurant after kissing her female partner. Quickly gaining followers and support on social media – largely via Facebook – the *Ruta de Beso Diverso* protest is now an annual event involving thousands of people. The 2012 *Marcha Invisibles*, on the other hand, joined several disparate protest groups together and motivated 100,000 people to march down the central streets of the capital, San José, in favour of gay rights, the recognition of ethnic minorities, the right to IVF, and the creation of a secular state (T. Gutiérrez, 2012).

The existence of homophobia and the invisibilization of LGBTQ+ communities is still highly prevalent in Costa Rican society, however, with the 2013 case of the chair of the country's human rights commission an example of this. Justo Orozco was forced to step down when he stated that 'la discriminación en Costa Rica sinceramente yo no la veo … La homofobia es un mito, la discriminación real contra homosexuales no existe' (*Gente 10*, 2012, 39). The same issue of *Gente 10* which reports on this, however, also carries a two-page piece about one man's battle with homophobia, as he states that the worst insults one can give in Costa Rica are 'playo', 'maricón', and 'tortillera', and that this naturalized homophobia is so inherent and corrosive in Costa Rican society that many gay people will never openly share their sexuality with their families or friends (2012, 21), thus undermining Justo Orozco's assertion. Although the existence of LGBTQ+ individuals has begun to be recognized in the twenty-first century, then, these groups are not always accepted within society.

In 2015, this became especially apparent as the new advertisement for Costa Rican biscuit company Pozuelo caused uproar on social media as it depicted the different types of families it saw in contemporary Costa Rica, including a male same-sex couple. The debate surrounding this video was polarized, with many people happy that the company was embracing what they saw as modern Costa Rica, while others bemoaned the erosion of traditional, Catholic values surrounding the family (Pozuelo, 2015). The fact that this advert even existed, however, was a step towards the normalization of LGBTQ+ people in the country's official discourse; Jimena Cascante asserts that although it is not easy to have a 'different' sexual or gender orientation to the norm, globalization through the medium of television and film has made great advances for LGBTQ+ people in the country (Harvey-Kattou, 2015). These advances as well as the polarization of society around this issue became more apparent than ever and took on huge political significance in the 2018 presidential elections, however. In January 2018, the Inter-American Court of Human Rights, stationed in Costa Rica, ruled that all its signatory countries had to comply with its ruling fully to legalize same-sex marriage. This provoked jubilant scenes on the one hand and uproar on the other in Costa Rica. While the ruling Partido de Acción Ciudadana (PAC) officially supports gay rights, it also understands that in this religious society legalizing equal marriage would be a polemic move. In fact, soon after this announcement, a previously unknown candidate from minority Partido de Restauración Nacional (PRN), Fabricio Alvarado – a pastor and gospel singer – began a presidential campaign based solely on repealing this legislation and ridding parliament of homosexual politicians (Sequeira, 2018). The results were unprecedented: the PRN secured 24.91 per cent and the PAC 21.66 per cent in the first round, forcing a run-off. On 1 April, however, the PAC and its candidate Carlos Alvarado won with a landslide 60.66 per cent of the vote, demonstrating that perhaps more of the population is accepting of equal marriage than not.

Defining the Costa Rican Internal 'Other': Subalternity, Ethnicity, Gender, Sexuality

While it is clear that the 'official' history of the mainstream *tico* depicts a homogeneous nation in many ways, the history and existence of the Costa Rican internal 'Others' – citizens whose legal and, in many cases, patriotic identity lies in Costa Rican nationality – forcefully undermines this superficial representation. The binary of the *tico*/'Other', which is forcibly disseminated as the norm and which uses a colonial framework to self-perpetuate and exclude, is therefore seen to be flawed and simplistic when attempting to describe a national reality. Indeed, within this history of the 'Other' Costa Rica, it is possible for individuals and groups to straddle both sides of the supposed binary – for example, Afro-Costa Ricans – a marginalized, non-*tico* group – living in the Central Valley – the *tico* centre.

Owing to this more nuanced view of Costa Rican society which this history uncovers, then, constructions of 'Otherness' must be considered in order to examine the portrayal of norms and normative challenge in literary and filmic works. While Spivak accepts that the language of identity is necessarily signified by its own lack or opposition, she also contends that 'definitions are necessary in order to keep us going, to allow us to take a stand' (Landry and Maclean, 1996, 54). The 'Other' can only be recognized, and the norm challenged, through the articulation of both. The normative stance adopted by any one society is determined by Judith Butler as defining 'the parameters of what will and will not appear within the domain of the social' (2004, 42). In Costa Rica's case, the dominant discourse of the *tico* stands as the idealized norm, while its 'Other' is constituted by difference with this. Despite the prevalent rhetoric within this of exceptionalism on a global scale, perhaps this norm is less unique than the *ticos* would believe, as bell hooks frequently refers to the US normative stance in similar terms, denoting it as a 'white supremacist, capitalist, patriarchy' (2000, 19). The theoretical framework surrounding the subalternate, ethnic, gendered, and sexual 'Other' – which stand in contrast to the *tico* norm – must be evaluated in order to interrogate the identity challenges considered in later chapters.

As Gramscian discourse places hegemonic power at the centre of society, with civil society surrounding it and acting according to social norms, it also situates the subaltern at the very edge of civil society as a group which exists within society but without constituting part of it. Alberto Moreiras has termed this dynamic 'the hegemonic circle and ... its counterpart, subaltern force' (2001, 19), and it is this binary relationship which, according to Moreiras, is used as the core critical theory for much of the study of Latin American culture (Moreiras, 2001). Gramsci describes the subaltern as a disunited group made up of feudal peasants or subjugated workers (Hoare and Nowell Smith, 1971, 16 and 52–3), and within the Latin American context, John Beverley suggests that:

> Subaltern studies is about power, who has it and who doesn't, who is gaining it and who is losing it. Power is related to representation: which representations have cognitive authority or can secure hegemony, which do not have authority or are not hegemonic. (Beverley, 1999, 1)

According to this definition, subalternity in Latin America includes any people or communities who are disenfranchised socially, politically, culturally, or economically in some way. Building on this broad definition, Beverley believes that although the discipline of Subaltern Studies began with Ranajit Guha's Subaltern Studies Group in India, which attempted to re-present the Indian peasant into Indian history, the notion of the subaltern can still work for Latin American cultural studies as 'globalization is producing new patterns of domination and exploitation and reinforcing older ones' (1999, 28). He proposes that as Latin America emerges from a cycle of leftist crises and failed revolutions these notions of dominance, globalization, and exploitation are particularly pertinent to the study of the region (6–7).

The Subaltern Studies Group defines the subaltern as a very specific set of people, comprising those who were most harshly exploited during and immediately after colonization, inferred to be the rural classes and the peasantry (Guha, 1997, xv–xxi). Within Latin America, the term has also frequently been used to discuss social groups such as the indigenous and the urban poor who, like the Indian peasants, were the most marginalized groups during and after the colonial period. Owing to the existence of a rhetoric that creates a centre and periphery in Costa Rica, and within it paradigms of internal 'Othering', a discussion of the concept of the subaltern is necessary to understand this debate. While an essentialist reading of the term, as will be demonstrated, renders it misleading for the study of identity, a hybridized reading of the subaltern is key to the exploration of the interaction of national identity with Costa Rican cultural production. It is here that the value of subaltern studies lies when dealing with national identity in this context, and it is the concept of a hybrid subalternity which will be seen in the literary and filmic challenges analysed in Chapters 2 and 3.

As one of the foremost proponents of subaltern theory, Spivak contends that the subaltern stems from the feudal mass which was opposed to, and exploited by, colonial rule, not the native elite which went on to collude with, and profit from, colonialism. The subaltern as a signifier cannot exist without this notion of an elite group coexisting and opposing it, and according to Spivak the elite constantly attempts to take power from its Other (Landry and Maclean, 1996, 212). Spivak also argues, however, that the subaltern has long been seen as a collective consciousness, even though it is sometimes proposed to be a self-conscious state, and that 'the definitive accessibility of subaltern consciousness is counterpointed also by situating it in the place of a difference rather than an identity' (213). Spivak's claim (216) that the subaltern should not be considered as an identity in itself demonstrates her concerns with the potentially essentializing nature of this term.

When analysing the use of the term subaltern, however (chiefly in Spivak's and Beverley's works), it is often seen to become too reductionist, leaving its proponents contradicting their own prior assertions. Beverley, for example, questions Guha's rigid definition of the subaltern as only existing in opposition to the ruling classes, agreeing with Bhabha that in this postcolonial era many scholars call for an end to binaries (Beverley, 1999, 68–88). Despite this assertion, however, Beverley then makes a distinction between hegemonic civil society – which in Latin America he states is white and Eurocentric – and the 'community' – whom he refers to as the indigenous, rural peasantry, setting the two up as binary oppositions (119). Indeed, he concludes that, above all else, subalternity is wrapped up in class: 'class is the form of subalternity that structures the others' (166). Taking the definition of subalternity as something much wider and more far-reaching than Guha's in order to apply the debates it throws up across a global spectrum, I find that reducing the term to being fixed and rooted in class structure alone brings it back to a place of restrictive opposition as an 'Other' to the elite or ruling classes. Beverley therefore appears to reject this dichotomy in one chapter (86–88), before reinforcing it in his conclusion (166), leaving his use of the term subaltern open to essentialist critique.

Looking more broadly at subaltern studies, it has further maintained an inextricable link – throughout history and in academia – with its own 'Other': the hegemonic force. Groups without power do not write history books, and Spivak notes that the principle aim of Guha's Subaltern Studies Group was both to discover and to explore a 'true' peasant consciousness. She indicates the difficulties associated in researching a history that has never been recorded, or which has been written only by its oppressors (Landry and Maclean, 1996, 211). As such, she goes on to argue that the actual subaltern consciousness is 'always askew from its received signifiers' (212), while Beverley suggests (1999, 28–34) that if the subaltern is seen only via the lens of the European model of hegemony then the subaltern's 'Other' is always the one speaking for the group. Spivak adds, of the role of scholars, that 'our role is to produce and be produced by the *official* explanations in terms of the powers that police the entire society ... As we produce the official explanations, we reproduce the official ideology ... We are part of the records we keep' (Landry and Maclean, 1996, 34–6). This statement complicates the study of the subaltern somewhat as if there are no histories telling the story of the marginalized truthfully, with no agenda, and there is no way for a subaltern to speak in the mainstream or official channels of academia or elsewhere, then it should not be possible to recover a subaltern history at all.

This is a key issue in the work of subaltern studies' scholars, and one which has been faced by Spivak herself in her 1988 essay 'Can the Subaltern Speak?', where she considers what she terms to be the 'ventriloquism of the speaking subaltern' as the 'left intellectual's stock-in-trade' (Spivak, 2006, 28). In this essay, she considers ideas of power and disenfranchisement stating that 'there is no unrepresentable subaltern subject that can know and speak itself' so the intellectual must ask 'with what voice-consciousness can the subaltern speak?' (32). Thus, Spivak demonstrates the constraints of the essentialized view of subalternity as she notes that the actual history of the subaltern is unrecoverable and that the insistence of speaking on its behalf is a futile obsession of academia. In the same essay, however, Spivak goes on to answer her original question in the negative: the subaltern cannot speak. While in subsequent works she has called her first version of this paper 'inadvisable' (Landry and Maclean, 1996, 35) and asked that this statement not be taken literally, perhaps Beverley correctly sums up what Spivak meant when he states that 'Gayatri Spivak formulated the problem concisely: If the subaltern could speak – that is, speak in a way that really mattered to us – then it wouldn't be subaltern' (Beverley, 1999, 1). This interpretation is underlined by Spivak herself as she insists that in order for subaltern representation to be possible there must be an 'unlearning project' whereby the 'masculine-imperialist ideological formation', or the way in which we are all conditioned to see the world, must be challenged (Spivak, 2006, 32–3).

She further asserts that work on subaltern issues is really all about the insertion of the subaltern into the mainstream citizenry of space – be it academic or political – and thus brings about the undoing of this subaltern space to begin with (Landry and Maclean, 1996, 207). These statements appear to suggest that one's identity as a subaltern – as a Third World citizen, or as a woman, which are both examples that Spivak uses – somehow disappears if and when one enters the centre by, for example, studying at university. Beverley also states that once the subaltern speaks, they are in the mainstream. These assertions, however, are incongruous with previously stated ideas that individuals, groups, and communities can harbour different, coexisting, hybrid identities, and as such go a long way to essentializing who or what a subaltern group is. To claim that a subaltern is a person with no voice and no power in society does not mean that they do not have the potential to have a voice and power within the mainstream while still located in some way at the margins, opposing hegemony.

Spivak's claim that in moving from the margin to the centre one is disqualified as a subaltern is discussed in relation to her own experience of academia. Emphasizing her difference as a woman – stating that she is accepted because the centre 'welcomes selective inhabitants of the margin in order better to exclude the margin' (Landry and Maclean, 1996, 35) – she contends that her goal is to 'narrate a displacement' between margin and centre (35). In this way, Spivak claims a nuanced view of marginality for herself – she is still marginalized as a woman while working in academia – but does not extend this complexity to those she would label as subaltern. And in this way also, the term becomes no more than a negative label forced upon a studied group which can be used to marginalize it even further. Similarly, Beverley states in one chapter (1999, 42) that he does not consider Toni Morrison or Salman Rushdie as subaltern by virtue of their education, and yet he later states that he hopes that when university students read the work of an indigenous woman, *I, Rigoberta Menchú*, it will be with a feeling of discomfort, as the subaltern may be 'a component of their own personal identity' (71). He makes this statement despite the fact that they are studying at an academic institution, and therefore would not be classed as subalterns by his own prior definition. This demonstrates how holding on to the term subaltern as a rigid notion of class or social position refuses to allow for the articulation of the differences of identity encapsulated within each individual or group.

Moreover, specifically within Latin American studies, theorists such as Alberto Moreiras have contended that these traditional notions of difference have been worn out and no longer apply to the discipline. He states that 'what today are outdated concepts of identity and difference' (Moreiras, 2001, 4) must be questioned, even if it is uncomfortable for academics themselves to do so. Furthermore, Moreiras dismisses subaltern theory, claiming that in adhering to the hegemony/subaltern dichotomy the whole of Latin America becomes a homogenized area of study. With this, he claims, comes the 'active production of othering or abjection' of the subaltern (32–3). By so believing in the very concept of a subaltern group, the real people constituting it are ever more pushed to the periphery of society; they are 'Othered' even more. He also argues that looking at the changing way in which identity is formed and through which it evolves it is clear that, in many cases, neither is the imperial force trying to maintain control nor is the subaltern force trying to inflict social change. In his words:

> a critical perspective on the infinitude of the social is therefore a kind of absolute historicism and also necessarily a radical opening to the subaltern position, calling as such for the permanent destabilization of hegemonic ideology and the passage to thinking beyond hegemony. (Moreiras, 2001, 263)

With this assertion Moreiras' suggestion is not just that in the act of using one mode of critical thought to analyse Latin American societies is academia being essentialist, but that the actual mode of thought itself is absolutist in its own manner.

While a rigid or reductionist notion of subalternity is therefore inadvisable for the study of Costa Rican cultural production and challenge, when the subaltern is considered in its hybridized, nuanced sense many of the assertions around it become valuable for this project. Indeed, Spivak contends that the subaltern can be studied as 'a space of difference' without the 'implicit assumption of cultural supremacy' (Landry and Maclean, 1996, 293). This space in which marginal identities exist, then, is also a point of dialogue and mutual learning and this is far from the essentializing claim that the subaltern cannot represent itself. Spivak would now appear to be arguing for a more flexible definition of the term, allowing for hybridity within the very concept of the subaltern. Taking the subaltern to connote discriminated groups such as women, ethnic and cultural minorities, and LGBTQ+ communities, the notions of subalternity and hybridity can work in tandem. I therefore argue that the semantics of the word subaltern have become intertwined in a power play of political and cultural opposition where mainstream is associated with positive connotations, while the subaltern is a negative term, but where scholars simultaneously champion the reversal of these roles. Despite the pertinence of the useful observations made by subaltern studies' scholars to the study of disenfranchised or marginalized groups within Costa Rica, adhering to subalternity as an essential term means that it cannot be used to discuss the fluid, hybrid, and plural nature of identity. One individual may identify with some aspects of the *tico* – living in San José, ethnically identifying as white, for example – but not with others – they may also be a feminist and critical of the traditional, Catholic teachings of the family. The marginalized or those rendered powerless in some situations are not necessarily those existing solely at the periphery of society as subaltern theory appears to suggest.

While a hybridized discussion of the subaltern advances towards a more nuanced view of Costa Rica's power structures, then, it does not touch on the specific themes of 'race', gender, and sexuality, which are used to exclude some inhabitants of the nation. Although arbitrary distinctions of 'racial' difference form a persistent dialogue in the modern world, it has been pointed out by Henry Louis Gates that 'race ... as a set of irreducible differences within the human species – is a scientific fallacy' (Ashcroft et al., 2006, 211). He further contends that 'race' is a no more than a constructed trope used for economic or political practices, created by the Western world in order to invade and conquer other regions and justify discriminatory policies such as the slave trade (216–17). The notion of 'race' as a biological category or an essence which manifests itself in physical characteristics is therefore unfounded and redundant. When the creation of social and cultural global systems has presupposed the veracity of the category for so long, however, the understanding of this term as a historical falsehood becomes problematic when discussing groups of people who identify with, or have been discriminated against, because of their perceived 'race', such as Afro-Costa Ricans.

It is with this in mind that the term 'ethnicity' has been offered to speak about the different cultural practices that exist from one country to another, or from one community or tradition to another, regardless of 'race' or differing physical attributes. Stuart Hall writes extensively about the term ethnicity and its implications, using the constructed 'black race' as his example. In a co-authored 2001 book, he states that:

> 'Black' does not reference a particular group, with fixed characteristics, whose social being or artistic imagination is determined by skin colour, genetic make-up or biological inheritance. It does not invoke an essentialized cultural identity, frozen in time, which is automatically transmitted into the work, and can thus be held to 'represent' collectively all those who belong to a particular 'race', ethnic community, or tradition. 'Black' ... is a politically, historically and culturally constructed category; a contested idea, whose ultimate destination remains unsettled. (Hall and Sealy, 2001, 35)

Hall, then, establishes that 'race' is a manufactured term kept in existence by social norms and as such he rejects the use of the concept as a way of defining groups or communities. On this point he also considers representation, explaining that it is impossible to separate completely the political from the cultural. He states that 'the question of the black subject cannot be represented without reference to the dimensions of class, gender, sexuality and ethnicity' (Hall and Sealy, 2006, 201), demonstrating that the very nature of identity is intrinsically intersectional and must be treated as such – in opposition to how most national identities are constructed.

In order to consider cultural differences within multicultural societies, Hall does agree that some terminology is needed. He states that:

> Ethnicity *can* be a constitutive element in the most viciously regressive kind of nationalism or national identity. But in our time, as in an imaginary community, it is also beginning to carry some other meanings and to define a new space for identity. It insists on difference – on the fact that every identity is placed, positioned, in a culture, a language, a history ... But it is not necessarily armour plated against other identities. It is not tied to fixed, permanent, unalterable oppositions. It is not wholly defined by exclusion. (Hall, 1993, 138)

According to Hall, ethnicity is completely separate from 'race'. Although it is also a historical concept, it is a part of identity which each individual can construct themselves through their own culture, heritage, nation, language, and history. Although, as he asserts, ethnicity as a term has been used to foster a spirit of xenophobic nationalism in the past, he believes that the notion is being, and to some extent has already been, revalorized as a fluid, hybrid concept within which all people can situate their own identity. This idea is also expressed by Henry Louis Gates when he actively agrees with Hall's definition of ethnicity, stating:

> I want to stress the *departure* entailed by his [Hall's] call to separate the concept of ethnicity from 'an equivalence with nationalism, imperialism, racism and the state.' This proves one of the enabling gestures for a post-essentialist recuperation of identity. The problem with the post-structuralist critiques of ethnic absolutism was that they quickly led to a sort of post-modern universalism that foreclosed the possibility of a politics of identity. Stuart Hall's reinstatement of 'ethnicity' is meant to counter-balance this tendency. (Gates, 2010, 45)

This definition of ethnicity challenges deconstructionist attempts to create a dialogue around identity and culture which actually conclude in cultural and 'racial' universalisms: the very concepts the discipline seeks to annul. Instead, seeing ethnicity as a concept which is not defined by exclusion allows it to be described and expressed as an ever-changing state, and to illustrate the diversities it encompasses. It is this definition which can be used to encompass ideas of linguistic, historical, and cultural belonging of groups such as Afro-Costa Ricans or indigenous communities, as discrimination against these groups is multifaceted and intersectional.

Using a similar, deconstructive argument, Butler underlines her agreement with Hall, suggesting that 'race' is constantly reconstructed in modern society in order to maintain and control the normative discourse (Blumenfeld and Breen, 2005, 11–12). She aligns this argument with her own surrounding gender and sexuality theory. She asserts that, like 'race', the notion of gender as a natural and biological phenomenon is interpellated through dominant social rules (14). Although sex, she contends, is to some extent contained within the body,[3] cultural variations as well as overlaps take place: people do not always maintain the sex assigned to them by their bodies (13). This re-reading of sex as assigned but never assumed signals her move away from the presumption of essential sexual difference (13), while

---

3 A notion contested by trans theorists which will be seen in the analysis of *Abrázame como antes* in Chapter 3.

the dichotomy of sex as biological and gender as the 'cultural meanings that the sexed body assumes' (Butler, 1999, 10) is contested. This signifies that these two facets of identity – sex and gender – do not necessarily denote continuity. Indeed, the assumption that the gendered binary of man/ woman and male/female exists, implies that gender merely mirrors sex and is therefore restricted or prescribed by it. As identities exist that break with this rigid trajectory, however, Butler argues that this simply cannot be the case (Blumenfeld and Breen, 2005, 10).

Noting that 'gender ought not to be construed as a stable identity or locus of agency from which various acts follow; rather, gender is an identity tenuously constituted in time, instituted in an exterior space through a *stylized repetition of acts*' (1999, 179), Butler chimes with Hall's views of a fluid identity politics. She also uses this statement to assert that gender is one of many historically and politically constructed categories used to uphold the prevailing social discourses – in this case heteronormativity and patriarchy. She contends that 'gender is a matter of doing and its effects rather than an inherent attribute, an intrinsic feature' (Blumenfeld and Breen, 2005, 20) and that the norms associated with the constructed genders of femininity and masculinity operate by requiring the embodiment of the social ideals surrounding gender (1993, 22). Spivak also contends that 'nationalism was related to reproductive heteronormativity as a source of legitimacy' (2010, 13), further demonstrating the links between nationalism and patriarchy as the two go hand in hand in the rhetoric of patriotism. These gendered norms have been widely documented by feminist scholars, and Spivak further states that the emotional, sexual, and domestic have been privately constituted and related to the female, while power, society, and economics have been public discourses represented by the male (Landry and Maclean, 1996, 30). Butler adds to this discussion that 'the cultural associations of mind with masculinity and body with femininity are well documented' (1999, 17), while Mary Eagleton asserts that 'according to binary thinking, the male and the masculine constitutes the norm, the positive and the superior; the female and the feminine is the aberration, the negative, the inferior' (2011, 270). These contentions highlight the association of the woman with femininity, as well as defining woman as a subjected being who is told through the interpellation of gendered ideals that she is inferior to man. They also demonstrate the extent to which postcolonial power structures are mirrored within the concept of identity.

Butler, like Fanon, also asserts that this social norm maintains its dominance as it is internalized by its subjects before being outwardly performed by them. Similar to Bhabha's concept of mimicry, she describes this notion of performativity as the 'practice by which gendering occurs, the embodying of norms is a compulsory practice, a forcible production, but not for that reason fully determining' (Blumenfeld and Breen, 2005, 22). The norm is, therefore, exposed as 'exclusionary and its ideality as normative' (20); it enforces performativity while at the same time masking it as a consequence of the 'natural' binary of man/woman and male/female. Due to the unchallenged consumption of this ideal, gender is constantly performed by individuals without them willing it to happen; it is a situation of constraint where the individual chooses neither their own gender nor the rules associated with it (Butler, 2004, 1). This notion of performing an identity without being fully able to represent or even identify with it is a core concept when dealing with the challenging of the *tico* norm through cultural production. As certain groups internalize the ideal, subconsciously internalize their own inferiority, and then perform their prescribed social role, others, according to Butler's ideology, consistently challenge normative assumptions.

This debate around the constructed and performed nature of gender, sex, and sexuality, according to Spivak, does not argue for the reversal of this male/female dichotomy, but to reflect what she calls a 'shifting limit' (Landry and Maclean, 1996, 31) between the two. Indeed, Butler's solution to the deconstruction of this binary coincides with Spivak's, as she also argues that:

> If one 'is' a woman, that is surely not all one is; the term fails to be exhaustive, not because a pregendered 'person' transcends the specific paraphernalia of its gender, but because gender is not always constituted coherently or consistently in different historical contexts, and because gender intersects with racial, class, ethnic, sexual, and regional modalities of discursively constituted identities. (Butler, 1999, 6)

This statement rejects gendered essentialism, demonstrating that although gender norms exist and are labelled as masculine and feminine, no man or woman can fully embody these social ideals. Many other aspects of identity always come into play, and one cannot be defined by a gender – whether identifying with it or not – because of the multiplicity of personhood. This leads her to contend that hybridity is experienced by all, as 'even if we accept the descriptive viability of terms such as "masculine" and "feminine", who among us has identifications with just one?' (Blumenfeld and Breen, 2005, 24). In this way Butler clearly demonstrates the possibility to live out more than one sex, gender, and sexuality at once, and reflects the constraining nature of gender stereotypes which, in fact, make it impossible for an individual to live out the idealized norm. This assertion interlinks with the notion of the glorified identity of the *tico* which is so specific in its formulation and articulation that it is has become entirely unattainable for most, if not all, Costa Rican citizens.

The hybridity of individuals, therefore, signifies that sex does not anticipate gender, and that neither gender nor sex direct sexuality. Butler argues that sexuality is a desire stemming from the body – both imagined and lived – which comes from the body's sense of possibility. Sexuality does not derive merely from the type of body one has, nor from the gender traits one associates with (Blumenfeld and Breen, 2005, 17). Although the dominant stance of heterosexism attempts to preclude the notion of homosexuals or transsexuals as a part of the mainstream, no person can fully inhabit the gendered name given to them as part of their sexual and social identity, thereby destabilizing the concept of sex–gender–sexuality as an interlinking and rigidly prescribed path (Butler, 1993, 18). This does not mean, however, that identity categories are no longer available, and Butler makes it clear that people must be allowed to group together under one banner in order to challenge social norms, despite the very real differences between them (Butler, 1993, 23). This argument leads Butler to revalorize the term 'queer' and the notion of a 'queer space' where different identities can meet in order to reflect on a shared experience of being marginalized, as well as to confront the social norms that push these identities to the periphery (19). The promotion of this queer identity as one which is fluid and capable of moving away from history and tradition strikes a chord with the Costa Rican context: the *tico* identity has seemingly remained unchanged and, often, unchallenged, since the birth of the independent nation. If this queer space is one of protest and non-conformity, then this is where much Costa Rican cultural production lies.

Within this queer space, then, there are many possibilities concerning ethnicity, sex, gender, and identity, and, as Butler states, the list usually ends with an 'embarrassed "etc."', which is 'a sign of the exhaustion as well as of the illimitable process of signification itself' (1999, 182). This demonstrates that although social norms and dominant ideologies will always exist – be they concerned with ethnicity, gender, sexuality, or other facets of identity – it is not their presence which must be called into question, but their composition. Ashcroft et al. have concluded (2006, 234) that feminist, queer, and postcolonial theories have in common their desire to 'reinstate the marginalized in the face of the dominant' through the questioning of normative concepts of identity which can be seen in cultural practice. This undoing of the restrictive normative concepts of gender, sexuality, and ethnicity forms part of the struggle for the right to be conceived as a human when one does not form part of, or identify with, the social norms associated with these concepts.

Although these notions of the deconstruction of rigid identity categories all hold counterhegemonic aims at their core, however, recent scholarship has noted the failure of identity theory to highlight the multiplicity and plurality of individuals. As identities embody several different aspects which can include but are not limited to an ethnicity, nationality, gender, tradition, or sexuality, it is possible for one individual to exist within many different groups, signifying that one sole aspect of identity cannot define a whole being. Kimberlé Crenshaw added a new dimension to this discussion when she coined the term 'intersectionality' to deal with the dual and therefore disproportionate discrimination certain groups – in her studies African-American women – face. Many other theorists have since argued for the emergence of an intersectional discourse whereby it is recognized that individuals can be at once oppressed and oppressors – demonstrating that not even these labels are essential (hooks, 2000, 16; Puwar, 2004, 7–11; Lykke, 2010); and these ideas tie in with Hall's concept of ethnicity and Butler's of the queer space. This concern with intersectionality also coincides with Bhabha's and Moreira's assertion that globalization is altering both national and academic discourses, and it is these changing conceptions of identity politics in an ever-globalizing Costa Rica which are analysed in Chapters 2 and 3.

Although critical theory is the defining backbone of the analytical discussion of cultural production, Spivak reminds us that there is not a one-size-fits-all solution as she states that 'theoretical descriptions cannot produce universals. They can only ever produce provisional generalizations' (Landry and Maclean, 1996, 218). Interrogating the *tico* imaginary, then, demonstrates that although when grouped together through a shared national identity Costa Ricans as one community may portray a happy facade – perhaps the happiest in the world – beneath the surface several communities identifying as Costa Ricans are often excluded from the idealized concept of the *tico*. Bhabha states (1990, 4) that cultural production and creation happen in the space which lies at the margins of the nation-state, and it is this hybrid space – which attempts to change habitus and normative behaviours – which has produced fecund periods of literary and media challenge to the very idea of national identity in Costa Rica. The following chapters therefore demonstrate that hegemonic ideologies as well as their counterdiscourses can, and do, inhabit the same national spaces, each fighting for legitimacy.

CHAPTER TWO

Coded Messages: Costa Rican Protest Literature, 1970–1985

O wing to the power and prevalence of the traditional image of the *tico*, the Costa Rican internal 'Other' began to be discussed by national authors in the sociological revolution and literary 'boom' of the 1970s (Quesada Soto, 2008, 103). Following the birth of the *Segunda República* in 1948, Costa Rica found itself surrounded by civil war and protest movements. While Costa Rica's own sociological revolution of the 1970s was less pronounced than the Nicaraguan civil war or the US civil rights movements, for example – as protests and strikes in Costa Rica occurred but were uncommon[1] – the decade sparked the awakening of a new kind of social consciousness. This in turn saw a surge in literature used as soft power in the 1970s as it was written to question national identity, and several of the country's most famous and prolific authors published their first works in this decade (Quesada Soto, 2008, 103). It is common among this generation of authors – who had grown up hearing the promises of the Second Republic governments[2] – to underline their indignation when faced with social injustice with what Álfaro Quesada Soto describes as an 'énfasis en el análisis de las nuevas transformaciones en la vida urbana y el campo que nacían con el nuevo proyecto modernizador, y con una posición ideológica más cercana a la socialdemocracia al que comunismo' (2008, 104). The everyday existence of those living in both urban and rural areas in the country had changed since 1948, but many of the social

---

1 The only mass protests and strikes in this decade were associated with the student movement's demonstrations against the bauxite exploration works which were to be carried out by US company ALCOA in 1970 in San Isidro El General. For more on the ALCOA protests of 1970, see O'Neal, 2010.

2 The 1948 civil war was ignited by alleged government corruption – which included vote rigging – and Figueres' revolutionary government promised to put an end to a range of social injustices when in power. This included offering healthcare and education to all citizens, giving women the vote, and making Afro-Costa Ricans born in the country Costa Rican citizens. For more on the civil war, see Bell, 1996.

guarantees which the revolutionary government had advertised were still yet to be seen.

As such, the works published in the 1970s by the country's most distinguished authors of this era contain several references to the social development of the nation, especially the notion that what they saw and documented was at odds with the patriotic ideals of social reform and justice. Chiefly, they hold at their core the narrative of marginality which challenges the social norms enshrouding Costa Rica. It has been noted that the use of literature as a form of social protest became common in this era; as Seidy Araya states: 'La novela costarricense en la década 1960–1970 se desarrolla por los cauces de una visión de mundo burguesa-existencialista y otra de índole popular y socialista' (Araya, 2003, 199) – the author of the latter, she argues, 'supera los límites de la crítica reformista, traslada al futuro la feliz culminación de la lucha y elabora una protagonista de complicada organización anímica, que supera la soledad y busca la solidaridad humana' (199). Costa Rican literature of the past had focused on the traditional figure of the heroic labourer, and this rural space is depicted as the norm in several works of the early twentieth century.[3] This new wave of 1970s literature, however, put the urban community at the centre of the narrative while also revalorizing the internal 'Others' who were found at the margins of society.[4] As such, this generation of authors who first published in the late 1960s and 1970s came to be characterized by the new social voices and concerns found in their works.

Although Quesada argues (2008, 105) that some marginalized groups, or Costa Rican 'Others', may have had a presence in literature before the 1970s, it is clear that this presence was previously manifest predominantly in terms of stereotype or caricature.[5] In the protest literature of the 1970s, not only did

---

3 The best-known example of this is Carlos Luis Fallas' *Mamita Yunai* (1941), which tells the story of a rural activist who challenges government corruption and unfair labour practices. Other examples include *El moto* by Joaquín García Monge (1900), *Concherías* by Aquileo Echeverría (1905) or *Ese que llaman pueblo* by Fabián Dobles (1942).

4 Abelardo Bonilla's detailed 1957 anthology of Costa Rican literature, *Historia de la literatura costarricense*, demonstrates this through a close analysis of both the history of Costa Rica and the literature published in the country. For more on this trend, see also Sotela, 1920; 1923; 1927; 1942 and Abreu Gómez, 1950. For works on Costa Rican literature in the second half of the twentieth century, see Portugés de Bolaños, 1964; Castro Rawson, 1971; Chase, 1975; and Quesada Soto, 2008.

5 The most salient examples of these can be found in the works *Puerto Limón* or *Cocorí* by *limonense* author Joaquín Gutiérrez, who wrote extensively about community relations and the Afro-Costa Rican population of Limón from a *mestizo* point of view.

the protagonists hail from a position of social marginality, but the themes contained within the works were also taboo – Carmen Naranjo's titular story from the collection *Ondina*, for example, narrates an act of bestiality. As with any form of protest, writing against commonly held beliefs and values in Costa Rica at this time was associated with risk-taking. Authors had to think not only of their reputations but also of their professional and family lives. It was entirely possible that they could be blacklisted for life, unable to publish works of fiction if they established a reputation for airing non-conformist views. Additionally, many national authors of this era also worked in academia or for the government – both tenuous public positions which they could easily lose. These potential concerns explain the frequent use of allegory and code in the protest literature of this period. The use of allegory as a literary device has a long tradition, and allegorical texts are often employed by authors for social, narrative, and aesthetic reasons. As Angus Fletcher points out, 'In the simplest terms, allegory says one thing and means another. It destroys the normal expectation we have about language, that our words "mean what they say"' (2012, 2). He also asserts that allegory adds to the 'fundamental process of encoding our speech' (2012, 3). When considering the use of allegory in the Costa Rican context, then, it is clear that authors could use the technique to completely encode, partially mask, or attempt to soften the impact of the social agenda behind their texts.

While the most extreme version of this use of allegory or code turns a text into what Fletcher terms 'the ironic aenigma [enigma]' – or one written entirely in code so that the state cannot understand what the masses can (2012, 8) – it is more likely to involve a narrative story and a subtext, which could be made as transparent or as opaque as the author wishes. While the surface narrative must always tell a story which can stand alone, the subtext imbues the text with a secondary or dual meaning – one which the author may struggle to utter openly for fear of censorship or reprisal. This leaves readers to play a more active role in the work itself, forcing them to uncover clues in order to find the ambiguous, hidden, or encoded message left by the author. Debra Castillo claims (1992, 71) that this type of narrative makes the readers themselves protagonists in the work, enabling them to take what they want from literature in the same way a chef takes what s/he wants from a recipe. I would add that when a reader has worked hard to uncover the hidden meaning in a work it forces them to participate in the author's protest message: they either mobilize in agreement with the author by challenging the prevailing ideology or they are made to be complicit in the perpetuating of the norms against which the author stands. Quesada alludes to this when referring to Costa Rican authors as he notes that this generation of the 1970s wrote 'un tipo de escritura que exige un nuevo tipo de lector' (2008, 108). This new reader is one who seeks out the social message behind the text. These critical texts were easily accessible in the 1970s, and several authors of this era sought to highlight themes which were considered to be unpatriotic or un*tico*, such as gender inequality, sexual difference, racism, prejudice, class injustices, and government corruption. This generation of authors, known as the 'generación de los 70' includes renowned and prolific authors Quince Duncan, Carmen Naranjo, and Alfonso Chase, who all narrate their works from the margins of society due to their ethnicity, gender, or sexuality.

Allegories of Identity
in *Los cuatro espejos* by Quince Duncan

Born in 1940, Quince Duncan Moodie is a third-generation Afro-Costa Rican author of Jamaican and Barbadian descent who grew up in the *limonense* town of Estrada on the country's Caribbean coast (Mosby, 2003, 3). Duncan is Costa Rica's first published Afro-Costa Rican author and his first novel, *Hombres curtidos*, appeared in 1971 after he had studied for his BA and MA at the Universidad Nacional in Heredia in Costa Rica's Central Valley, before moving to St Olaf's, in the USA, to complete his PhD on human rights. Moving back to Costa Rica upon completion of his doctorate, he has since become one of the country's most prolific authors, having written short stories, novels, essays, and children's literature. As a result – and because of his incisive critique of national culture – Duncan has been described by literary critic Ian Smart (1984, 51) as the most important Costa Rican author of the twentieth century. In addition to his literary career, Duncan has also occupied various academic positions in Costa Rica and the USA, while remaining politically active in government initiatives to increase integration between the Afro-Costa Rican community of Limón and the rest of the country. In 2015, at the age of 74, he was appointed *Comisionado de Asuntos de la Comunidad Afrocostarricense* by the Solís administration which was also the first to declare Costa Rica to be a multiethnic and pluricultural country (Sequeira, 2014).

When naming Quince Duncan, academic literature, newspaper articles, and television presenters always point out that he is *afro-costarricense* (Smart, 1984; Martin-Ogunsola, 2004; Sequeira, 2014). Clearly taking an essentialized view of an author whose works cover such a variety of themes could be described as narrow, but it is actually a denomination that Duncan welcomes, and it certainly becomes a central theme of many of his works (Q. Duncan, 2009). The distinction between being Costa Rican and Afro-Costa Rican is important for Duncan not just because he feels his own very acute sense of ancestral history, as well as the sense of living in a racialized, postcolonial world, but also because his ethnic heritage has shaped his literature – and the reception of it – profoundly.[6] His works from the 1970s are particularly enveloped in social critique, having been influenced by both the US civil rights movements and the changes in Costa Rica's official attitude towards Afro-Costa Ricans after the 1948 revolution (Q. Duncan, 2013). Of the themes in his work, Duncan himself states that 'yo sigo un militante por la justicia social' (Q. Duncan, 2013), demonstrating his preoccupation with the integration and acceptance of ethnic and cultural difference within the country.

Duncan therefore formed a core part of the shift of consciousness towards a protest literature in 1970s Costa Rica, choosing to use his soft power as an author to bring an awareness of the history, traditions, and struggles of the Afro-Costa Rican population to a wider, pan-Costa Rican audience (Q. Duncan, 2005). Indeed, his novels often conclude that Afro-Costa Rica forms a valid and diverse – but not separate – part of national society, and as such should be accepted by the rest of Costa Rica and more widely integrated into the 'official' national imaginary. Due to the prejudice which Duncan argues is present within Costa Rican academic and literary practice, however, his works have seldom been recognized in his home country,[7] with his most significant critics hailing from the USA and the Caribbean. As such, academics such as Richard Jackson, Ian Smart, Dorothy Mosby, and Dellita Martin-Ogunsola have written extensively about the ways in which Duncan depicts Afro-Costa Rican traditions, describing his works as forming a part of a pan-Caribbean, or Afro-diasporic, literary tradition rather than in relation to Costa Rica as a nation.[8]

6 In a 2013 interview (Q. Duncan, 2013), Duncan stated that he has made the conscious decision to write short stories and novels where Afro-Costa Ricans played the main characters, and where racial prejudice influenced the narrative, up to and including *Un mensaje de Rosa*, which was published in 2005.

7 Duncan's much used example of this prejudice can be seen in his choice to write and submit his novel *Final de calle* (1980) (which takes place in the civil war and makes no mention of the Afro-Costa Rican community) anonymously to the committee of the *Premio Nacional de Literatura*. When this novel (which Duncan maintains is one of his worst) won the prize, he noted the committee's dismayed reaction upon finding out the true identity of the author. He also claims he had never been awarded a prize for his other works because of the excuse that his Spanish was simply not up to scratch due to his 'condition' as an Afro-Costa Rican (Q. Duncan, 2013).

8 For more on this, see Smart, 1984; Mosby, 2003; Martin-Ogunsola, 2004; and Jackson, 1998.

Duncan's works generally portray the interplay between different cultures inhabiting the same space, narrating the psychological and cultural damage that prejudice causes the individual and the community. Within Costa Rica, although official racism had been discredited by law following the 1948 revolution, the topic of the nation's 'racial purity' and issues of prejudice have continued. Indeed, his characters often display the harmful consequences of the Eurocentric inferiority complex imposed on them as narrated by Fanon. This focus has come about because of Duncan's belief that all authors are shaped by their own background and viewpoint. He states that writers must:

> reconstruir la realidad a partir de su particular visión del mundo. Pero en esa reconstrucción, uno está socialmente programado, y no puede evitarlo. Esa programación es natural, tiene mucho que ver con tu ambiente, tiene mucho que ver con la sociedad en que te crías, y tiene mucho que ver con el impacto que estas dos cosas realicen en tu psique personal. (Q. Duncan, 2013)

Duncan's position as an Afro-Costa Rican originally from Limón but now living in the Central Valley, and as a member of the academic elite, means that Duncan's own lived experience of these cultural clashes is often narrated in his works. Moreover, by using Spanish, rather than his mother tongue of English, Duncan writes for a pan-Costa Rican audience – not just an Afro-Costa Rican one. His use of allegory also further helps a non-Afro-Costa Rican reader gain a deeper understanding of the dangers of segregation and discrimination since in this decade perceptions of Costa Rican national identity were in flux, and the traditionally prescribed model of what it was to be *tico* was openly beginning to be questioned. Through his writing, then, Duncan attempts to undermine dominant definitions of the ethnically European and monocultural *tico*, with his novel, *Los cuatro espejos*, a prime example of how normative society is viewed through Duncan's eyes and how he uses the novel to challenge this norm.

Written in 1973, Duncan's novel *Los cuatro espejos* uses a non-linear narrative to detail the journey of its protagonist and narrator Charles McForbes from his home in San José back to the province of his childhood and early adult life, Limón. Although the account begins in San José where Charles, an Afro-Costa Rican, lives with his *mestiza* wife Ester, the plot starts in a small village in Limón where Charles had worked as a farmer and a Christian priest alongside his Afro-Costa Rican wife Lorena. This portion of his story is told entirely through flashbacks, and it soon becomes clear that Charles left this life in Limón after a curse was put on Lorena which eventually caused her death. While Lorena was still ill, Charles moved her care to a hospital in San José and he remained in the city permanently after her death. After meeting Ester – the daughter of Lorena's doctor – the reader is told by the omniscient narrator that Charles fell in love with her white skin and social status, and the pair married. He then began to forge a life for himself as a professor of English literature at the *Universidad de Costa Rica* in San José, where he lives among the white elite. It is here that the novel begins – the morning after an event about the place of Afro-Caribbean and indigenous people in the nation, which Charles organized, despite feeling detached from the issue himself – as Charles looks in a mirror but cannot see his own face. Initially thinking he may be going blind, or mad, Charles wanders the streets of the capital to clear his head, reminiscing about his past in Limón, before, impulsively, catching the train to go back there. Once there, however, he is confronted with the realization that he no longer knows who he is or where his roots lie. Upon arriving in his home town once more, looking for continuity, he finds that the lives he was once a part of have moved on. This sudden understanding forces him to accept that his life is, in fact, in San José, and when he returns to Ester and his life in the city he resolves to stay and make his home there, asking Ester to accept her life married to an Afro-Costa Rican and all that comes with that. It is only then that he is able to see his face reflected in the mirror once more.

Through Charles' first-person narrative and via an omniscient narrator whose voice enters the novel periodically to offer an alternative viewpoint, several key aspects of Costa Rican identity and national life become apparent. It is also immediately obvious to the reader that there are two stories being told. On the surface, *Los cuatro espejos* gives the reader an insight into life in Limón and San José, as well as Afro-Costa Rican culture and traditions, while also telling the story of a philanderer who has something akin to a mid-life crisis. Beneath this superficial reading, however, lies the allegorical story of a man marginalized because of his ethnicity and all the associations that go with it. Duncan's use of four mirrors signals his employment of a self-reflexive code in this work, as they demonstrate both the instability and changing nature of identity as well as the theme of self-understanding which encompasses the novel for both Charles and the reader. Indeed, beneath the superficial reading we see a man in the midst of an identity crisis caused by Fanon's notion of the internalization of racial prejudice, and it is in this way that Charles stands in for the entire Afro-Costa Rican population. This reading not only highlights the plight of the 'nowhereans' – to borrow Perry and Sawyers' term (1995, 218) – but also gives the reader a clear depiction of Duncan's ultimate solution: the challenging of what constitutes the national norm.

Normative Discourses

Within *Los cuatro espejos* Duncan sets up the normative, *tico* discourse before subverting and undermining it in order to allow his readers to question and critique it. Indeed, the mainstream is described as 'white', racist, patriarchal, and existing only in the Central Valley. The question of ethnicity and discrimination is detailed in considerable depth, and Duncan narrates incidents ranging from the propagation of harmful ethnic stereotypes to cases of overt racist abuse through Charles' first-person accounts. These even occur within his own family, as Charles' wife Ester and his father-in-law Dr Centeno are seen to be prejudiced. Indeed, on one occasion Dr Centeno says to Ester, 'ya se sabe: no es lo mismo ser negro que ser hombre. Porque los hombres son blancos' (122). This demonstrates the normative belief that humanity and masculinity are preserves of one 'race' and that Dr Centeno equates whiteness with personhood, an idea originally constructed to uphold the legality of slavery, as, if only the 'white race' is human, then it can use others as it pleases. This also sets up in the narrative a Eurocentric hierarchy within Costa Rican society where 'whites' are men and superior and Afro-Costa Ricans and women are inferior.

The instilling of these beliefs as 'normal' also occurs at a young age: Ester recalls tormenting the only Afro-Costa Rican boy in her class at school saying, 'Blaky solo entiende de cacao y banana' (105), thereby mocking the agricultural roots of the Afro-Costa Rican population. Duncan also points out that her attitude was developed in childhood: 'era su realidad: "el negro descendiente del mono es un ser en estado de evolución permanentemente inferior" y punto' (107). This acceptance of the very notion of the existence of biological 'races', and then the animalization of a 'race' purported to be inferior, allows her and her father to see Afro-Costa Ricans as a sub-human species (120). This clearly ties in with Said's assertion that 'Orientalism' – or the negative 'Othering' of people of colour – is a prominent social discourse, one which means that the idea of white supremacy is subliminally assumed – through habit or the unconscious interpellation of ideals – from childhood.

The notion that Costa Rica is a nation ethnically descended from Europeans is also highlighted by Charles as he speaks to his first wife, Lorena, to whom he recalls pointing out that Independence Day in the country only celebrates 'el indio asesinado y sus propios descendientes mestizos cantan la gloria del conquistador' (88). This statement creates a view of Costa Rican society which mirrors Charles' own journey: so desperate for progress and to fit in with the Western world, the country preaches outward celebrations of diversity – through the *Día de la Raza* – while actively and purposely rejecting its real history of indigeneity. This contradiction in the nation's behaviour demonstrates Butler and Spivak's contention (2007) that the nation-state actively excludes those it does not wish to recognize as a valuable part of the nation while also exhibiting the idea that Costa Rica must always officially present itself as a stable, happy, peaceful country.

This narrative of an inharmonious nation continues as Charles recounts his encounters with discrimination on the streets of the capital, San José. After a brief altercation has broken up on a street corner and Charles walks away from the scene, a young girl shouts after him 'negro desgraciado' (31), a heinous insult in Costa Rica, but one which does not seem to shock the passers-by. In another incident, when on a bus in San José, Charles hears a Costa Rican shout repeatedly at a black man in English, asking him to move, assuming that he cannot understand Spanish. When the man replies in perfect Spanish, she immediately assumes he is Panamanian and not *limonense*, showing that in the mindset of the *tico*, *limonenses* are separate from the nation and are expected to be English speakers only (20). This prompts Charles to recall the words of the speaker from the previous night's symposium; 'Si una persona latina emplea mal el género, la audiencia comprende que fue un error sin importancia. Si un negro comete la misma falta, provocará la sonrisa irónica del público' (20). This statement highlights the fact that the perceived difference between *ticos* and Afro-Costa Ricans goes further than skin colour and culture: they have also become a linguistic 'Other'.

This discussion of multifaceted elements of identity – and therefore also of discrimination – strengthens Hall's contention that 'race' is often too reductive when combating racism, as one's ethnicity encompasses other aspects outside an idea of 'race' based on skin colour, and racism can take many forms. Ethnic background in this first instance denotes that a negative cultural stereotype of Afro-Costa Ricans exists in *tico* society while the second demonstrates linguistic prejudice. Moreover, from the anecdote provided by Charles we learn that an Afro-Costa Rican speaker has been brought into the space of the academic and cultural elite only to be privately derided. This is reminiscent of Spivak's view that the 'centre welcomes selective inhabitants of the margin in order better to exclude the margin' (Landry and Maclean, 1996, 35), as though the motivation for the speaker's invitation is to prove that he is indeed inferior. The effect of this habitual linguistic discrimination is observed and internalized in Charles who makes an effort to use typical *tico* words and phrases such as 'pucha carajo', 'cursi', and 'maje, hijuemialma. Maje, sos un cabrón' (16). Indeed, he notes that he purposely stops using any *limonense* terms like 'va pa' or 'ónde' when he is in the capital in order to fit in, making himself more palatable for a *tico* public (27).

Within this normative stance of the Central Valley, Charles also depicts a clear culture of materialism and class-based hierarchy into which he also desperately attempts to insert himself. Although the very notion of class is often dismissed in the country's 'classless' or 'entirely middle-class' society (Biesanz et al., 1999, 102), Duncan observes that it actually forms a very real part of the central provinces. Class distinction in San José is narrated as going hand in hand with a materialist culture, undermining the idea of the nation as an ecological paradise. *Josefinos* are described as dependent on their possessions, using them to show off in front of others: 'la gente no compra cosas para su uso, sino para impresionar' (11), while Charles himself lists everything he owns including his house and car, which he hopes situate him highly in society (24). Indeed, he even describes San José's philosophical motto as 'tenía, luego era' (15). When Charles enters the room hosting the debate about minority cultures which he has organized, he states that he and Ester 'caminamos despacio, como correspondía a nuestro papel social. La gente esperaba eso de nosotros. Uno no tiene problemas cuando hace lo que se espera de uno' (16), thus also demonstrating the existence of Bourdieu's concept of habitus as creating a set of commonly understood social rules. Duncan also describes San José as 'un mundo superficial ... en donde el sueño mayor era un viaje a Miami' (24). Not only does Duncan include this theme in the novel because of the dominant consumer spirit he sees growing in Costa Rican society at this time, but also as a way of questioning and perhaps undermining the government of the day which still claims to hold true to the socialist ideals of the Second Republic, but which consistently subverts these principles with its actions.

While listing his middle-class possessions such as a car and a gardener, Charles also includes his wife in the list, adhering to the patriarchal culture of the city. He initially states that he married her in order to further his cultural and social standing in San José, and it is made clear that he has internalized the *tico* view of women as another material commodity. This aspect of normative culture is also seen as Charles and Dr Centeno sit in traffic in his car and a *mestiza* crosses the street 'casi desnuda', leaving the doctor to exclaim, 'qué copita de helados' (24), objectifying the girl's body and reducing her to a sexual object. When another girl crosses the street, this time an Afro-Costa Rican, he declares 'qué descaro de negra' (24), showing the intersectionality of dual prejudice endured by a citizen who is not only an ethnic, but also a gendered, 'Other'. These incidents also demonstrate a facet of the habitus involved in the *tico* norm as neither incident is commented on as uncommon by the narrator. Through these examples of how *tico* society behaves – excluding ethnic, gendered, and class 'Others' – Duncan's vision of the country appears to at once accentuate normative *tico* views while also being morally opposed to the rhetoric that usually surrounds this idealization of mainstream Costa Rica. Just as Charles is forced to look in the mirror four times until he sees his true face, the reader is also forced into a journey of self-reflexivity where they must recognize the active 'Othering' in the country.

These incidents therefore set up in the narrative a common experience of racism, sexism, and classism in Central Valley society, with attitudes ingrained in society displayed through habitus: the use of racist and sexist language, the employment of negative stereotypes, and the objectification of women. Present within the novel is also the notion of geographic 'Otherness', and, in the eyes of the *tico* in San José, Limón is an 'Other' with its supernatural beliefs and Afro-Costa Rican traditions derided in the rational and progressive capital. This idea of the *tico* as only dwelling in the Central Valley is cemented by Clarita de Duke, a *limonense*, Afro-Costa Rican nurse who trained in San José but moved back to Limón to work in the hospital there. Her experience is used to narrate a clash of cultural values and practices as she attempts to impose Western medicine on a community that prefers to rely on traditional herbal and spiritual cures. As such, she describes Limón and San José as 'dos mundos irreconciliables' (42), as African spiritualism and curses abound in one, and science and Catholic prayer in the other (42). This clash of cultures is also keenly felt by Charles, who asserts that 'es lo que dice aquella poetisa Africana: "aquí estoy, atrapada entre dos culturas"' (66–7). Through the use of racist incidents and in setting up Limón and San José as binaries, the reader is forced to question his or her own habits and attitudes in relation to the place of the ethnic 'Other' within the nation and therefore the role of the individual in the perpetuation of damaging norms.

Duncan thereby demonstrates that it is not merely skin colour but also geographic belonging and the cultural significance of this which divides Costa Rican society. As the narrative is set in both San José and Limón, the distinction between the rural and urban classes is portrayed, and Duncan critiques the Eurocentric capital city and the class-based hierarchy to which it subscribes, as well as the infrastructure gap apparent between the city and the province. Limón is distinguished by its communal spirit, but also by its lack of scientific education; Clarita de Duke constantly tries to force Western medicine on its inhabitants. When Charles goes back to Limón, he encounters his ex-lover and former neighbour, Ruth. Upon telling her that his new wife is from a good family, she immediately asks if he is insinuating that his first wife, Lorena, was not from a good family. By way of explaining what he means by 'good', he replies that Ester is 'burguesa' (148), demonstrating that San José attributes positive imagery to high social status, according to European tradition. When Ruth misunderstands him – not knowing the term bourgeois – thinking he has described Ester as 'turquesa' (148), the divide between the rural and urban social classes is highlighted, with the rural dividing people according to their spiritual and agricultural worth, and the urban creating a hierarchy based on education, family background, and financial wealth.

Furthermore, this class divide is tied to Charles' identity crisis: as he had high social value when living in Limón as a landowner and Christian priest, when he arrives in San José, he yearns for the same social status there. Although he was educated in the capital, he arrives having worked only in agriculture and is therefore unable to play the part of the cultured urbanite as well as he had hoped. In order to combat this, just as he tries to 'overcome' his ethnicity, he throws himself into playing the part of the *josefino*. He even decides to resolve the problem of not being able to see his face in the mirror according to the social rules of San José: 'actuaba como me había enseñado en la capital: dejar las cosas que resolviesen por sí mismas' (8). In order to allow the situation to be resolved on its own, he initially believes that he must tie himself even more firmly to his wife, stating that he must 'recoger los cabos sueltos de mi existencia y atarlos; atarlos a ella' (9), or, in other words, he must tie himself to the new elevated status he holds in San José because of Ester again using the unspoken rules of society.

The internalization of the idea of racial hierarchies and between differing cultures by both Afro-Costa Ricans and *ticos* is seen in this novel as the consequence of the perpetuation of colonial habits and attitudes. This recalls Fanon's experiences of a negative consciousness being forced upon the colonized subject which then becomes latent in postcolonial society. An example of this internalized image is seen as Charles recalls that, in Limón, older generations of Afro-Costa Ricans discussed the notion of *blanqueamiento* – or the whitening of one's hereditary lineage over six generations – as a positive goal. Charles' neighbour, Cristián, remembers his father as being proud of his European blood and telling his son off for being 'más negro que un condenado salvaje africano' (61). Charles also recalls his own grandfather having very fixed ideas about whitening, as he used to tell his grandsons, 'no quiero a ninguno de ustedes casado con una negra. Búsquense una mulata o una inglesa. Hay que subir de color para escapar de esta cochinada en que estamos ... Hay que ir blanqueando, esa es la solución' (130). This demonstrates the very real internalization – both insipid and overt – of the colonial notion that black skin equates savagery while white skin equates civilization.

Charles carries these beliefs with him to the capital where he sees everyone around him as superior because of their skin colour – leading to his own employment of prejudice against other Afro-Costa Ricans. When he describes an Afro-Costa Rican woman attending a party in *La casa amarilla*, Charles declares that 'nadie se sintió ofendida por su presencia ... la negra era linda a pesar de su color' (12–13). Here Charles highlights the difference, or 'Otherness' of Afro-Costa Ricans among white Costa Ricans in the capital, and at a high-culture event. His unwilling acceptance of the woman, who was lucky to be pretty despite her skin colour, does not stretch to others, however, as when an Afro-Costa Rican man on the bus in San José proves he cannot move down any more, Charles thinks 'así son de necios' (20) about all Afro-Costa Ricans. Not only does he not appear to count himself as Afro-Costa Rican with this utterance (he does not exclaim 'así somos de necios', for example) but his internalized discrimination and complete lack of self-awareness does not endear Charles to the reader. In turn, the audience is further persuaded to agree with Duncan that denying one's cultural background is a harmful betrayal of identity and that life in the nation's capital should not force Charles to act in this manner.

Charles' refusal to identify as Afro-Costa Rican in the capital is also underlined as he misunderstands racism directed towards him. In one incident he confuses a passer-by's motive for asking him for a match in English; rather than recognizing it is because he is *limonense* and the person has assumed he cannot speak Spanish, he asserts that 'todos tenemos complejo de gringos' (19). The reader, however, infers that Charles has been addressed in English because there exists the expectation that Afro-Costa Ricans cannot speak Spanish. The fact that Charles has narrated the entire novel in perfect Spanish, however, undermines this perception and compels the reader to recognize the falsehood of stereotypes and the negative consequences of their perpetuation.

Within *Los cuatro espejos*, just as Charles begins with negative essentialist – and even racist – views about Afro-Costa Ricans, he also expresses similar prejudice against women. Whereas the protagonist slowly comes to terms with the error of his ways and accepts that racial discrimination is incorrect – on both a personal level and a wider, moral level – he does not dismiss his gendered views. Rather, these are cemented as the female characters within the novel are one dimensional and appear as no more than bodies designed for male sexual pleasure and potentially to bear their offspring. This recalls Crenshaw's assertion (1991, 1242–6) that not only is all power – or lack thereof – intersectional but an individual discriminated against in one situation can turn to be a discriminator in another.

Charles' first wife Lorena, who died in San José, and his second wife Ester, are both afforded short chapters, narrated in the third person – Charles is the only character with first-person authority in this novel. While Charles is portrayed as an eloquent, if hypocritical, character, these two women only display jealous or racist behaviour, and are described solely in terms of their looks and function for Charles. Ester is introduced to the reader as merely 'el cuerpo de mi esposa' (14) who states over and over, in her sleep, 'no me despeines' (15). Furthering this depiction of her as no more than a body that belongs to Charles and is only concerned with her looks, he states of her: 'mujer, su ser abierto, su voz "un no me despeines amor" constante; una larga luz inundando el cuerpo, y una palabra débil tragada por el sueño' (15). In this description, Ester becomes a woman, a voice, a body, and a word, but never a person. Charles also narrates how he came to be incorporated into San José's high society, noting that by marrying Ester he incorporated himself into it: he knows that he has 'ganado bastante con el matrimonio' (13) in terms of status. When reminiscing about meeting Ester, he states, 'me fui enamorando de la blanca piel de Ester' (133), and he is clearly proud of her fair hair and light eyes, as well as the fact that she knows how to dress the part of the upper-middle-class wife:

> Mi esposa era de porte galano, elegancia griega, grandes ojos y un ligero rasgo germánico … vestía elegantemente. Ella sabe hacerlo. Es una de las cosas acerca de ella que me gustan más. Me gusta mucho una mujer que sepa vestirse bien. Vale la pena mirarla. Siempre he dicho que si una mujer no sabe vestir bien y tampoco está dispuesta a escuchar consejos, debería andar desnuda y economizar el ridículo. (10–11)

Charles reduces Ester to no more than a commodity which helped him to achieve his social aims, demonstrating the inferior and powerless position of the woman in *tico* society, as women, according to Charles, should learn to dress well and do as they are told – presumably by men. Ester began life being told what to think by her father, even if she was a genetic mistake – Doctor Centeno had 'fallido genéticamente, engendrando una mujer y no un varón' (70) – before being chosen by Charles to be his wife (87). She is presented as his possession which made her leave behind her vocation of spinsterhood (89) – the only option open to her if she remained unmarried. When stating '¿cómo se le dice a *una* esposa que uno se volvió negro en la madrugada?' (89; emphasis my own), Charles further comments on her disposable quality: she is no more than '*a* wife', an item he could procure more of. Although, at the end of the novel, Charles proclaims that his life is with Ester and that he is chained to her, she still never crosses into the realm of personhood in his eyes, and the humanization which Charles so desired is only afforded to the male protagonist.

Duncan, then, uses this novel to expand upon several facets of discrimination, and the hierarchy of gender is also clearly seen as women equate with the private, powerless domain while men stand as the public face of the nation. This dialogue is complicated by Duncan as, unlike other social norms he points out, he seems unquestioningly to adhere to this dichotomy without challenging or critiquing it. As Spivak has noted, the 'male subaltern and historian are here united in the common assumption that the procreative sex is a species apart, scarcely if at all to be considered a part of civil society' (Landry and Maclean, 1996, 228), and through Duncan's dismissal of the issue of gender bias – and his actual employment of it to further his conclusion – this statement appears to hold true. While using this novel to further the counterhegemonic struggle against ethnic stereotypes and hierarchy on the one hand, he underlines essentialist gender difference on the other. As Rita Felski points out:

> patriarchal power pervades verbal and visual systems of meaning. Within such systems, woman is always connected to and inseparable from man. Men's ability to symbolize the universal, the absolute, and the transcendental depends on the continuing association of femaleness with difference, otherness, and inferiority. (Felski, 2011, 38)

These incidents, then, demonstrate the pervasive nature of the *tico* norm as assumed through habitus and the interpellation of ideals. Through these examples of how *tiquicidad* excludes ethnic, cultural, geographic, and gendered 'Others', Duncan's vision of the country appears at once to accentuate normative *tico* views while also being morally opposed to some of the rhetoric that surrounds the idealization of the nation. He also highlights the intersectionality of both identity and prejudice, undermining the view that Costa Rica is a peaceful, egalitarian haven. As Charles is forced to look in the mirror four times until he sees his true face, the reader is also forced into a journey of self-reflexivity where they must recognize and question the place of internal 'Others' in the nation. However, *Los cuatro espejos* does not just underline the dominant view that 1970s Costa Rica was a Eurocentric, patriarchal society ruling culturally and economically from San José; Duncan also uses this novel and its protagonist to subvert this assumption.

Charles McForbes' Life as Allegory

Charles lives an exaggerated version of the ideal *tico*, and yet he is still excluded from the nation due to his ethnic heritage. Through writing out against this prescriptive, narrow view of inclusivity Duncan wants his reader to begin to question societal norms. At the same time, it is made clear that Duncan's chief concern with this novel is the revalorization of Afro-Costa Rican culture and ethnicity as an authentic and valued part of the nation. To achieve this, Duncan uses Charles' life and identity crisis as an allegory: his protagonist's journey from Limón to San José represents internal, metaphorical, and physical displacement and embodies the struggle of someone attempting to move from the margins to the centre. His physical move also has historical echoes; just as urban migration from Limón was rife in post-1948 Costa Rica, generations before Charles moved from Jamaica to Costa Rica, and their ancestors were forcibly moved from Africa to the Caribbean colonies as part of the slave trade. This theme of displacement and a questioning of belonging resonates with many of Duncan's other works, although none other takes on the internal, personal struggle to assimilate as directly as *Los cuatro espejos*.

As Charles is faced with the realization that he no longer knows where his identity lies or with which culture he belongs, it is made clear that the ramifications of his loss of identity are severe. He is portrayed as a hypocrite, so ashamed of his ethnic background that he internally rejects it, refusing to see his face in the mirror because of the colour of the skin looking back at him. This use of Charles' reflection is demonstrative of the power of the gaze within postcolonial power formations. When Charles looks at his reflection in the mirror, it is from a point of view of total internalization of the assumptions implicit in the *tico* mainstream. As he works to be a member of this dominant elite, he believes he will see the face of the *tico* ideal gaze back at him in the mirror. When all he can see is dark skin, his disillusionment with the gap between his imagined and actual self is so overwhelming that he prefers to believe he is going mad than that he is black. Indeed, he is so far removed from his own sense of identity that he only exists as a person in his own imaginary. When he looks in the mirror, then, he sees his own perceived lack, or the absence of his desired self – what Lacan terms the ego-ideal (1994). The extent to which Charles has begun to mimic and internalize stereotypes of the *tico*, as well as his desperation to embody this ideal at all costs has impeded his own power of self-reflection and recognition.

Through the use of Charles' identity crisis, Duncan also uses his reflections on Limón to revalorize both the province and Afro-Costa Rican culture in the eyes of the reader. Indeed, Afro-Costa Rican culture punctuates the majority of the narrative in *Los cuatro espejos*, and this coincides with Duncan's own adherence to the literary theory of Afro-realism which states that the cultures of the African diaspora should be celebrated (Q. Duncan, 2005; 2009). I would also argue, however, that Duncan goes further than this in *Los cuatro espejos*, and that he adheres to the three-stage subculture-structure of writing, as Elaine Showalter maps out:

1. the imitation of dominant traditions and the internalization of these standards;

2. the protest against these values and the advocacy of minority rights and values;

3. the journey's end of self-discovery whereby the search for one's identity turns inward. (Showalter, 2011, 13)

The internalization of the *tico* standard is made apparent as not only has Charles adopted racist attitudes, but he also loses his identity because he does not feel that he can reconcile two such different histories, traditions, and societies into one, individual identity. His attempt to do this is so problematic, in fact, that he loses his own sense of self. It would appear that Duncan condemns those who, like Charles at the start of the novel, go about this reconciliation of differing cultures in the wrong way – by mimicking the mainstream. Duncan criticizes his protagonist's moral values and decisions by painting him as a hypocrite only interested in material possessions and social status. After trying to fit the mould acceptable for an Afro-Costa Rican in the eyes of the *tico* mainstream – educated, Eurocentric, patriarchal – Charles then actually begins to believe himself to be 'white' Costa Rican. When describing his appearance, he states: 'ustedes pueden ver mi piel: pucha, no es negra. Es decir, si no fue por mi pelo y mis facciones yo podría pasar en cualquier parte como latino', desperately attempting to will himself to become the dominant ethnicity (128). Although his light skin colour may have allowed Charles to develop a relationship with Ester, however, it does not allow him access to mainstream society more widely. His belief that it does allow this, though, chimes with Fanon's assertion (1986, 110) that the ethnically marginalized may forget about the discrimination inherent in society until it is forced upon them in a violent or overt manner.

As Charles looks in the mirror the first time, he prefers to think he is going mad rather than seeing his own face. He describes the incident as 'una sensación extraña, como si estuviera fuera de mi cuerpo ... una traicionera demencia' (7) whereby 'una inexplicable negrura sepultaba mi rostro' (10). I assert that this blackness that appears to have buried and betrayed him and which – when he looks in the second mirror – turns into 'un rostro negro' (30), is, in fact, not just *a* face, but *his* face – one which he refuses to accept as his own. He therefore breaks the mirror before wondering if it can be that his skin is changing colour, referring to his condition as 'mi repentina mutación' (31), asking himself '¿cómo se la dice a una esposa que uno se volvió negro en la madrugada?' (31), as though he sees a doppelgänger in the mirror instead. Indeed, it is the gap between Charles' actual – black – face and his ideal – white – face which is described by Duncan via the lens of the mirror here, and his reaction to his real reflection allows the reader to gain a fuller understanding of what it means to deny, or forcibly to lose, an ethnic identity. In this way the novel is a politicized re-writing of stories involving doubles, with a racial dynamic added to the Romantic mirror trope.

In order further to persuade the reader of his agenda, Duncan also portrays Charles as a hypocrite who denies his own background in order to climb the social ladder while at the same time criticizing the notion of social stratification: 'el proceso evolutivo se había detenido inesperadamente por la estratificación absurda e irracional de un mundo desviado por una ilusión: la de creer que un grupo es superior por el simple hecho de ser más poderoso' (34). Furthermore, Duncan uses the omniscient narrator to describe Charles as 'siempre un hipócrita profesional' (55) in order to undermine his internalized beliefs. Moreover, even his marriage is based on hypocrisy: Ester claims that when they first met 'era la primera vez que veía en un negro algo que valiera la pena', 'había encontrado en su negritud una profunda humanidad' and, 'él la había hecho consciente por la primera vez de la humanidad de los negros' (101). These affirmations of her perceived tolerance work on a purely ironic level as Ester clearly does not actually see Charles as 'negro' because of his light skin and the fact that he constantly tries to fit into her world. She even asserts that 'Charles es una persona extraña; no es ni negro ni blanco. Está más allá de esas definiciones' (111). Despite this level of hypocrisy, however, Charles' own views are set in ironic contrast: not only does he recognize social hypocrisy, but he criticizes others for practising it. In Limón, Charles notes that a sense of pride is felt among the Afro-Costa Rican population as they speak English at home, failing to accept that the language was only passed onto them by British slave masters: 'nos sentimos orgullosos del inglés, idioma de criminales' (89). Charles also reflects upon the meaning of the *Día de la Raza* – or 12 October – which is celebrated in Limón but was created on the back of brutal acts of colonization: 'en Limón hacemos carnaval ... para celebrar el día de la raza que introdujo estacas en el año del indio en el nombre de los Reyes Católicos' (89). Owing to this initial portrayal of Charles as a hypocrite, then, the reader comes to understand the tension existing between the *tico* norm and its 'Other' as in Charles' desperation to fit the mould of the former he is forced to undermine himself.

It is at this point that Duncan's novel enters Showalter's second stage of subculture writing as these *tico* values which he has internalized are subverted, leaving the 'Other' normalized. Duncan does this by making frequent reference to the African and Afro-Caribbean religious traditions in Limón, treating them with sincerity and sympathy. This is most evident when Charles thinks back to his life with Lorena, as it is mentioned by various members of the village that a 'dopí'[9] – a type of evil spirit common in Caribbean folklore – had attacked her, causing her illness (40), and that the only way to reverse the effect of this would be to contact the local 'obeahman', or spiritual doctor (39). It is also widely acknowledged within the village that the years that Charles' crop failed and Cristián's grew while they were competing as farmers was down to a curse that Cristián put on Charles' land (77). These supernatural beliefs are coupled with cultural traditions such as membership of a lodge, or traditional Caribbean brotherhood.

Charles recalls that on his father, Pete's, deathbed, he stated, 'cuando me haya muerto y está en peligro, haga este señal; la de la logia' (46). When Lorena becomes ill, Charles summons the ghost of his father using this sign, and it is through this visitation that Charles discovers that 'un hongo en el estómago era la causa de su mal. Y Bowman era el responsable' (52) and that the curse will end up taking Lorena's life (85). These traditions, which have been carried along on the Middle Passage on slave ships from Africa, and merged and distorted across generations in the Caribbean, are proposed by Gates as creating a New World Pan-African culture, which serves to give the ethnic subaltern in postcolonial societies a joint identity and understanding due to their common ancestry. Although it could be argued that Duncan's use of these themes is no more than a journey into a dead or forgotten history, he makes it clear that not only are the traditions and beliefs that he documents alive and well, but that they remain important in the discussion of Charles', and perhaps Duncan's own, family history. Although a wider Costa Rican audience may read about supernatural occurrences with scorn and disbelief, Duncan does not mock them. In fact, he often gives spiritual practice and its believers more credibility than science: although Charles is a Christian priest and he takes Lorena to a hospital practising Western medicine in San José, neither his prayers nor private medical care can overcome the power of the curse (51).

Within Duncan's revalorization of Afro-Costa Rican identity, the San José–Limón binary also plays an important role. In the same way that Afro-Costa Rican culture is exalted, Limón – and its inextricable link to Caribbean culture – is also praised. Limón is depicted as a tropical paradise, where community spirit persists and where the people live off the land. Indeed, the *limonenses* are described as small-time farmers who can use the land to

---

9 The duppy – here translated into Spanish by Duncan as *dopí* – is a Jamaican word meaning: '(1) the soul of a dead person, manifest in human form; (2) the soul of the dead manifest in a variety of fabulous beasts, and also in the forms of real animals like lizards and snakes; (3) an order of supernatural beings only vaguely associated with the dead' (Leach, 1961, 207). For further discussion of the folklore surrounding duppies, see Leach, 1961.

their advantage and whose spiritual beliefs give them power. In San José, however, materialism and hypocrisy rule among the middle classes, while it is also home to the underbelly of society: prostitutes, drug users, and the homeless (118). Duncan narrates the differences between the two in a type of moral *Bildungsroman*: Charles begins his journey from the capital to the province of his past which also signals the start of his cathartic journey of self-rediscovery. Although reflecting on his life while walking the streets of San José, it is only once he slips onto the train to go back to Limón that Charles suddenly gains an insight into the identity crisis he is experiencing. He exclaims that living as he has in San José, ignoring his previous life completely 'era una manera de escapar mi realidad' (19), and he eventually accepts that 'nunca me había podido quitar del todo mi condición de limonense, a pesar de todo' (75). Although still speaking about being *limonense* as though it were a disease, terming it his 'condition', the reader begins to sympathize with Charles' predicament, blaming society rather than him for his lost identity. It is not until he is on his way back from Limón, having realized that there is no longer a life for him there, that he acknowledges the truth of his situation, claiming that:

> La conferencia escuchada en el Teatro Nacional, de pronto me reveló su sentido pleno. ¿En qué momento preciso perdí mi propia identidad? ¿Qué cúmulo de sueños me pusieron en conflicto con la cultura mamada en los negruzcos pechos de mi madre, y sorbida gota a gota desde la pálida rodilla de Pete McForbes? ... Me crié entre un pueblo negro ... Pucha carajo, la verdad es que no puedo entenderlo y no es que me estoy haciendo el cursi ... realmente no sé lo que me ha sucedido. (128)

It is made clear in this passage, then, that ethnically dominant cultural norms have been so ingrained in his psyche that he has buried his own ethnic and cultural background in order to assimilate. This is a dilemma that Fanon discusses extensively, stating that when a dominant culture is internalized, an inferiority complex is created. Indeed, Charles feels so inferior that he has unconsciously attempted to rid himself of his 'Otherness' by hiding it even from himself. This also demonstrates what Georg Lukács terms a 'false consciousness', where one acts in line with the dominant belief system, but against one's own interests (1971, 50–1). Throughout the majority of the narrative it would appear that Charles has been possessed by this false consciousness as he acts according to a belief system that works against him. It is this mimicry of the dominant group, detailed as common by Bhabha in his discussions of postcolonial resistance, which he eventually has to face and conquer.

After the realization that he had lost his identity and was living in opposition to his cultural background, Charles begins to consider his reaction to the incident, later stating, '¿en dónde, pues, había perdido mi identidad al punto de redescubrirla con tanto horror?' (132). It is at this point that Showalter's third stage of writing comes to the fore. This occurs when Charles recognizes the belief system behind his mimicry as having negative consequences for him as an individual, and for Afro-Costa Ricans as a group. In this way he begins to uncover and then question his false consciousness, and his dilemma is used as an allegory of all young Afro-Costa Ricans who attempt to bridge the gap between two cultures and two identities in a quest to find a place for themselves in Costa Rica. As discussed by Mosby, the 1970s was a time of urban migration from Limón to San José for many young Afro-Costa Ricans. Writing *Los cuatro espejos* in 1973, Duncan plays with the socially prevalent themes of lost identity and rejection of origin as they were issues pertinent to the Afro-Costa Rican population, but which were yet to be recognized or accepted by the *tico* centre. Through Charles' own journey from a lack of self-awareness towards a realization and acceptance of his cultural and ethnic heritage, he is saved. The identity which he takes on at the end of his journey, however, is not a romanticized version of his *limonense* roots, but one which takes into account all aspects of his life: his Caribbean background, his job as a professor, his wife in San José, and his life in the capital, thereby creating a new version of his own, individual, ethnicity. With Charles' own self-acceptance, Duncan adheres to Showalter's third stage of subculture authorship which demonstrates self-reflection and acceptance.

Spivak has argued that 'in literary discourse there is a playing out of the problem as the solution' (Landry and Maclean, 1996, 55), and this is certainly true of *Los cuatro espejos*. The final solution that Duncan proposes for the national reader involves a change in attitude and habitus in order to begin a shift in power. In agreement with Butler, Duncan does not suggest that the concept of normative society is removed, however. Rather, he demonstrates that the norm itself must change in order to accept different facets of Costa Rican identity by challenging the mythical history of whiteness that it holds at its core. The fact that Charles recognizes that his life and identity are no longer in Limón does not signify that Charles should forget or deny his background in the future. The implication of this coming-to-consciousness for Charles is reminiscent of Stuart Hall's call for a revalorization of the term ethnicity as a concept which is open to change and difference, then, as in this novel Charles accepts his ethnic and cultural background as Afro-Costa Rican but vows to continue living his life in the capital. He therefore demonstrates how a change in norms begins within the consciousness of the individual. Duncan clearly considers there to be major societal conflict between the 'white' centre and the Afro-Costa Rican periphery – an issue of which he has first-hand experience. His message for 'white' Costa Rica is to recognize, accept, and include difference into the national rhetoric, while the implication for the Afro-Costa Rican population is that they should not feel under threat and be forced to lose their cultural background in order to integrate with the dominant social group.

As Charles acts as a hybrid of the two cultures, his decision to go back to San José at the end of the novel demonstrates the possibility of norms changing. While his return could appear contradictory to the process he has had to go through in order to regain his identity, Duncan uses this to declare that a reconciliation of a disenfranchised identity into the dominant social ideal is possible. The final passage, a conversation between Charles and Ester, reflects this notion as he asks, '¿Te das cuenta que al encadenarme te encadenarás vos misma?', to which she replies, 'todos estamos encadenados. Son cadenas de Dios' (163). Despite the theme of romance barely emerging throughout the work, it is interesting that Duncan chooses to end the novel on this note. According to Doris Sommer, nineteenth- and twentieth-century Latin American novels – or the 'foundational fictions' of the region – often used romantic unions to allegorize the nation, pointing toward a harmonious national future (1991, 6). While the remainder of Duncan's novel displays very few of the characteristics discussed within Sommer's work, this ending is certainly reminiscent of the allegory of love and marriage as encoded signifiers of national and ethnic unity. Marriage, according to Sommer, can serve as a sign for national and ethnic consolidation, which she terms the 'redemptive capacity of cross-over romance' (22), where the female body stands in for the national territory (38). When reading the conclusion in this way, Ester represents Costa Rica: she began her life internalizing racist assumptions and conforming to racial hierarchies, she learnt to overcome these and see beyond ethnicity and skin colour, before finally realizing that the only differences between herself and Charles are purely cultural, and should be embraced rather than rejected. When Charles states so emphatically that he will be chained to her, he is therefore also stating his hope that Costa Rica will change and that a new, inclusive nation will emerge – one to which he wishes to belong. In this way Duncan uses this novel and his influence as an author to persuade the reader round to his ideological vision of inclusivity and integration for Costa Rica.

It is this recognition that leads to Charles' final glance in the mirror. This time he discovers that 'una sonrisa profunda iluminó el color de mi piel' (63). It is now also clear that he has accepted his own ethnicity, no longer describing it as 'negritud'. This recalls Spivak's suggestion that 'all such clear-cut nostalgias for lost origins are suspect, especially as grounds for counterhegemonic ideological production' (2006, 34), demonstrating that Charles' journey was not into the past but into the future. Moreover, Eagleton points out that in order to counter exclusive normative discourses one's habits need to change (2011, 239). Indeed, Charles no longer refers to his appearance negatively, instead recognizing it as merely 'the colour of my skin'. This also fits with Hall's revalorization of the term ethnicity, which does not suggest essential similarities between people of the same skin colour or ethnic background, nor does it imply absolute differences between ethnicities. In terms of *Los cuatro espejos* forming part of a movement demonstrating counterhegemonic ideological production, then, it is clear that, in terms of ethnicity, Duncan portrays a Costa Rican society where prejudice exists but can be challenged, and where dominant modes of viewing cultural identity can be overcome to include marginalized members of the nation.

In writing a novel which at once documents the mainstream, cultural discourse of the concept of the *tico* in the 1970s while also attempting to highlight and revalorize the place of the marginalized, cultural 'Other' in the country, Duncan demonstrates his integrationist agenda. He aims this story at a national audience, using his protagonist's identity crisis as an allegory for all Afro-Costa Ricans in this era. At this time, the Afro-Costa Rican community was facing a bicultural dilemma which has been highlighted by Fanon: leave behind a tradition and culture in order to assimilate as thoroughly as possible, or segregate in order to exalt a cultural heritage to such a point that it becomes essentialized and unable to develop (1994, 45–6). Through the use of Charles' life as a symbol in *Los cuatro espejos*, Duncan appears to suggest another way. He posits that the normative discourse needs to change and adapt – the myth of the white *tico* nation must come to an end. At the same time, marginalized cultures must recognize both their value and their capacity to essentialize: Duncan uses Charles to warn an Afro-Costa Rican audience against opposing the natural process of change within their culture too. Although the mimicry of mainstream *tico* society may have been ingrained in the lives of much of this generation of the 1970s, *Los cuatro espejos* demonstrates the potential pitfalls of this approach. In this way, Duncan uses his soft power as an author to bring about changes in habitus for both the mainstream and the Afro-Costa Rican population which he suggests can begin the process of social change in Costa Rica.

The Use of Subtext for Feminist Critique
in the Short Stories of Carmen Naranjo

Like Duncan, Carmen Naranjo has also been inextricably linked to the field of Costa Rican literature since her first publication appeared in 1964. Judy Bravo states that Naranjo is 'among those whose names are readily recognized abroad' (1993, 154) and Luz Ivette Martínez asserts (1987, 15) that she is counted among the best writers in the Hispanic world. Born in Cartago in the Central Valley in 1928, Naranjo moved to San José in 1931, witnessing the 1948 revolution and *Segunda República* first hand. A supporter of the movement and of the new revolutionary government, she was among the first generation of women allowed to attend university. Graduating in philology from the University of Costa Rica, she went into the civil service and later became one of the first women to occupy various political positions in the country (Martínez, 1987, 154). As Minister for Culture from 1974 to 1976, she was known as an activist for social justice who, in her own words, created problems for the Costa Rican establishment (Miranda, 1981, 121). Indeed, she resigned from politics altogether after the central government urged her to censor a documentary critiquing its policies which was made using funds from her department in 1976 (Martínez, 1987, 126). She went on to work for a number of charities fighting for human rights in Central America before her death in 2012.

Naranjo also produced a steady stream of literary works from the 1960s onwards, including novels, short stories, and poetry. Totalling 31 published works, she is among the most prolific authors in the country (Paul-Ureña, 2007, 425). Her works can be situated within the wider body of literature written by other female Latin American authors of this same generation, such as Rosario Castellanos, Elena Poniatowska, and Luisa Valenzuela, and the comparisons between Castellanos' and Naranjo's works are widespread. Many of Naranjo's works are characterized by a focus on the themes of social justice and as such Judy Maloof contends that her works have 'played fundamental roles in shaping national and cultural consciousness' (2000, 247), while Jeana Paul-Ureña notes that Naranjo was among the first authors in Costa Rica to use literature as a means of protest (2007, 423-6). Indeed, in Borloz Soto's 2007 anthology of Naranjo's work, she asserts that:

> Carmen Naranjo surge para obligarnos a replantear una definición de poder, para invitarnos a recorrer con ella la metáfora del poder, del lenguaje y el poder, del poder y la sexualidad, del poder y la dominación masculina, del poder y la mujer-palabra dentro de esa relación de poder. (Paul-Ureña, 2007, 4)

Although this evaluation places paramount importance on the theme of gender, the topic is generally omitted from Naranjo's early novels whereas it is prevalent in the collections of short stories *Ondina* (1983) and *Nunca hubo alguna vez* (1984), in which her protagonists are faced with the internalization of, and rebellion against, certain social norms. The short story has a long tradition of being used to discuss polemic social issues, with authors as diverse as Ernest Hemingway, Angela Carter, and Luisa Valenzuela having used this form.[10] Within Latin America, the short story was used first by indigenous groups to tell oral stories in order to keep their culture and traditions alive under colonial rule, and has gone on to be frequently reproduced, from the *costumbrista* folk tales of the nineteenth and early twentieth centuries to Borges' fantastic fiction (Balderston, 1992).[11] In Costa Rica, Candide Carrasco notes (2003, 86) that it has been used for protest because its stylistic possibilities mean it can break with literary order, thus serving as a metaphor for a break with accepted social order.

It is interesting, then, that while Naranjo used much of her writing to openly critique several aspects of Costa Rican society, she wrote no explicit critiques of the disregarding of women until much later in her career. Diane Marting points out (2001, 7) that this is typical of the region, as in Latin American narrative women's desires were portrayed as dangerous, and the author is often identified with the penned experience. Many assume that it was only with Naranjo's essay *Mujer y cultura*, published in 1989, that she joined the feminist cause, so that by the time she published *Más allá del parismina* in 2000 – her first explicitly feminist fictional work – she was a well-known advocate for women's rights. While this view of the social agenda behind her works is certainly applicable on the surface, I would argue she used subtext in order to critique patriarchal norms much earlier in her career, primarily using the short story as a vehicle for this protest. Considering the national context in which she wrote, perhaps it is little wonder that Naranjo chose to protest in an understated manner. In fact, Castillo notes (1992, 31) that many Latin American female academics in this era actively disassociated themselves with feminism due to its subversive nature. Moreover, the overwhelmingly patriarchal nature of Costa Rica has a long history, and undermining male authority and heteronormative discourse has been, and to some extent still is, seen as a dangerous act.

10 For more on these authors' short works of fiction, see Benson, 1975; Cavallaro, 2011; and Magnarelli, 1988.

11 For more on the history of the short story in Latin America, see Leal, 1966 and Peden, 1983.

The issues facing Naranjo were not uncommon, and María Lourdes Cortés contends that the idealization of the traditional family unit – which is the historical centre of the Costa Rican nation – is to blame for this, stating that:

> El discurso de lo nacional costarricense se construyó a partir de la imagen de una familia, metáfora de nuestra sociedad ... La patria era vista como la gran madre de todos los miembros de esta sociedad, convertidos, a su vez, en moradores felices de esta familia patriarcal. (M. L. Cortés, 1999, 81)

The roots of patriarchy, as discussed by Cortés, explain why Naranjo felt compelled to leave her works unpublished until her father died: she did not want to cause him the shame of having a daughter who wrote books pertaining to the male domain of the public sphere (Arizpe, 1979, 102). Indeed, even after having published for some time, Naranjo maintained her distance from the feminist movement in Costa Rica and in interviews appeared to dodge questions about her views on the topic. In a 1979 interview, she stated: 'I did not want to write "feminine" literature because I do not believe in "feminine" or "feminist" culture' (Arizpe and Naranjo, 1979, 101). Her position as a feminist was not publicly clarified until a 1999 interview, when, asked if she was a feminist, she eventually replied: 'Sí, pero es más que solo teoría: yo me defino como feminista humanista. Me interesa el ser humano que está en condición de discriminación, minusvalía o deterioro social' (Díaz, 1999). Although she felt she had to maintain the silence that patriarchy imposed on her – a condition discussed in detail by Castillo (1992, 38–44) – publicly for some time, I use the following analyses of the text and subtext of her short stories to argue that Naranjo actually did construct a 'revolutionary response' (40) to male domination in her early writings too.

'Simbiosis del encuentro'
Naranjo's 1983 collection of short stories, *Ondina*, is an example of the use of the short story to open discussions about the role of women in patriarchal society in Central America, a common occurrence according to Jaramillo Levi (1991, 14). Indeed, within it she reveals female passions hidden behind closed doors and Martínez points out (1987, 164) that the entire collection demonstrates irony, the fantastic, and ambiguity. I also contend, however, that Naranjo uses these tools to construct a reflection on the social issues that she sees present within contemporary Costa Rican society. The fourth story in *Ondina*, 'Simbiosis del encuentro', is her most explicit exploration of the roles of sex and gender. In it, Naranjo uses the

fantastic to explore and critique these as normative, essentialist notions. Told by the first-person narrator Ana, 'Simbiosis' recounts the story of her encounter and relationship with Manuel. While at first the story appears to be a classic tale of 'boy meets girl', the tone soon begins to change as the boredom of daily routine sets in. After an argument about this, Ana's and Manuel's lives take a fantastical turn in which they begin to take on the sex and gender of the other – Ana becoming a physical man, and Manuel becoming a physical woman – to the extent that Manuel becomes pregnant with their child. The notions of what constitutes sex, gender, and sexuality are dealt with in this story while Naranjo also uses 'Simbiosis' to form a critique of Costa Rican society, the parameters of the *tico* norm, and to construct a protest against gendered prejudice.

'Simbiosis' begins by setting up the *tico* norm – a heterosexual love story – before then undercutting it using the fantastic. Indeed, the title suggests a meaningful, two-way interaction described not as *an* encounter, but *the* encounter, implying a monogamous, long-lasting relationship. The 'boy meets girl' narrative is furthered in the first words of the story: 'Nos amamos' (35). Even the binary of sexual difference is strongly reaffirmed as the narrator states: 'Mi nombre es Ana. El de él es Manuel' (35), making it clear to the reader that Manuel is indeed a man. The differences in perceived gender roles within the relationship are also seen in this opening passage, as Ana is seen to wait for Manuel to take the lead; she writes: 'Alguien le habló a Manuel de mí' (35), explaining that he chose her. However, that this idea forms part of Ana's narrative demonstrates the extent to which she has internalized and normalized gendered stereotypes.

Gender difference is also apparent as Ana introduces herself to the reader. She states that 'la noche me abre los ojos y me embellece', unable to describe herself other than as an outward representation of beauty (35). She goes on to assert that 'hablo poco unas veces y otras nadie me calla ... hago novelas de monólogos interminables' (35) thereby setting herself up as the female enigma, timid and shy at times, but gossipy and vociferous at others, mirroring the Madonna/whore complex where the female is either associated with purity and virginity, or ascribed the oppositional qualities of promiscuity and treachery (Conrad, 2006, 310). Araya notes (2003, 197) that this dualistic view of the female is prevalent in Costa Rican society, where Catholic values are often used to describe women as either dangerous to men – as Eve was to Adam – or, conversely, as maternal and protective like the Virgin Mary.

Further demonstrating the disparity between the expectations of female and male roles in society, Naranjo uses irony to draw attention to Ana's gendered assumptions and the performance of her role as woman. When

Ana attends the party where she has been set up to meet Manuel, she avoids him on purpose and prefers to speak to her female friends about the latest cookery recipes. Ironically, Ana makes it clear that – with little awareness of the gender stereotyping apparent in this decision – despite all the time she took getting ready for the party in order to meet him she would have left without even introducing herself if he had not initiated contact. These assertions therefore not only place the female in the realm of the domestic and private, even when physically in a public space, but also demonstrate Butler's contention that gender is performed; Ana has learned the expectations of her gender and unconsciously chosen to accept and perform them (Blumenfeld and Breen, 2005, 22).

Moreover, Ana recounts that upon leaving the party before having spoken to Manuel she thought: 'Qué gusto da el respirar libre ... era mejor ... el escoger al ser escogido' (36). On the surface it could be said that the pronouncement shows Ana positively affirming her distance from ascribed gendered roles. However, in the paragraph that follows, it is clear that Manuel is the only one actually allowed to do the choosing. As Ana walks away, she feels a hand on her shoulder, and he says to her: 'Se me escapaba, pero vine por usted', while she tells the reader – perhaps by way of apology for her short-lived independence of thought – 'Su voz fue imperativa y convincente. No dejó alternativa' (36). Naranjo uses irony here to subvert convention: as soon as Ana states that she prefers to be free to make her own decisions, the masculine imperial voice of the story speaks for the first time, directing the narrative and curtailing this right. Moreover, while Ana remains a woman in the first half of the story, she is also not given sexual agency or pleasure outside romance. Although she states: 'Nos quedamos [en el apartamento] toda la semana' (36), implying a mutual initiation of the sexual encounter, there is a lack of sexually explicit language used to describe Ana's desires. It would appear that Naranjo makes the decision to exclude sex from this story consciously, as other stories in the collection – notably 'Ondina' – do contain erotic references.

Delving further into the gendered implications of the *tico* norm, Naranjo begins to shift the tone of the narrative from that of a romantic fairy tale – Manuel running after Ana as she leaves the party early, saving her from a life of loneliness – to look beyond the happily ever after. The relationship is narrated as morphing into a habitual routine, encompassed by household chores. It now becomes reminiscent of Rosario Castellanos' 'Lección de cocina' (1971), where the female narrator of this story recounts the minutiae of her daily tasks as a housewife, gradually turning on her husband and their marriage as she cooks – and burns – his steak dinner. Like Castellanos, Naranjo notes that the everyday chores fall to Ana as is the habitual expectation of both Ana and Manuel. Indeed, in order to maintain peace, Ana must to keep silent about domestic inequality, and, as Debra Castillo points out, 'the function of women is not only to mask themselves in myth, but also to provide a comfortable, silent, malleable mask for their men as well' (1992, 40).

Naranjo is not silent about inequality, however, choosing instead to highlight it. When Ana cannot remember what colour Manuel's eyes are, she notes, 'Nunca lo había visto ojo a ojo' (37). Although this could refer to her being shorter than him, it also serves to highlight that, due to Ana's condition as a woman, she is not allowed parity with Manuel in the relationship. Moreover, Ana states that with everything she pays for 'ya era suficiente para garantizar mi independencia y libertad' (37), suggesting that, in being in a relationship, independence and liberty are rights denied her by the unspoken laws governing social conduct. Naranjo goes on to describe Manuel as living 'con casa gratis [y] mujer gratis' (37), showing his belief that women are men's possessions. Indeed, both Ana's and Manuel's beliefs and attitudes towards the relationship affirm the internalization of gender roles and expectations: that Ana does not leave Manuel or complain to him about her inferior role in the relationship underlines her acceptance of this, and for all Manuel's talk of a belief in utopian politics, his world-view does not appear to extend to include gender equality. The showcasing of these attitudes therefore underscores the idealization of *tico* society as overwhelmingly patriarchal, affirming the protagonists' internalization of gender roles and expectations, and demonstrating their perpetuation through habitus.

With the fictional woman's focus firmly set on domestic matters in the first half of this story, Naranjo appears to adhere to the stereotype of women's writing in Costa Rica, rather than undermining it. Not only do her protagonists conform to dominant gendered roles but her style of writing appears to as well, as the narrative contains romantic overtones, along with the suppression of any description of Ana's sexuality or desires in favour of monologues about mundane domestic chores. Although Biruté Ciplijauskaité notes (1988, 66) that women's writing of the 1970s often uses these typical feminine trappings to raise awareness about the plight of the woman in patriarchal society, Naranjo's aim is quite the opposite in this story. Rather than describing the trappings of domesticity to elicit sympathy or even solidarity, Naranjo actually sets up the story in this way in order to establish the importance and implications of the more subtle gendered critique which is to come. Indeed, it is necessary to construct and portray the social norms that the story will undermine in order to begin their deconstruction and subversion. Naranjo spends less time considering the obvious gender inequalities seen behind the closed doors of relationships, and instead chooses to use the fantastic to build a more indirect examination of the position of sex and gender within wider society.

In 'Simbiosis', the reader is alerted to the initial blurring of boundaries between established binaries when, after the first night Ana and Manuel stay together, Ana writes that they stay at her flat all week, 'sin distinguir el día y la noche' (36). This phrase also suggests that Ana goes from being a passive object of Manuel's desire to a subject who also has the agency to desire, and to choose what she does with her sexuality, thus undermining the sexual dichotomy set up in the first half of the story. This notion is explored by Castellanos who argues that 'Through the male mediator, woman finds out about her body and its functions, about her person and her obligations' (Ahern, 1988, 241), and this authorial role is clearly assumed by Manuel prior to his change in sex. Indeed, once the relationship has begun, the responsibilities of everyday life and habits lead to arguments between the two – perhaps Ana is not fulfilling her role as Manuel would like – and she now sees a mix of 'dulzura, asombro, reproche, resentimiento' (38) in his eyes. This quickly undoes the notion set up in the title of 'el encuentro' – the perfect meeting of two strangers bound to fall in love and live happily ever after. Even the innocent-sounding comment made by their mutual friend before introducing them – 'sé que ambos harán nido' (37) – appears to come true, but is turned on its head as it is Manuel who is the one who begins nesting, making ready for the child he is to bear (39). The unravelling of the fixity of these accepted oppositions is, however, most apparent in Naranjo's treatment of sex, gender, and reproductivity, as, throughout the account, the reader witnesses the physical and emotional changes that lead to Ana becoming a man, and Manuel becoming a woman, eventually giving birth to a baby.

This normative viewpoint therefore shifts in the second half of the story, as Naranjo employs the use of the fantastic to undermine *tiquicidad*. As Roberta Johnson argues (1980, 15) of Naranjo's entire body of works, they force the reader to enter a world of different rules in which they see their own, familiar, surroundings reflected through a distorted lens. Naranjo's use of everyday spaces which are then cut through with the announcement of social taboos or fantastical elements blur the boundaries between established binaries and align her with other Costa Rican writers of her generation such as Quince Duncan and Alfonso Chase. The sexual and gendered narrative which has appeared to inhabit the realm of the real so far, then, becomes fantastical, a concept that Cynthia Duncan defines (2010, 5) as containing elements of the inexplicable or impossible. She argues that the fantastic is used in Latin American fiction for social critique and protest, asserting that 'In Spanish America, the fantastic is wedged into a space where cultural tensions come together, smoothing over surface divisions while at the same time threatening to undermine the foundations on which the culture rests' (2010, 6–7). Naranjo is not the only author to play with the idea of fantastic metamorphoses in Latin American fiction, and Miguel Ángel Asturias in *Hombres de maíz* (Guatemala, 1949), Alejandro Carpentier in *El reino de este mundo* (Cuba, 1949), and Julio Cortázar in the short story 'Axolotl' (Argentina, 1956) are other well-known examples of the use of this technique. Where Naranjo's use of a fantastic metamorphosis diverges from that of her predecessors, however, is in the gendering of the fantastic whereby woman and man morph into one another and thus challenge social norms. Duncan notes that the short story 'lends itself to the kind of tension required to bring the fantastic to life' (2010, 7) as being a source of both destabilization and renovation (10). The juxtaposition between the real and the fantastic is experienced by the reader of 'Simbiosis' thereby ensuring their questioning of the social implications of gender imbalance.

Within the narrative, the boundary between the real and the fantastic is ambiguous at first. When Manuel arrives at Ana's flat 'con cara de goma[12] y mal aliento' (38) and is soon vomiting, the reader assumes he has been drinking. Even when Ana describes how 'le crecían los pechos y se le abultaba el vientre' (39), she appraises his body according to the social rules of beauty, stating that 'a los seis meses tenía ... el cuerpo más horrible que se puede concebir en un hombre' (39). These rules of physical appearance are usually applied to the female body (Ahern, 1988, 236–40) which gives the reader the first clue as to the fantastic turn the story is about to take. This obscuring of the lines between the real and the fantastic whereby no clear indicators are given about the cause of Manuel's condition, chimes with Duncan's contestation that the real is a necessary part of the fiction of the fantastic, as one must inform the other in order for the fantastic to have any impact (C. Duncan, 2010, 5 and 48).

In 'Simbiosis', the fantastic replaces the real as the narrative 'truth' towards the end as Manuel is told by his doctor that 'el niño está bien, nacerá en diciembre' (39). The process of supernatural change is then accelerated as, after the birth of the baby, Ana notes that her words 'me salió con voz ronca. Empecé a sentir el peso de un bigote mientras hablaba' (40) and that she now has to shave her beard twice daily (41). This rapid advance into the field of the fantastic, which had only been hinted at previously in the story, firmly denotes the 'juxtaposition of the real and the unreal', which, according

12 'Goma' means 'a hangover' in Costa Rican slang (Quesada Pacheco, 2007, 205).

to Duncan, is the relationship needed in fantastic literature to allow the dominant belief system to be violated, literary conventions to be challenged, and the boundaries of nature to be broken so that an author 'can threaten to undermine the norms that prop up their view of the world' (C. Duncan, 2010, 48). In using just one unnatural and inexplicable element in a story which holds so many other realistic representations and depictions, Naranjo creates a literature of protest which highlights and questions the gendered and sexual norms taken for granted in *tico* society.

Furthermore, Duncan points out that the fantastic also has the 'subversive capacity ... to undermine patriarchal authority and disempower male discourse' (C. Duncan, 2010, 180). Through Naranjo's questioning of the biological rules which are seen to bind physical appearance and procreation, it could be argued that she uses the fantastic to explore feminist thought and subvert gender difference. There are several aspects of this story that adhere to this notion, and Willy Muñoz is adamant that this is the case in 'Simbiosis'. He claims that Naranjo's work closely mirrors feminist movements which assert that the only difference between the sexes is linguistic (Muñoz, 2000, 106). He contends that, within 'Simbiosis', this can be seen through Naranjo's undoing of the dominant/subordinate male/female relationship at the core of this story (100). He concludes that 'Naranjo va más allá de la realidad y construye mundos alternos motivada por el deseo de contribuir a la construcción de una sociedad más benigna, impelida por su anhelo de mejorar el contexto que motivó su escritura' (108). There is certainly evidence from the text that supports this last statement, as it is clear that Naranjo wishes to describe the linguistic aspect of perceived gendered difference. After the moment occurs when Ana's and Manuel's sexes begin to swap after their 'orgasmo de miradas' (38), Ana claims 'recobré la voz' (38) – the voice that had been silenced as a woman and which denotes the beginning of her turn towards masculine language patterns. Similarly, Manuel then 'pidió perdón, no volverá a pasar, hoy fue mi día de mala leche' (38), immediately taking on the traditional female role of peacemaker, taking the blame for their argument, and claiming it was not his day – using a phrase very similar to the adage 'it's my time of the month'.

This switching of ingrained gender patterns continues in their relationship, whereby Ana states that 'Fui detestando sus detalles, el exceso de ellos, la parquedad de algunos, lo amanerado de otros, lo femenino de varios' (38). Moreover, Manuel begins to moan about everything, stating that he feels repulsive, and has a negative body image (39) – all associations attributed to women in relationships. Reversing that, Ana takes on the role of the non-committal male, stating that 'lo aguanté más allá de la repugnancia que me daba', eventually telling him that he disgusts her (39).

Ana even claims, after she assumes the child has been born but she can find neither it nor Manuel, that she feels like a father whose possession has been taken from her (40). The crux of Muñoz's argument, then, centres on his contestation that as Ana and Manuel are able to learn, unlearn, and relearn feminine/masculine language patterns, this must imply that these are no more than learned behaviour, and are therefore not roles intrinsic to individuals (Muñoz, 2000, 106). He states: 'la capacidad de Ana de aprender el lenguaje hegemónico masculino, y con él todo el sistema de dominación patriarcal, indica que tanto "el lenguaje del hombre" como "el lenguaje de la mujer" no pertenecen esencialmente al hombre y a la mujer respectivamente' (106). I argue, however, that Naranjo makes it very clear that neither Ana nor Manuel consciously act out these gender roles, as neither was aware they were switching sex or gender. Further, both are confused when the doctor tells them that Manuel is pregnant, Ana exclaiming, '¿Yo? ¿Madre de un hijo de Manuel? ¿O padre de un hijo de él?' (39). This consequently signifies that as their physical sex began to change, so did their gender, including their language use and emotions, thereby implying Naranjo's belief in a causal link between sex – man or woman – and gender – male or female, the antithesis of Butler's theories of gender seen in Chapter 1.

Indeed, Ana claims that the cause of the swap was 'aquel orgasmo de miradas con que nos desnudamos, la verdad nos llegó y jugó algún horrible ente diabólico un enredo de papeles tradicionales sobre la simple y automática división sexual' (40). Although I would argue that it is this automatic division of the sexes into traditional gender roles that Naranjo is calling her reader to question, then, it appears that she is not ready to go as far as to adhere to Butler's proposal (1999, 179) that gender is merely learned, rather than something intrinsic to human beings. Despite this, it does still clearly question accepted notions of what it is to be sexed and gendered, and which gendered assumptions are made below society's level of consciousness. Indeed, the ongoing male/female binary is set up, broken, and then reversed in 'Simbiosis', which, although not in adherence with later theories of gender such as Butler's, does undo the notion of the female as the inferior gender. This awareness is brought to the fore via the protagonists' gaze, hinting at the undermining of a visual system of meaning. Indeed, as Rita Felski points out:

patriarchal power pervades verbal and visual systems of meaning. Within such systems, woman is always connected to and inseparable from man. Men's ability to symbolize the universal, the absolute, and the transcendental depends on the continuing association of femaleness with difference, otherness, and inferiority. (Felski, 2011, 8)

It would therefore appear that with 'Simbiosis' Naranjo narrates this gendered system of meaning whereby the male and female live in opposition to one another in an unjust hierarchical system. She undermines its basis despite also maintaining the view that there are essential qualities associated with sex and gender. This stance reflects not only the era in which she wrote, however, but also the fear of reprisal in a country which did not wish to promote feminist thought or campaigns, as well as Naranjo's own point of view that there is a specifically female voice which is different from the male voice.

Although Naranjo rejected the notion of *écriture féminine* – as promoted by French critical theorists such as Hélène Cixous – when pushed to speak on the subject in an interview with Chalene Helmuth (1996), she did argue her belief that the female authorial voice is full of concern for social inequality and human rights on a wider scale than gender politics (Helmuth and Naranjo, 1996, 47–8). Moreover, she states that when she writes, 'estoy muy convencida de que está hablando la mujer, quien está analizando el mundo. Es decir, lo siento mucho, carnalmente lo siento' (47). In this way Naranjo situates herself with the third camp of gender-specificity in women's writing as detailed by Stephen Hart (1995, 335–6). This approach asserts that women's writing is different from men's because their lives are different (336), whereas *écriture féminine* would fall into the fourth camp which argues that women's writing differs from men's both thematically and structurally.

Although Naranjo does not entirely subscribe to theories of feminine writing, then, 'Simbiosis' does embody a dialogue on the traditional role of women in *tico* society, discussing their silence and passivity. Ana's antipathy towards Manuel when he is pregnant and plays the part of the nagging wife is a notable consequence of the reversal of their sexes. It has been pointed out that stories of motherhood were frequently used by female Latin American authors in the 1970s as a way of creating a space for women in the fictional realm (Ciplijauskaité, 1988, 63–6), and Naranjo's depiction of this through the eyes of Ana who holds the dominant gaze when she begins to be male serves to give the reader an awareness of a traditionally female situation from another perspective. Ana's attitude towards Manuel and inner thoughts about him at this point have even been described by Evelyn Picon (1987, 299) as misogynist and thus could be considered as the technique, elaborated by Laura Mulvey (1985, 804–5), of re-writing the male gaze. Moreover, Marting argues (2001, 16) that female sexuality has a very different role from male sexuality because of the power implications;

if the woman falls pregnant, her body produces the child, and she may have to raise it alone – an irreversible life change with social implications. The fact that it is Manuel who must suffer the consequences of childbirth and pregnancy gives the reader a new perspective on what it means to become a mother, rather than putting the role on a sacred pedestal. That Ana has now been allowed a voice – albeit as a man – shows Naranjo's commitment to breaking with the silent role handed to female authors. Castillo points out (1992, 44) that 'only in breaking silence ... can the writer hope to establish any form of critique, any potentially revolutionary opposition to the oppressive system', and by harnessing the power of the male voice and channelling it through Ana, Naranjo speaks out.

This challenging of traditional *tico* norms continues as Ana's repugnance towards Manuel during his pregnancy leads the reader to question if his/her reaction to this scenario would be the same if Manuel were relating his thoughts about a pregnant Ana in this way. With this reversal of roles, Naranjo not only exposes a typical attitude that a man may express about a pregnant woman, but also considers the way in which masculine ideals negatively affect men; Manuel is expected to conform to the strong, decisive, provider image of the typical *tico* patriarch. When he is reduced to a whiny, sick mess he loses all respect in Ana's eyes. Moreover, as Ana ends the story assuming that Manuel has had the child and run away to raise it by himself, the reader is left wondering what will become of Manuel as a single mother, thus leading to further questions around traditional male and female familial roles. I therefore argue that this reversal of stereotypes leads the reader to challenge the dominant and unsympathetic public position of the male in Costa Rican society and the silent passivity of the female. Through the use of irony and the fantastic Naranjo creates a reflection of society which is undermined and then turned on its head in order to expose gender stereotypes, inequality, and harmful suppositions.

With 'Simbiosis' Naranjo creates a dialogue around the injustice and damaging nature of gender inequality, constructing a compelling critique of *tico* norms. Although Naranjo's approach may not tie in with French feminist theory (such as Cixous', which promotes a female authorial voice writing solely about female concerns, or with later theories such as Butler's, which write against essential notions of gender difference), we are reminded by Castillo (1992, 1–2) of the dangers of applying the parameters of Western feminist theories to Latin American works too rigidly, as their historical and social contexts must be taken into account. Through her articulation of gender difference, and her subtle highlighting of its inequality and the detrimental effect it has on both women and men, Naranjo certainly works to uncover normative stances and destabilize notions of gender inequality and prejudice in Costa Rican society. Although this attempt remains solely in the realm of the fantastic, this is perhaps, as Castillo contends, because 'any radical breaking of silence remains a utopic exercise' (1992, 45).

'A los payasos todos los quieren'

Naranjo's short story, 'A los payasos todos los quieren', from the collection *Nunca hubo alguna vez* (1984), also details the ways in which gender stereotypes are inherent in *tico* society and in this story Naranjo uses a child narrator to underline this point. The use of this technique aids the creation of the dual narrative, immediately forcing the adult reader to see past the words of the child into the subtext beyond the child's comprehension. The core motives for choosing to use a child narrator include the creation of distance between the author and the message, the establishment of a new viewpoint, and the exposure of accepted truths as irrational. Although writing about Macedonian literature, Michael Seraphinoff makes an observation that chimes well with Naranjo's fiction:

> A child narrator can, among other things, create a degree of distance between the adult author and his or her message that serves to lessen hostility to that message. Readers tend to be more accepting of a child rather than an adult who gives voice to certain uncomfortable or controversial truths. (Seraphinoff, 2007, 2)

The use of a child's voice in order to make a controversial statement more palatable for the reader is employed by Naranjo as she subverts convention and gives a platform to a new way of seeing the world. Both Seraphinoff and María Elena Soliño write about this use of innocence as creating sympathy for the narrator and Soliño contends that works 'use the purity of the child narrator to highlight the truths that are often hidden or ignored by adults in repressive societies' (Soliño, 2008, 353). The debunking of the myths surrounding accepted social truths can therefore be brought about by a child in a way denied to an adult narrator. Although the children in Naranjo's stories may not fully understand the choices made by the adults or the rules that govern them, the reader certainly will, and the negative effects that the adult's decisions have on the innocent children are highlighted through this contrast.

The vision of Costa Rican society as a space in which the sexes have differently defined roles and where essential gendered qualities are seen as inextricably tied to sex certainly puts the national ideal at odds with arguments such as Butler's which contest fixed notions of gender identity. Butler suggests that individuals perform their gender based on society's expectations of their sex – whether intentionally or subconsciously – and the process of learning and mimicking behaviour patterns begins in childhood. It is on this basis that *Nunca hubo alguna vez* is best placed to deal with Naranjo's concerns around the instilling of social roles in future generations – thus creating a perpetual recycling of social norms – as it deals solely in child narrators. Within Naranjo's stories, the choice to use a child narrator also allows Naranjo to use irony to undermine the accepted world-view – that of the adults in the stories – through the innocent depiction of the child's viewpoint. Of irony, D. C. Muecke has pointed out that 'the basic element is a serene, confident unawareness coloured … by innocence' (1970, 30) and the child narrator is certainly able to reflect upon a situation without their judgement being clouded by socially accepted norms or stereotypes. While the title of the collection points towards the fact that these are stories told by children, they are not stories *for* children: the fact that the 'once upon a time' construction is rejected in the title indicates the absence of any 'happily ever after' endings within the collection.

'A los payasos todos los quieren' from *Nunca hubo alguna vez* is the first-person monologue of a young girl who narrates the trouble she has had answering the question that adults always ask her: 'What do you want to be when you grow up?' When she states she wants to be a nurse, an adventurer, or a shop owner, all her ideas are mocked. As such, she decides she wants to be something that makes people laugh – a clown (*payasa*). When her family ridicule her, stating that there is no such thing as a *payasa* – a female clown – she decides that she must therefore be a *payaso* – a boy clown – and she begins to dress like one all the time, painting her face, telling jokes, and doing tricks. She then narrates the trips she is forced to make to the psychologist and her eventual realization that her parents will only talk to her again if she conforms to what society expects of a little girl like her. As soon as she takes off the make-up and clown suit, and puts on a dress, her family accept her once more.

The childlike tone used in 'Payasos' is set up from the start as the child narrator bounces from topic to topic and as such highlights the social pressure to perform the *tico* norm from a young age. The narrator has an imaginative way of seeing the world, and her innocence is highlighted as it stands in stark contrast to the negative consequences of being raised in a gendered society. This is demonstrated as she describes garlic as 'envuelto en papel de regalo que cuesta un gran esfuerzo quitar' (39) before her thoughts quickly move on to the animals she likes. The gendered narrative starts immediately as she notes that lizards are her favourites because they are 'alegres … escondidas y presentes', while the lizard she observes is 'nerviosa y ligera … curiosa y traviesa' (39). These adjectives all denote an age where the protagonist is unsure of herself and what is expected – or perhaps demanded – of her. She wishes to be happy, curious, graceful, and mischievous like the lizard, but she too feels nervous and wants to fit – or blend – in. Not only do these adjectives aptly describe the process of growing up, but Naranjo also chooses the parallel of the lizard and the girl for this story because the *lagartija* as a noun takes the feminine pronoun in Spanish, meaning that the adjectives used to describe the lizard can more readily apply to the girl too.

Furthermore, it is clear that the girl already has a very certain sense of gendered expectations, answering the question of what she wants to be when she grows up with 'enfermera', 'paseadora', 'dueña', and 'payasa' – all in the feminine form. The use of gendered wordplay to highlight and undermine the gender difference found even in everyday language is a common tool used by authors of Naranjo's generation to draw attention to, and subvert, the rules of patriarchy,[13] but in using a child narrator Naranjo covers up this subversion with humour. Indeed, the girl's linguistic decisions appear to be made below her level of consciousness as her reasons given for choosing these professions range from never having to get injections to having everyone like her, rather than because they are jobs women can do, thus demonstrating Althusser's theory of interpellation of social ideals. Even when she is told there is no such thing as a *payasa* she does not reason that this is necessarily because of her sex; instead, she simply states: 'Como no podré ser payasa, seré payaso' (42). It is with the narrator's naive disruption of the accepted norms of gendered segregation in the professional world that Naranjo employs irony to make her point. Muecke states that one of the core elements of irony is 'pretending to be what one is not and pretending to be what one is' (1970, 25). This definition chimes with Butler's notion of gender performativity, and it would appear that the narrator in this story will pretend to be a clown in order to be one, while at the same time the reader is made aware of the girl being told to perform her gender, even though this means she cannot be a male clown – *payaso*.

Owing to this underlying pressure to perform her social role, the narrator makes several gender-based decisions without recognizing them as such, thus signifying that the interpellation of ideals and social norms – as noted by Althusser (1971, 174–81) and discussed in Chapter 1 – is at play within *tico* society. Naranjo also indicates that these attitudes stem from imitating the habits of others, pointing towards the importance of the role of habitus and mimicry in forming social awareness and maintaining set social roles. Indeed, the girl states that, when peeling garlic, 'sudo las desgracias de una cocina desordenada que me toca ordenar' (39), demonstrating that

---

13 For more on this, see Hart, 2008.

the chores she has to do already fall within the domain of the private and domestic, including cooking and cleaning. Additionally, when she states, 'jugamos la casita' (40), she is also imitating the social role of women, who must tend to the house and aspire to look after one.

It is also apparent that these sorts of social rules are instilled in the protagonist through the actions of her mother as when she arrives home from the supermarket armed with the latest clothing catalogue the event is described with reverence, as the dresses are contemplated slowly because 'hay decisiones muy serias' (40). Up to this point in the story, the choosing of clothes is the only desire of the girl's which has been taken seriously by her family, as her potential life choices have merely been laughed at. Felski argues that 'our sense of … how women look, talk, think, and feel, comes from the books we read, the films we watch, and the invisible ether of everyday assumptions and cultural beliefs in which we are suspended' (2011, 38) demonstrating that the perpetuation of stereotypes occurs as the girl imitates her mother in showing concern about her outward appearance. Motherhood, while a revered role in Costa Rica, is also, according to Naranjo, a burden that often curtails women's sense of self, as gender inequality in child-rearing is common (1981). She states, 'Dichosa la lagartija que tiene vestido por vida y es el mejor que podría tener, le va a la perfección' (40), clearly demonstrating her jealousy that the lizard has the ability to feel good in its own skin, not having to perform a social role assigned to it by normative discourses.

The parallels drawn between the girl and the lizard continue to be brought to the reader's attention as girls – like lizards – are encouraged to camouflage their true colours in order to blend into the background. However, just as the girl describes these creatures as happy, and mischievous as well, it is also made clear that she has not quite learned to accept the role assigned to her just yet, as she shows signs of curiosity and rebellion. It is interesting to note that as she begins to discount several animals which are not her favourites she claims she would not want to be a dog or a cat because 'nunca logran pensar que lo distinto es respetable' (39), intimating that at this point – at the beginning of the story before she is forced to accept what her fate as a woman must be – she believes that being different can be respectable. This same sense of boldness is demonstrated when she states that she wants to be a 'paseadora' as she would like to travel and see new things.

Moreover, she eventually settles on being a clown, despite its non-conformist implications: 'Sí, quiero ser payasa' (41). The female appellation of the word *payaso* does not exist, and thus the neologism *payasa* strikes the reader who begins to question why this profession – like many others – does not have a linguistic feminine equivalent. This linguistic strategy of 'feminization' is discussed in depth by Anne Pauwels, who states that it is a strategy used in languages such as Spanish which contain gender-specific nouns. She argues that as a means of achieving gender equality it is a more powerful tool in many cases than the gender-neutralization of words, as feminization effectively showcases the increasing number of women in certain professions (1999). It could therefore be argued that in her creation and employment of these new nouns, Naranjo's work offers an example of a feminist linguistic technique. Moreover, through the use of these gendered pronouns to describe professional roles, Naranjo purposely chooses to denounce the notion of 'female jobs' and 'male jobs', forming a critique of the fact that *enfermeras* exist while *enfermeros* do not, and vice versa with *paseadores* and *paseadoras*, *payasos* and *payasas*.

While the *tico* norm in relation to gender is established within the overt narrative, it is then critiqued in the subtext. Not only does this occur in terms of the feminization of professions, but 'Payasos' also opens a dialogue on the rules of beauty. The girl's mother states that she should find a job which is 'bonito' and 'alegre' (40), adjectives which are associated with the female form, both in terms of how the woman is physically expected to look and with regards to her social comportment. Castellanos states that 'beauty is an ideal composed and imposed by men' (Ahern, 1988, 237), and in 'Payasos' the women are told to be more concerned with their outward appearance than their inner desires or goals. This idea is then subverted, however, as women are seen to be negatively objectified by the male gaze. As Mulvey contends, 'women are simultaneously looked at and displayed, with their appearance coded for strong visual and erotic impact so that they can be said to connote to-be-looked-at-ness' (1985, 809). Although Mulvey, writing these words in 1975, had in mind women on film, this depiction of women as created to be looked at is an appropriate idea for the study of Naranjo's work, as her female characters have been coded, through the learned behaviour of social norms, to consider their visual aspect as their social value.

Naranjo's underlying critique of women as objects of beauty is evident as the girl's father takes no interest in the girl's thoughts, caring only about her appearance: 'Papá dice que no me va la ropa con vuelos, se le caen de flaca que está y se nota que con unos rellenos para disimular lo que le falta' (40–1). Her father therefore asserts his judgement over her appearance, assuming his right to do this, using prescriptive language to establish his – male – dominance from an early age. His words have also had an impact on the girl as she states, 'por eso me brinco los vestidos con vuelos, aunque son lindos y las niñas que los llevan se ven preciosas' (41), affirming that already she places less value on her own judgements and preferences than those of patriarchal society. This notion is underlined by Castellanos' critique of the myth-making of women – as 'the creator and spectator of the myth no longer see a woman as a flesh-and-blood person' (Ahern, 1988, 236) – instead, making her into a creature or possession useful to them.

Naranjo also critiques the double standards by which men and women live in the *tico* norm. Although Tío Jaime is loved when playing the clown, the girl is derided. Her mother dismisses her, stating, 'eso [payasa] ya sos' (41), before the girl notes that 'papá me explica que no hay payasas, a las mujeres nadie les contrata para eso porque son payasas siempre, se pintan y se disfrazan, nadie va a pagar para verlas porque sin entrada se ven de gratis en las calles y en los parques' (41). This ingrained world-view – which remains notably unchallenged by any characters in the story – is the accepted norm which has been passed on through the interpellation of ideals and become part of learned behaviour, even in childhood. This failure of the characters to contradict or question the patriarch's words serves to frustrate the reader, who, in turn, is forced to challenge these conceptions themselves.

As Borloz Soto reminds us with reference to Naranjo's works, 'vale la pena recordar que no siempre esos espacios [nacionales] se presentan como idílicos o paradisíacos' (2007, 92). Women as no more than their outward appearance – having to be beautiful and pleasing to men on the one hand, while also being ridiculed for this being their only role on the other – is the message that Costa Rican society sends to future generations.[14] This is an area of gender criticism prevalent among Latin American women writers in the 1970s and Castellanos explores the notion of woman as myth, created by and for men and to aid patriarchy, in her essay 'Woman and Her Image' (Ahern, 1988, 236). In answer to this outpouring of gendered prejudice, the girl thinks: 'Me da una rabieta enorme, pero en vez de ponerme furiosa me pongo muy triste y quisiera ser una lagartija con su propio mundo, sin que nadie la obligue a ser otra cosa' (41–2). Thus, Naranjo leaves the episode as an open-ended experiment, one through which I argue she posits questions to her audience: what should the girl's reaction be? Should the reader be angry about this treatment of women? Should this gendered approach to child-rearing be the norm? As these questions and answers are not openly discussed in the story itself – it is implied that the narrator is too young fully to formulate them – the emphasis is placed even more firmly on the reader

---

14 María Lourdes Cortés demonstrates this in 'El polvo de los sueños: Aproximación a la nueva narrativa costarricense' (1999) through her reading of literature as often containing the social norms ingrained in the Costa Rican nation where women are subject to the playing out of the Madonna/whore complex.

to delve into this issue and come to their own conclusions, thus using the narrative to push them towards a rebellion against habitus.

Naranjo furthers this experience for the reader as she unpacks the consequences of this imposition of gendered beliefs. When the girl stands firm, she is met with negative reactions as 'papá pone el ceño fruncido, mamá la cara amarga, la misma que pone cuando no le alcanza la plata' (42). She is also derided by her parents as they tell her 'es muy estúpido ... sos muy desconsiderada, nos ponés en ridículo' (42), demonstrating the parents' concern with upholding social norms. Even her psychologist states that 'si querés ser payaso pues a serlo todo el tiempo para que te des cuenta que nadie los quiere y los aguanta apenas un rato' (42), highlighting the imposition of gendered norms as a forceful and overt exercise as well as something implicit which is maintained through learned behaviour. The final conclusion of this episode, however, has tragic overtones which push the reader to want to take action. The girl looks in the mirror one day and tells herself 'al fin aprendí' (43) and then 'pongo los zapatos blancos que van con las medias azules, mi falda de paletones con cuadros blancos y azules y la blusa de organdí celeste' (43). The reader now sees that the girl has sacrificed herself in order to conform to the *tico* norm and has been praised by her family for it: 'ya me conversan, se ríen y sonríen conmigo' (43). Just as Duncan's Charles McForbes acts out Lukács' idea of a false consciousness – colluding with society in its prejudice against him no matter how negatively this affects the individual – so the girl in this story also decides to adhere to the dominant system which is opposed to her own choices. Naranjo again employs irony to critique gender imbalance – in this instance the irony of self-betrayal – described as something a character 'throws away' only later to find it 'indispensable' (Muecke, 1970, 66). The narrator throws away her dreams, individuality, and ability to challenge stereotypes, all of which are fundamental to the feminist discourse that Naranjo explores in this story.

A final irony is employed by Naranjo, however, as the girl states: 'Cuando me vuelven a preguntar qué voy a ser de grande, contesto que lo que ellos quieran ... Y para que me quieran de verdad, sé que debo ser payasa como quien no se da cuenta de que lo es' (43). This assertion reveals the culmination of the dramatic or situational irony prevalent throughout the story whereby 'two co-existent meanings are opposed' (Muecke, 1970, 22) within the same story. The girl innocently narrates her decision to conform to social stereotypes by suggesting that she will be whatever she is told to be. Ironically, however, the profession or persona she is told she cannot embody – being a clown – is exactly what her parents, the psychologist, and wider society have made her: she must now perform her accepted role in society so that she can be outwardly acceptable in the part she is to play. The irony, then, is not lost on the innocent child narrator, but on the dominant parties she is at odds with, as it is they who are, as Muecke puts it, 'unaware that the situation as [they] see it is the contrary of the real situation' (1970, 73). This statement also demonstrates that the *tico* norm is constructed in such a way that the social pressure to conform to the cultural ideal – be it gendered or otherwise – is ever-present in Naranjo's world-view. When the narrator states that she knows she must always be a female clown now, she is no longer using this term for the purposes of individuality and empowerment, as before. She is also establishing that, as a woman, she now knows she must paint her face, dress up, and pretend to be something she is not.

As Borloz Soto notes:

la condición de subordinación, de invisibilidad, de vejación o de maltrato en la cue han vivido y continúan viviendo inmensas mayorías de mujeres en el mundo, es reiterativa y fuertemente denunciada a lo largo de toda la producción literaria naranjeana porque 'las mujeres son siempre payasas' pero ni siquiera el disfraz les permite ser 'persona', ser ellas mismas y tener voz propia. (Borloz Soto, 2007, 13)

'Payasos', then, is not an innocent account of a young girl who begins to consider the big life question of what she wants to be when she grows up – as the Cuban animated adaptation of the story would have the audience believe (Recuerdos TV Cuba, 2011). Rather, it is a narrative that explores the impact of the rigidity of gendered roles, the subordination of women in mainstream *tico* society, and the devastating effects of this on future generations of Costa Ricans who will go on to perform and perpetuate these expectations. By using the child narrator who does not fully comprehend the weight of the words spoken to her alongside techniques of defamiliarization, Naranjo shocks the reader into recognizing the extent to which gendered socialization and learned behaviour patterns occur and collude to create harmful social norms, thereby challenging her audience using the tools of gendered language and irony to take action on behalf of future generations. Just as in Duncan's *Los cuatro espejos*, then, the problem that Naranjo deals with is laid bare, and the reader is forced either to react against habitus and challenge gender inequality or become complicit in it.

Encoding the Gay Experience in Costa Rica: The Fiction of Alfonso Chase

Another of the protest authors who began to publish in the 1970s and who also uses subtext and the short story as vehicles for this protest is

Alfonso Chase Brenes. Chase has been described by literary critic and author Alexander Obando as 'reconocido como uno de los innovadores de las letras en nuestro país' (2008, xxxii), and this contention is certainly present in both his writing style and the themes that he develops throughout his works. Born in Cartago in 1944, Chase completed a BA in literature and social sciences at the University of Costa Rica before undertaking postgraduate study in the USA and Mexico. His first work, a collection of poetry entitled *Los reinos de mi mundo*, was published in 1966, and since then he has gone on to publish 16 further works of fiction, including novels, short stories, poetry, and children's books. Testament to Chase's important role in the world of Costa Rican letters are the numerous national and international literary prizes that he has been awarded, such as the 1999 *Premio Magón* for his contribution to literature (Editorial Costa Rica). In addition to his literary career, Chase has also occupied various political and academic roles and currently works for the *Universidad Autónoma* in Heredia. Despite his notable career as an author, however, Chase's literary works remain largely unstudied both within Costa Rica and internationally.

Chase's fiction often encompasses techniques used by the generation of Latin American boom writers as well as socially engaged themes (López, 2012). He notes that Julio Cortázar and Miguel Ángel Asturias are his literary influences (López, 2012), and the theme of identity writing – or the discovery of selfhood through narration – is apparent in Chase's works. As a homosexual author in Central America, however, Chase also narrates his works from this standpoint. As David William Foster notes, homosexuality in Latin America was seen as being both a disease and a crime until the 1960s and 1970s – coinciding with the era in which Chase started to publish. He states that:

> With the emergence of the medico-legal concept of the homosexual at the end of the nineteenth century ... a personality or psychological type is created, whose nature, character, worldview, and total life experience are marked by same-sex preference. This preference is universally viewed as a compulsion, a depraved weakness, and a fatal alienation ... this ideology prevailed from the latter decades of the last [nineteenth] century until the 1960s and 1970s. (Foster, 2002, 75)

Although some authors have attempted to construct a canon of queer literature in Latin America, Foster notes (2002, 3) that progress towards this is tentative as homosexual fictions have often been viewed as standalone acts rather than attempts to construct an entire identity around sexuality. He goes on to point out that there is a tendency in some texts towards a demystification of homosexuality as a valid expression of a natural desire (48), a motif employed by Chase in his stories. This technique is used by Chase in code, however, as Obando notes (2008, xvii) that openly aligning yourself with the LGBTQ+ community in public spaces is dangerous even in the twenty-first century and was especially so in the 1970s.[15] Based on this, it is perhaps little wonder that Chase was able to do no more than allude to the homosexual experience in Costa Rica in his early works. Indeed, just like Naranjo, it was not until the 1990s that Chase found it was possible for him to make homosexuality a core theme of his writing, as he does in *Jardines de asfalto* (1994) and *Cara de santo, uñas de gato* (1999).

It is my contention that his early works can, however, be classed as the beginning of pro-gay literary production in Costa Rica, with Obando noting that *Mirar con inccencia* cannot be termed as 'exclusivamente heterosexual' (2008, xxii). For this reason, Candide Carrasco includes Chase alongside Naranjo, Uriel Quesada, and José Ricardo Chaves as the only authors to confront themes of sexual 'Otherness' in their works (2003, 84). He also notes, however, that these authors were forced to explore these issues in an implicit or even obscure manner, as 'en Costa Rica ... con dificultad algún autor se presenta como escritor gay ...' (81), as 'en un país donde aún los valores religiosos, católicos y otros influyen sobre casi todas las clases sociales, resulta atrevido y debilitante declararse gay' (82). He also notes that subtext was often used to present a homosexual point of view in works of this period (84) while Obando notes in his anthology of gay and lesbian writing in the country (2008, xxii) that Chase's more explicit works on the subject of homosexuality were published from the 1990s onwards. The use of coding – which will be explored in his earlier works – is suggested to be common to the gay experience by Eve Sedgwick (2008, 67–90) as, unlike with other marginalized identities, a work of fiction has to 'come out' as being gay. Claude Summers also notes (2002, 2) that homosexual literature often uses code as a means of disguising the sexual element of the work, while Foster asserts (2002, 431–4) that in Latin American fiction this is particularly common.

In reference to his 1975 collection of short stories, *Mirar con inocencia*, Chase stated in 2012 that: 'se refiere a usted mismo como personaje de su propia historia, siendo una persona gay en una sociedad donde haber sido gay en ese tiempo fue muy duro y se tuvo que enfrentar a muchas

---

15 Obando asserts (2008, xxvii) that many works of literature which contain topics such as homosexuality which are said to 'offend' the official, national values are readily dismissed by the academy as 'no edificante', 'pachuco', or 'carente de principios constructivos' in order to curtail their study or promotion.

dificultades' (López, 2012). It is a collection which encompasses several different themes such as religion and mental illness, and although the theme of sexuality is not evident in the collection based on a superficial reading, when delving deeper into the subtext of the stories within *Mirar con inocencia* many do contain a critique of the country's heteronormative ideology. In these stories-within-stories, Chase plays with the contention that sex, gender, and sexuality are independent of one another and do not form a straight-line trajectory – for example, one that would read man–male– desire for women. This standpoint forms the basis of Butler's conception of queer theory; she contests the ideals of patriarchal and heteronormative societies using this rationale. Indeed, Sedgwick further points out (2008, 9–10) that a queer viewpoint can be used to challenge the very notion that homosexuality and heterosexuality exist as binaries, and queer literature therefore may discuss the normalization of homosexuality and the rejection of patriarchy, considering the role of the 'Other' within the text.

Chase's works are certainly therefore examples of queer literature in Costa Rica, and it is further apparent that he deliberately breaks with the *tico* norm in his writing by attempting to narrate this 'Other' experience and the impact of normative discourse on it, a concept that Sedgwick terms (2008, 91) the universalization, rather than the minoritization, of the gay experience. Chase is not, of course, the first author to do this,[16] but within Costa Rica he is certainly a part of the first generation of writers to show a preoccupation with issues of non-hegemonic sexual identities. Considering the context in which Chase wrote *Mirar con inocencia*, then, the following analysis of his work will explore the codes used implicitly to examine the gay experience in Costa Rica.

'La lluvia. El silencio. La música.'

As has been pointed out about Naranjo's *Ondina*, Chase's collection of short stories, *Mirar con inocencia* (1975) also explores several social taboos using dark humour and, often, shocking themes. One such story is 'La lluvia. El silencio. La música.', which has rarely, if ever, been commented on by critics of Chase's work. This may well be because of the sexually explicit nature of the text, as well as its polemic theme of three people sharing a sexual encounter as an issue academics in the nation have not traditionally wished to consider. It is, however, Chase's most overt exploration of both hetero- and homosexuality, and as such merits further consideration. As previously mentioned, writing about sexual encounters has been considered dangerous for Latin American authors in the past, although perhaps more so for female

---

16 For a detailed study of a queer literary tradition, see Summers, 2002.

than male writers, which could explain why Chase felt less inhibited when writing this story. He did not, it would seem, feel that it was possible to include references solely to homosexual relationships in this collection, however. As such, while this story is about young people's discovery of their own sexuality which does not fit the heteronormative mould, Chase is careful to include both men and women in the actual sexual experience.

'La lluvia. El silencio. La música.' is a first-person narrative told as a stream of consciousness and reported speech with the entire story forming one sentence. The narrator is a young man who begins the tale stating that it is raining and that he is sitting in his room not speaking while listening to music. Indeed, the rain, silence, and music of the title of the piece are frequently mentioned, and become intertwined with the scene that plays out. The reader soon discovers that the boy-narrator is not alone, and that there are two others with him lying on his bed naked – a boy and a girl. The three begin to talk about having seen each other around their neighbourhood and having desired each other from afar, and soon these admissions lead to sexual exploration of the physical bodies of the three protagonists. The language is rarely sexually explicit or erotic, however, and the boy links the three bodies with the three sounds – rain, music, and silence – that pervade this experience. The inner monologue ends as the boy describes his contentment at having been able to discover himself through this experience, noting that every time it rains in the afternoon and he sits in silence listening to music, he remembers this encounter. These three concepts create a type of *roman à clef* as they are the key to unlocking the codes used by Chase to present an experience of a sexual 'Other' in Costa Rica through the use of subtext and ambiguity.

Although Chase does not use overtly sexual language in this story, just as he shies away from writing an entirely homosexual affair, the content certainly pushes the boundaries of normative Costa Rican ideals of sexuality. In order to allow himself the space to write about the sexual encounter, Chase constructs a *Bildungsroman* as the young protagonists discover themselves, their bodies, and their desires. In many ways, it is the typical tale of a first sexual experience and resonates with the audience in a similar way to Naranjo's love story in 'Simbiosis'. The boy states that the three are 'cuerpo a cuerpo' (71) but also 'los tres en un mismo espacio, muertos de miedo, temblorosos, llenos de lluvia interna' (71). The mixture of fear and anticipation that they feel helps to set the story up as a site of discovery and as such it is made more palatable for a *tico* audience. Moreover, it is clear that the encounter has romantic overtones and is not just about sexual pleasure. Indeed, the only element to break the heteronormative code of the new, happy, relationship is the fact that there are three people involved, not just two. The narrator states that 'el primer día que nos vimos: él, ella y yo, como si no nos conociéramos desde siempre y así empezamos a hablar de música y de lluvia y de plantas y todas esas cosas que tanto nos gustan' (71). Just like Naranjo, Chase uses the typical language of the 'boy meets girl' encounter to describe the threesome's first meeting as they felt they had known each other forever and found topics of conversation in common. Even when the three do begin their physical encounter, Chase states: 'tomé las manos de ambos entre las mías y las besé, juntas en mi boca' (72), again creating a romantic, rather than erotic, tone. The boy then notes that 'ustedes me decían, mudamente, cosas que yo no entendía pero me encerraba en sus miradas y olvidaba los versos' (72), thereby demonstrating the silence around non-normative relationships and the consequential confusion the boy harboured over his own desires.

Aware of the constraints of writing a sexually explicit piece in 1970s Costa Rica, Chase also offers descriptions which are more anatomical than erotic: 'las tres cabezas juntas, muy cercanos los cuerpos, el sexo hacia abajo, las espaldas extendidas como una piel' (71). Indeed, the most explicit scenes of the story are narrated in a practical manner that appears to eschew all erotic imagery: 'acerqué los dos cuerpos hasta mí, y allí estaban: jóvenes, blancos, duros' (72) and 'acercamos más los cuerpos y nos estuvimos juntos y ya no hubo más lluvia o música y solo el sonido de los cuerpos se escuchaba por el cuarto' (73). The adjectives 'jóvenes, blancos, duros' (72) used to describe the bodies of the narrator's two lovers are a far cry from even the romantic language he has used so far to describe their relationship. Moreover, the acceleration from their shared kisses to the point at which 'acercamos más los cuerpos y nos estuvimos juntos' (73) demonstrates that Chase knows he must not give too much detail about the practicalities of this threesome; noting solely that the three were together must suffice. What Chase does make clear, however, is that this is not just a homosexual affair, as from the start the girl is included both sexually and emotionally in the threesome. Every utterance refers to 'them' and 'we' in the plural – 'seguía besando sus manos', 'ellos ... besaron mis labios', 'los hice uno con mi cuerpo' (73) – whereby if these pronouns were changed to the singular, the narrative would depict a traditional, heteronormative sexual encounter.

Though the fact that there are three participants is evident from the beginning of the story, it is not until halfway down the first page that the reader discovers that the narrator is male, as he describes himself using a gendered adjective, 'desnudo' (71). As it is clear that the other two are a boy and girl – described as 'él' and 'ella' (71) from the start – the reader is now alerted to the possibility of a homosexual encounter which would break with social – and religious – norms. The inclusion of the girl in the trio denotes that Chase did not feel able to write simply about a same-sex couple in this scenario, and this inhibition also becomes apparent when considering the sexual language found in the story. When the boy describes his actions with the girl, they are the most sexually detailed of the entire narrative: 'bésenme dijo ella, y los dos la besamos por los muslos ... nos subimos por todo el cuerpo y la sentimos' (73). When the boy describes his sexual encounter with the other boy, however, the language once more becomes ambiguous, and the narrative rushed: 'nos besamos los dos y nos besamos los tres y las bocas se encontraban, él y yo, yo y ella ... yo lo amaba a él y yo la amaba a ella' (73). The same-sex kiss is only allowed to enter the reader's imagination for a split-second, before heteronormative order is restored and the female once again enters the account. Chase thereby uses his female character to broker a same-sex encounter between two males. It would appear, then, that the use of the forbidden threesome is actually used as a smokescreen to explore bi- and homosexuality – or the sexual 'Other'.

This notion of the performance of a forbidden act that must be kept secret is one that Chase maintains throughout the narrative, perhaps to alert the reader to the fact that as an author he has been forced to conceal his true intentions beneath the superficial text. The first line of the story points the reader towards this fact, as does the silence of the title, as the boy notes 'no nos es permitido hablar, pensé' (71). The reader soon infers that this is the enforced silence of the sexual 'Other' living in *tico* society. Indeed, rather than choosing to be silent, it is clear that the protagonists are actively being silenced as Chase describes them as: 'callados' and 'mudos' (72) rather than enjoying a peaceful or comfortable silence. Moreover, they all utter that 'la tarde cae sobre todos los rincones de la ciudad, dijimos' (71), implying that their liaison or entire relationship can only take place under the cover of darkness, again underlining its forbidden nature within the boundaries of the *tico* norm. This understanding is highlighted as, in the final part of the story, the boy notes that he will always remember them 'en estas tardes en que el aire se detiene para mirarnos y la ciudad desciende, por una leve pendiente, para olvidarse entre ruidos, pasos y gestos' (74). The narrator suggests that their relationship can only occur when society is looking the other way or too busy with other tasks to notice them, allowing them to carry on in secret. While Chase continually makes it clear to the reader that the encounter narrated to them is taboo, then, he also appears to use this language to signpost his audience towards the subtext of his story which refers to all non-heteronormative relationships as forbidden by society. In this way, not only are the characters mimicking heteronormative relationships while performing some semblance of what is expected of their genders, they are also internalizing the dominant notion that what they are choosing to do with their bodies is wrong. Although Fanon's thesis on the internalization of negative stereotypes centred on tropes of racial hierarchies, it is also seen here to apply to the dominant discourse surrounding sexual norms.

This idea is also showcased as the silence imposed on the trio carries with it a sense of threat. The boy says, 'yo soñaba con ustedes y pensaba en sus ojos, y en sus cabellos', and he goes on to state: 'pero tenía miedo de encontrármelos por la calle y decirles lo que pensaba' (72). Although this could be taken to mean that the boy was scared of what the boy and girl would think of his feelings, it also indicates his fear around what other people – or *tico* society – would think of this relationship. The other boy also notes this fear, asserting that 'cuando los que se aman están juntos hace frío, es el pánico de estar juntos' (72). The panic and cold that he claims are normal repercussions of being with the ones you love stands in stark contrast to traditional romantic descriptions where love connotes warmth and contentment. The fact that their relationship subverts the norm, then, is cause for fear. This notion can also be seen in the combative language used by Chase to depict the scene. They are described as 'escondidos en la música' (71), not simply lost in it or listening to it, but actively hidden in it, as well as 'fugados por un instante del cuerpo' (71). The consequence of describing them as 'fugados' and 'escondidos' conjures up visions of warfare, where the protagonists are being hunted down. This image is continued by Chase as he narrates the rain trying to get in as though someone is breaking through the door: 'los sonidos de la lluvia que ya empezaba a golpear con fuerza los cristales de la puerta de mi cuarto' (71). This notion of the music hiding them and their affair while the rain tries to get in is then furthered as he describes 'la música batallando con la lluvia' (71). The juxtaposition between the *tico* norm – or the outside world – and the relationship instigated by these three, then, is set up using these code words of rain, music, and silence.

These external elements – the rain, the people, the city – are thereby seen as the enemy of the gentle, romantic relationship portrayed in the story, demonstrating how the sexual 'Other' is demeaned by the rest of Costa Rican society and constantly feels under attack from the *tico* norm. These three symbols – rain, music, and silence – then, are the keys to the subtext of the story. While the rain at once provides the cover for the illicit affair, it also embodies a society which is too busy to notice what they are doing, although, when it finds them, beats down their door trying to put a stop to it. The music is their protection – it is ambient and fluid, just like their sexuality and Hall's concept of the fluidity of identity, and allows them to keep the sounds of the rest of the world at bay. The music could be said to be the pro-gay rights voices which began to make themselves heard in the 1960s and 1970s: while the rain and music – or social norms and pro-gay supporters – battle it out externally to the trio, silence is maintained by the protagonists. It represents both the gay or LGBTQ+ experience in Costa Rica which cannot be fully articulated for fear of reprisal, while at the same time demonstrating the author's inability to formulate a homo- or bisexually erotic narrative. The absence of the full realization of the sexual act within the text perhaps speaks louder than its inclusion possibly could.

In order to combat this sentiment of non-heterosexual, monogamous, relationships as 'Other' or abject, Chase then uses the images he sets up in the title – the rain, music, and silence – to parallel the trio of protagonists, making the argument that their actions are entirely natural. In the opening of the story, the narrator thinks of silence, the girl states that music is taking over her body, and the boy notes that it is raining outside, and immediately the characters are bound up with these elements. While at times the outside influences appear to be at war, at others they are personified in positive terms, as a part of this sexual and romantic encounter: 'la música picoteando por los muslos, la lluvia detenida en el cerebro' (72), 'la música también allí estaba, entre la mirada y la lluvia' (73), 'por la sangre va la música con su sonido claro' (73). In this way these three elements become not only their protectors from the outside world but also their intermediaries. The narrator states: 'nos amábamos los tres en las tardes de lluvia y con música y con silencio' (73), demonstrating the reliance of their encounter upon the rain and music that shielded them from sight and sound, and the silence that they had to maintain.

It is also made clear that, although they felt they had to hide their relationship, they themselves understood that it was as natural as the rain splashing against the windows: 'los tres entendimos de esos encuentros en las tardes y de la lluvia salpicando los cristales de las puertas de mi cuarto' (73). Chase also chooses to naturalize same-sex desire in the story as the narrator states: 'besé primero uno y luego a la otra, y no descubrí ninguna diferencia en el sabor de la saliva o en la intensidad del tacto' (72). With this pronouncement Chase makes it clear that whether the boy kisses the girl or the other boy there is no difference in his desire towards them, which makes the reader question why one of these kisses would be viewed as normal, whereas the other would be vilified. The boy also points out that 'ellos me amaban los dos igual' (73), again evidencing the natural quality of sexual desire, and the absurdity of the constructed and imposed binary of homo- and heterosexuality.

Through the creation of a story which revolves around a sexual act involving three people – albeit one which is never fully articulated – Chase is already undermining several ideals which are bound up with both *tico* social norms and Costa Rican literature. Without using explicitly erotic language he depicts a sexual image, one which is at odds with the patriarchal and Catholic normative ideology prevalent within the country. The notion of sex as only being acceptable within marriage and for procreation is also undone in this exploration of adolescent desires. Through the construction of a three-way relationship, Chase creates a same-sex encounter, something rarely attempted in Costa Rican literature before the end of the twentieth century. Rather than setting up the *tico* norm in order to subvert it, Chase assumes that normative attitudes towards sexual behaviour will be ingrained within his reader's imagination and he therefore undermines them through his use of sexual language, parallels with nature, and a dialogue of the forbidden which stands in contrast to the romantic innocence of his narrator. This radical breaking of habitus by the characters in 'La lluvia', however, occurs only once, leaving the reader of the story questioning why the narrator should have to be left with his memories, rather than being allowed to maintain the relationship he desires. 'La lluvia' therefore forces the reader to reconsider the prescriptive nature of the *tico* ideal, seeing it as both harmful and repressive.

'El hilo del viento'

Like 'La lluvia', Chase uses the short story, 'El hilo del viento' – also from the collection *Mirar con inocencia* – to narrate the dangers of the internalization of social norms and the impact of these on the Costa Rican sexual 'Other'. 'El hilo' is told by a child narrator who, like Naranjo's, is naive when it comes to deciphering the thoughts, motivations, and actions of those around him. Indeed, while the text tells of a physical journey of the boy and his family, the subtext points towards an encoded reading of the boy's sexual journey and the attitudes he encounters towards sexual 'Otherness' as symbolic of all Costa Rican society. In a similar way to Naranjo's 'Payasos', then, Chase also uses the child's voice to make the subtext visible as the reader looks beyond the limited understanding of the narrator.

'El hilo' tells the story of a boy, his brothers, and his father waving goodbye to their mother and starting a long journey into the Costa Rican jungle. The boy begins by narrating the physical journey as a stream of consciousness, using long sentences and little punctuation. During the journey, the family meet Luis Esteban Curti who hitches a ride with them, in return regaling them with stories about life in the jungle. Luis Esteban soon becomes a permanent fixture in the boy's life, and they grow closer as the years pass, spending all their time together and sleeping side by side. The boy soon notices that his brothers and father act in a hostile manner towards them both, making up lies about Luis Esteban and claiming that he has a tail. Although the boy does not take this seriously, he is awoken one night by screams emanating from the forest and he follows the sound to find his brothers violently beating Luis Esteban, leaving his dead body in a river. After committing the murder, the brothers find that their bodies begin to rot, but never die, and the boy states that a whole community has now grown around them in the jungle, a community from which he distances himself.

The two layers of this story – the tale that the boy narrates and the subtext beyond this – work together to create a critique of how sexual 'Otherness' is viewed in contemporary *tico* society. In a similar way to Naranjo's 'Payasos', Chase alerts the reader to the youth of the narrator, at once underlining his innocence and informing the reader that they must look beyond his words. The story begins mid-sentence 'Y empezamos el viaje en la mañana' (75) and the long sentences which punctuate the story – and the majority of sentences beginning with 'Y' – point towards this being an oral tale. The boy's age is highlighted as he talks about his toys and stamp collection: 'yo iba en el altillo del coche, con mis soldados de plomo y los muñequitos de paja y el libro de estampas viejas' (75). The fact that he does not know why they are going on this journey or where they are going also points towards his young age, suggesting that his father does not yet think him old enough to understand. His innocence is also highlighted as he is excited by the thought of journeying into the jungle, and notes that he sleeps, at first, 'entre los brazos de mi padre' (75), clearly still requiring his protection and comfort.

In order to further force the reader to engage with the story's subtext, certain ambiguities are also set up within 'El hilo'. It is with a childlike fascination that the boy first recalls his meeting with Luis Esteban, as he marvels at the new world shown to him by his friend. This innocence enshrouding his character from the start of the story sets up these ambiguities as the narrative continues. The reader is alerted to his growing up as he states that his trousers are too big for him, while he also states that Luis Esteban has taught him to 'hacer muchas cosas ahora con mi cuerpo' (77), such as 'andar como los monos y desnudo' (77). However, the potentially sexual connotations of walking naked and being able to do new things with his body are curtailed by the innocence that permeates the account, as the boy goes on to say that Luis Esteban has also taught him how to climb trees and pick flowers. It is this constant affirmation of the boy's innocence that leaves the reader profoundly struck by his cruel treatment at the hands of his family when he states, 'y empecé a sentir que mi padre me regañaba por gusto y que mis hermanos no me daban la comida suficiente o me molestaban con Luis Esteban, y él nada decía' (76). This sudden depiction of cruelty prompts the reader to question why the boy is being made to feel different and victimized. The narrator, however, remains ignorant of both his family's motive and of the full height of their feelings, until Luis Esteban's death. Even after seeing the body, he says: 'yo nada decía porque estaba mudo y se sentía como si nada tuviera ya en el cuerpo' (78). To the adult reader it is apparent that he is grieving for his friend, unable to form the words which could help him make sense of the situation.

Through the highlighting of the boy's naivety and innocence, then, the reader is forced to play detective in order to uncover the implicit reasons behind this act of violence that the narrator seemingly finds incomprehensible. Reading between the lines of Chase's story, using pieces of the narrative that remain unsaid as well as inferences from the text itself, it would appear that the motive behind the crime is a hatred of difference and the possibility of Luis Esteban's homosexuality. As the story begins, Chase sets up the narrative within the parameters of a patriarchal order into which women will rarely feature. The reader is told in the opening paragraph that the journey will include the boy, his father, and his brothers as 'mi madre quedó en casa' (75). The first woman to be mentioned in the story is quickly left behind, and soon forgotten by her family (76), while the only other women entering the narrative are the prostitutes who sleep with the brothers (78). The journey is regarded by the boy with the solemnity of a rite of passage and the concept of the patriarchal prism – the lens through which society is viewed from a patriarchal point of view – can be seen as the boy is taken away from female influences by the powerful men in his family to whom he must look for instruction and survival.

The relationship that the boy starts with Luis Esteban, when viewed from the point of view of his position within the patriarchal hierarchy, can therefore also be seen as having dual layers. On the surface, the way in which their kinship progresses seems like a friendship. The young boy is fascinated by Luis Esteban's magical stories and tricks. Their relationship could also be read, however, as the showcasing of another lifestyle and belief system outside of the patriarchal prism. Indeed, the boy states that 'cada día aprendía algo de mi amigo' (78). This mirrors the covert learning experience that the homosexual community of Costa Rica went through in the 1970s as announcing oneself as 'different' had the potential to uncover violent consequences. When the boy speaks of the types of things that Luis Esteban teaches him, he notes that 'mi amigo me enseñaba suertes y palabras nuevas y sonidos para practicar con los labios, y flexiones de cuerpo que me hicieron crecer más el tórax, adelgazar la cintura y aumentar el tamaño de mis brazos' (76). Again, this statement can be read on two levels. On the surface, this pronouncement demonstrates learning how to adapt physically to life in the jungle as Luis Esteban teaches him not only how to survive but also how to thrive in this environment. On another level, however, the boy is learning about a new way of living in the society and world that surrounds him which insists upon the learning of a new mode of expression both vocally and physically.

Chase includes these descriptions to show that the boy actually has to relearn the rules of his own body and passions in order to discover how he really wants to live. Although Chase does not explicitly align Luis Esteban with any notion of sexuality, the language he uses to describe their relationship points towards the possibility of homosexuality. Soon after the boy meets Luis Esteban, he notes that their relationship progressed from playing together to them sleeping side by side: 'mi amigo dormía ahora cerca de mí' (76) and that, often, 'nos íbamos a bañar al río, mi amigo y yo, desnudos y alegres' (76). Moreover, after Luis Esteban's death, the boy does not sleep with the prostitutes that visit his brothers, perhaps further demonstrating that he has no interest in a female partner (78). Claude Summers notes that the recurrent themes in gay and lesbian literature which are frequently coded or constructed in the subtext of a story include: 'self-realization, erotic longing, alienation from society, and the celebration of beauty and forbidden pleasures' (2002, 1). The narrator of this novel displays all these elements as in the text he finds he has new abilities and a new friend to whom he is close, as well as distancing himself from his family and society. Within the subtext, all of these can be read as aspects of the gay experience as they are unexplained in the surface narrative.

This duality of the text continues as the boy's family – the patriarchal gender regime – displays displeasure with the relationship after the boy states that he and Luis Esteban bathe naked together in the river. This is Chase's most overt hint that the pair may have a sexual relationship, and after it is recounted the boy notes 'mis hermanos refunfuñaban y mi padre, muy pensativo, golpeaba con el látigo a los bueyes' (76). Although the reason for their discomfort is not clear to the boy, it is apparent to the reader that they do not approve of the nature of his relationship with Luis Esteban. Their reactions continue to sour as the pair become closer: 'mis hermanos me miraban con odio y mi padre con indiferencia, y yo entendí que ya nada había entre nosotros' (77). It is interesting to note that while the boy seems to pick up the nuances of his relationship with his family very clearly, he does not overtly reference the motivations for their hatred. The authorial reasons for this appear to be twofold: first, Chase cannot disclose a sexual relationship between the two boys for fear of censorship and, secondly, the fact that the reader has to dig into the subtext even further in order to understand their motives makes both the violence and the senselessness of the brothers' crime even more shocking.

Although Chase cannot explicitly mention the boy's sexuality, then, the reader's task in cracking the code of the subtext is made somewhat easier by the linguistic clues that Chase drops into the story. At the beginning, the boy states that they left home 'llenos todos de tristeza por dejar lo que teníamos y por no saber lo que nos iba a pertenecer' (75). This statement could easily be appropriated by any group fighting against social marginalization, as the decision to choose to live an 'alternative' or 'non-normative' lifestyle is always a leap into the unknown. Moreover, at the end of the story, the boy states that although a community is formed in the jungle, 'me fui alejando de todos' (78), isolating himself from normative society.

Another clue left by Chase can be seen as the brothers' actions mirror wider society's treatment of the homosexual community as they victimize Luis Esteban, suggesting that he has a physical deformity. As David William Foster notes (2002, 75), throughout the nineteenth and twentieth centuries homosexuality in Costa Rica was often associated with physical illness and mental depravity. Even in the twenty-first century, the stance that homosexuality is an abnormality that can and should be cured is prevalent, most notably in the Catholic Church. Chase appears to play on this notion in both the text and the subtext as the boy's brothers begin to tell their father that Luis Esteban has a tail: 'y un día mis hermanos dijeron que habían visto a Luis Esteban bañándose y que tenía rabo' (77). Within the narrative of the story they are voicing their displeasure with Luis Esteban and attempting to bring about an end to his relationship with their brother. They are also, however, marginalizing him as an 'Other', animalizing him, and making him seem different, while playing with the notion that society's view of homosexuality is that it is not natural – just like having a tail. The use of the word 'rabo' rather than the word 'cola', which is more common, also acts as a coded wordplay. The Real Academia Española (RAE) recognizes the word to mean, in a vulgar context, 'pene del hombre', while in Costa Rica specifically the same dictionary defines it as having the colloquial meaning of 'trasero (nalgas)'. Considering this context, the passage takes on new meaning and the reader understands that Luis Esteban was not using his own penis in a way considered natural, or proper, by wider society.

The reiteration of something bordering on a sexual encounter between the boy and Luis Esteban also prompts fear and hatred in the eyes of normative society – the brothers and their father. The boy notes that 'mis hermanos tenían miedo de mí' and that, of his father, 'yo sabía que tenía también miedo de mis manos pero sobre todo de mis ojos' (77). These statements demonstrate a generalized fear of 'Otherness', and of something the family does not find socially acceptable occurring to one of them. As the boy notes that his father was afraid of his hands, but even more so of his eyes, Chase appears to show that the father cannot understand his son's desires – contained within his touch and sight. It is at this point that the full rupture occurs, with the boy and Luis Esteban on one side and the brothers and father on the other. This isolation is representative of the position of the marginalized 'Other' in the *tico* paradigm – especially of the sexual 'Other' who has had to create an entire community in which to feel at ease.

Indeed, the boy states that he and Luis Esteban 'dormíamos juntos, como para protegernos y me di cuenta de que cada vez estaba más lejano de mis hermanos y de mi padre y ellos insistían que mi amigo tenía rabo' (78). Not only does the boy now actively feel that he is in danger, but his family refuses to accept his side of the story. Chase appears to be saying that this is the contemporary position of the sexual 'Other' in Costa Rican society: it is isolated from the mainstream, pushed to the margins, and victimized for its perceived difference. The pointlessness of violence against 'Others' is then highlighted through the haunting picture painted of Luis Esteban's death: 'una noche me di cuenta de que estaba solo y me desperté completamente y oí ruidos y gritos en el bosque y cuando vi su cuerpo hecho pulpa, lloré amargamente y mis hermanos lavaron los palos en el agua cercana' (78). This arresting image is used by Chase to shock his reader into thinking about the very real presence of hate crime in society. Chase, then, uses this story to force the reader to see and understand the negative effects of being an 'Other' or of suffering marginalization in a patriarchal society, making it even more poignant as this violence – both physical and epistemic – is against children.

Chase goes further than merely attempting to elicit sympathy from his reader, however, and – as in 'La lluvia' – he also naturalizes the homosexual relationship. Taking the idea that homosexuality is a disease to be cured, he demonstrates that it is as natural as the landscape of which Costa Rica is so proud. Even the title of the story alludes to this as 'el hilo del viento' refers to the Yolanda Oreamuno quote which is printed on the title page: 'Sé que tengo que seguir el hilo del viento' (75). Following a piece of thread which is blown around by the wind ties into the dual narrative: on the one hand it represents Luis Esteban's lifestyle as he wanders around the jungle, this way and that, but on the other it is also a more powerful refrain showing that one should follow one's own path in life, no matter where it leads. Clearly, Luis Esteban's and the boy's choice not to break up their relationship has led to Luis Esteban's death, but Chase makes it clear that neither of them contemplated living life differently because of fear of the consequences.

The role played by the natural landscape is also used to associate the body of Luis Esteban with the country of Costa Rica through his deep connection with nature. Indeed, he is introduced to the reader as a part of the boy's natural surroundings: '... y las noches eran iguales a los días por el sonido monótono de los insectos, por la locura desbocada de las chicharras y por la alegría de encontrarnos con Luis Esteban Curti ...' (75). The reader is then told that Luis Esteban can also talk to animals and use flowers and plants as natural cures. He also teaches the boy and his family how to live off the land by drinking boiled rainwater and eating the correct herbs, plants, and fruits. The connotations created by Chase between Luis Esteban and the natural world are intentional, and his harmonious interactions with nature are meant to develop his favour with the national reader. They also imply that he is at one with both nature and his own body, as he teaches the boy how to use his body to its best advantage in the jungle. His potential homosexuality when created in the subtext of the story is also seen as a natural part of his being and, by extension, as a natural part of being Costa Rican – thereby contesting the idea that it is non-*tico* and to be condemned. Indeed, it is *tico* society which is condemned in this story as after the murder the brothers' bodies 'empezaron a pudrirse, unos y otros, y mi padre tuvo miedo ... y ellos no morían de su pudrición y olían horrible ...' (78). The decomposition of the brothers' bodies depicts their corruption, the self-destructive nature of patriarchal culture, and the corrosive nature of prejudice for society. The fact that the boy ends the narrative stating that he has moved away from the village in order to pass this story on to new travellers implies Chase's hope that the discrimination he depicts will find an open dialogue in Costa Rica.

With this story, then, Chase chooses to use the child narrator in order to construct a dual narrative. On the surface, this is a semi-fantastical short story about a family's journey into Costa Rica's jungle and the friendship between two boys. The subtext of the narrative, however, is used to create an allegory of Costa Rican society where anyone living outside of the boundaries of heteronormativity is marginalized and victimized. Perhaps feeling unable explicitly to pen a defence of gay rights when seeking to publish *Mirar con inocencia*, it would seem that Chase instead aimed to create a subtle critique of society's reaction to perceived 'difference' and 'Otherness'. Through the creation of an innocent and naive narrator who does not try to seek out the motivation for his family's hatred of his relationship with Luis Esteban, Chase forces his reader to consider the situation using their own social and cultural understanding of the text. Thus he attempts to use literature to change the habitus – or accepted world-view – of his audience regarding same-sex relationships, creating an awareness that did not previously exist and about which he could not, at this point, openly write.

These powerful works of protest fiction by Quince Duncan, Carmen Naranjo, and Alfonso Chase stand on the platform of identity politics, demonstrating both a recognition of, and an opposition to, the *tico* norm in 1970s Costa Rica. Despite all three authors portraying normative society in a similar fashion – it is undeniably white, Central Valley-centric, patriarchal, and heterosexist – they each take up a specific stance in order to critique certain aspects of it. In this way the postcolonial power structures at work within Costa Rican society are made clear, and a counterhegemonic stance towards them is taken through the soft power of literature. These positions focus on specific and singular issues in order to challenge a facet of the rigid notion of *tiquicidad*. Quince Duncan uses allegory and self-reflection to discuss ethnic and geographic prejudice in *Los cuatro espejos*, demonstrating the negative effects associated with the internalization of racist stereotypes for Afro-Costa Ricans. Carmen Naranjo and Alfonso Chase use the short story as a means of exposing and exploring gendered and sexual identity within Costa Rica, and the discrimination and violence which is part of *tico* society. While Duncan's ideology is perhaps thinly veiled behind allegory, Naranjo and Chase's stances as authors are carefully hidden in subtext and code. All these works thereby invite the reader to uncover and consider his or her own habits and to question the attitudes often instilled in childhood, as seen through the experiences of the child narrators in Naranjo and Chase's stories. Despite their differing focuses, then, these works all unite in their rejection of *tiquicidad* and rigid, oppressive cultural norms.

Despite the 1970s as a decade of social protest and the questioning of norms, it is clear that Costa Rica's official position regarding national identity and normative society did not change as a result. In fact, these areas of opposition continue to be explored in twenty-first-century Costa Rica through the use of new media and digital technologies, harnessing the power of the visual, virtual, and viral. This 'digital revolution' throws up very similar definitions of normative society, but offers more nuanced portrayals of internal 'Others'. While geography, ethnicity, gender, and sexuality are all prominent themes in the 2010s, ideas about Costa Rica's external-facing image are also constantly considered and questioned. Indeed, the similarities and differences between lived realities and the tourist image of the nation which is sold beyond its borders is especially prevalent in Costa Rican film, as will be seen in Chapter 3.

CHAPTER THREE

Reflecting the Nation: Costa Rican Cinema in the Twenty-First Century

D espite challenges to the prevailing hegemonic ideology of the *tico* espoused by authors through the soft power of literature in the 1970s, it is clear that at the turn of the twenty-first century this dominant rhetoric remained largely unchanged. What has unfolded in this new millennium in Costa Rica is mirrored in countries across the world: the rise of digital technologies and the subsequent globalization of knowledge has mobilized the powers of protest, breaking down physical borders in the digital world. As noted in Chapter 1, these new technologies have brought about the first changes – both official (government legislation) and unofficial (the mobilization of large parts of society) – to *tico* identity. While literature, of course, is still written in Costa Rica, counterhegemonic productions are no longer the preserve of the written word, and the digital revolution of the twenty-first century has created an unprecedented cinematic boom in Costa Rica.[1] This chapter considers the ways in which this visual and narrative medium has been used to destabilize *tiquicidad* and the ways in which the centre and the 'Other' are presented in this period. Indeed, it will be seen that although national norms still stand, fresh challenges are brought up by national films, with marginalized stories brought to the fore for the audience's consideration. Interestingly, a nuanced approach to discrimination and marginalization – that in some cases focuses on the intersectionality of dual discrimination – replaces the more rigid identity politics that was the stance of the protest authors of the 1970s, and a broader view of society can be seen in twenty-first-century Costa Rican film.

1 The national newspaper *El País de Costa Rica* reported that in the year 2010–11, although 98 per cent of Costa Ricans could read, only 49 per cent had read a book in the last twelve months, and only 41 per cent had bought a book in this period (Anon, 2012a). A 2013 study, reported on in online magazine *RedCultura*, however, showed that 96 per cent of Costa Ricans had watched television in the previous week (Jiménez Arguedas, 2014), while *El financiero* reported in 2012 that cinema audiences had increased by 30 per cent from 2007 to 2011 (Brenes Quirós, 2012).

To say Costa Rican cinema has undergone a transformation in the new century is an understatement: in the whole of the twentieth century, nine feature-length, fiction films were made in the country; between the years 2000 and 2016, 36 such productions were released. This increase is staggering. While Hart suggests (2015, 8) this radical change is a global phenomenon, it has certainly affected the cinema of small nations more than the strong cinema industries, such as Hollywood or Bollywood. Primarily, the turn towards digital has meant that filming can be low-cost. For a few hundred dollars, anyone can pick up a high-resolution camera which can be used to make full-length films. Moreover, these films can be edited digitally using software that is a fraction of the price of analogue editing materials; and digital films can be bought and distributed easily via the internet. Film-making is therefore no longer the preserve of those with enough capital – won through sponsorship or self-funding – to actually produce a piece of cinematography. Even dissemination through online channels such as YouTube or Vimeo is either free of charge or very low-cost, and means that any film made can potentially have huge global reach.

The relative accessibility and reduced cost of film-making are not the only effects of the digital turn, however, and inextricably linked to these consequences is also the trend towards the portraying of a new world vision on screen. Hart contends that with the possibility of film-making open to anyone, grand narratives can be renounced in favour of a focus on 'everyday lives' (2015, 8); this in turn has opened up a new space for small nations' cinema in the global world. The impact of digital in Costa Rica can be seen not just in the volume of films made but also in the sharply rising number of cinemagoers since the year 2000; between 2007 and 2011, the number of people going to Discine cinemas across the country rose by 30 per cent (Brenes Quirós, 2012). Moreover, despite being a country of fewer than 5 million people, Costa Rica is the largest cinematic market in Central America, being home to 26 per cent of the region's cinemagoers (M. L. Cortés, 2014). Given this renewed interest in film in the country, the productions considered in this chapter demonstrate how conceptions of the 'national' and the 'everyday' are dealt with on screen for this new audience.

The History and Infrastructure of Costa Rican Cinema

According to Samuel Rovinski, although film production was limited in the twentieth century, a love of cinema in the country was born when the first screen opened in 1900 as 'el éxito del invento fue tan espectacular que las salas de proyección empezaron a surgir como hongos en todo el país. El Cinematógrafo había sentado sus reales en Costa Rica como espectáculo comercial' (1985, 63). This trend has not decreased and Distribuidora Romaly – which owns many of the nation's screens – announced in 2015 that it would open 31 new cinemas in the country (Brenes Quirós, 2014). This increasing interest in film has led the country to join the *Conferencia de Autoridades Audiovisuales y Cinematográficas de Iberoamérica* (CAACI) and to host its own international film festival – the *Costa Rica Festival Internacional de Cine* (CRFIC) – as well as setting up a new fund – the *Fauno* – for national film-makers in 2015 (Sánchez, 2015). Interest in national film has also increased and most of the productions made after the year 2010 have seen over 100,000 local viewers fill screens (M. L. Cortés, 2014).

While the popularity of twenty-first-century Costa Rican film is astonishing given its near non-existence in the twentieth century, much has happened since the photographers Amando Céspedes Marín and Manuel Gómez Miralles began to make short films about political or newsworthy events in the 1910s. The first fiction film, *El retorno* (dir. A. F. Bertoni), was released in 1930 and tells a typical *costumbrista* tale of love and separation in the countryside and city. The amelioration of the rural, and tradition's triumph over the vices of city life, were also common themes in Costa Rican literature written during this period (Quesada Soto, 2008), and this film, written by author Gonzalo Chacón Trejos, certainly follows suit as well as mirroring the debates at the time about where the *tico* identity should lie geographically: the cities of the Central Valley or the *campo*. Despite the relative success of *El retorno* nationally, Costa Rica waited 25 years for its next home-grown production, and between 1955 and 1970, only three works of fictional film were released: *Elvira* (dir. Carlos Álfaro MacAdam, 1955), *Milagro de amor* (dir. José Gamboa, 1955), and *La apuesta* (dir. Miguel Salaguero, 1968) (M. L. Cortés, 2002, 21–3).

While the 1960s and 1970s saw a boom of film productions elsewhere in Latin America, just as in the literary world, the Costa Rican film industry was once again left behind. Although US productions remained extremely popular in Costa Rica, Third Cinema and the New Latin American Cinema increased in popularity in the region, and, desperate to keep up, in 1973 the Costa Rican government set up the country's first Department for Cinema (Rovinski, 1985, 63), the tagline for which was 'dar voz a quien no la tiene' (CCPC, 2015). The core projects funded by this department, however, came in the form of documentary, and while 75 such productions were made – mainly addressing similar social concerns to the literature of the decade and the ethos of the *Nuevo Cine Latinoamericano*, such as corruption, drugs, prostitution, social ills, and inequality – no fictional films were produced. By the end of the 1980s, however, like many other Latin American nations, Costa Rica suffered from the economic crisis and withdrew state funding for film-making activities.

Despite the years 1980 to 1987 seeing five films made, then, Costa Rica had to wait 14 years before the next national feature-length film was released. *Asesinato en El Meneo* (2001), directed by Óscar Castillo, is a detective comedy/drama which tells of corruption and class tensions with a purposefully 'Latin' vibe. Although not achieving the number of viewers or the popularity of other Latin American films of this era, it certainly broke Costa Rica's arid season of film-making. Indeed, in 2008, Roberto García of the Centro Costarricense de Producción Cinematográfica (CCPC) – the new name for the Department for Cinema – underlined how far Costa Rican cinema had matured, stating that 'sin duda alguna el salto más importante se ha dado del año 2000 para acá, en un plazo de ocho años se han filmado más películas que en toda la historia anterior' (Solano Gómez, 2011). This renewed zeal for film production has continued well into the 2010s, triggering wave upon wave of new directors trying their hand at feature films. And many have since been box office sell-outs, with four of these – *Maikol Yordan de viaje perdido* (dir. Miguel Gómez, 2014), *Italia 90* (dir. Miguel Gómez, 2014), *El regreso* (dir. Hernán Jiménez, 2011), and *Gestación* (dir. Esteban Ramírez, 2009) – staying in cinemas for 12 weeks or more (M. L. Cortés, 2014).

It is not solely the turn to digital which has caused this rise of national cinema, however, but also the persistence of a generation of film-makers who have studied abroad before returning to Costa Rica to make films, the new possibilities for academic study that this has now created in the country, and the CCPC's attempts to offer the infrastructure and support the burgeoning industry needs.[2] Despite this surge in both film-making and interest in Costa Rican film nationally, these productions have often never left the borders of their home country in terms of academic study or critical attention. In fact, even within Costa Rica there exists very little academic scholarship on the nation's cinema. María Lourdes Cortés' works on Central American and Costa Rican cinema have led the way in the field, while one academic journal – *Revista Comunicación* – dedicated a special issue to the topic in 2011. Although the issue of a lack of attention is common among 'small nations' cinema' more widely (Hjort and Petrie, 2007, 8–9), it has been noted that it is especially true of Central American cinema (Falicov, 2008, 1) – although the 2018 *Studies in Spanish and Latin American Cinemas* special journal edition on the topic seeks to begin to redress this balance. This is of particular interest when considering the visible nature of Costa Rica's global tourist brand, although it is rarely present as anything more than a tropical background for a Hollywood film.

---

2 For more on the landscape of Costa Rican cinema in the twenty-first century, see Harvey, 2017.

Situating Costa Rican Cinema

Despite the vast historical differences between the emergence of Costa Rican film and the broader context of Latin American cinema, the themes occurring within the former and the latter offer up interesting comparison points. While it is a misguided approach to attempt to consider 'Latin American cinema' as one fixed genre, the situating of films within the wider context of the Latin American cinematic market occurs frequently. The distinction is generally drawn between the cinematographic and overtly sociopolitical themes found in Third or New Latin American Cinema, and films made – digitally – in the twenty-first century. Michael Chanan notes (1997, 373–6) that Third Cinema is essentially anything which goes against the grain: it is anti-establishment, anti-Hollywood, anti-conventionalism. In contrast, Hart contends that Latin American films made in the early twenty-first century were the first to be made with private funding and as such made a conscious effort to reject the 'picture-postcard vision of Latin America and, in the process express a message which was, of course, intrinsically Latin American but also addressed wider, supranational issues, themes and problems' (2004, 13). This new wave of film-making has moved away from the theme of national allegory and towards issues of urban and youth cultures which Hart terms 'slick grit' (2015, 105), while genre films have also emerged.

Within Costa Rica these varying trends can be seen in films using non-actors and displaying anti-establishment (and especially anti-Hollywood) themes, mirroring Third Cinema trends. Moreover, Chanan's contention that Third Cinema 'inevitably constitutes a site of ideological contestation over definitions of nation, state, people, and country' (2006, 43) can be seen as many of Costa Rica's directors use film as a way of reflecting upon the nation, critiquing elements of national life. Although it has bypassed the making of an overtly political cinema, Costa Rica has certainly taken aspects of social and cultural reflection from Third Cinema and appropriated these for *tico* film. Costa Rican film is also strongly influenced by Hollywood convention, however, as 95 per cent of films shown in Costa Rican cinemas – even nowadays – are straight out of Hollywood (Calderón Quesada, 2013). This means that Costa Rica's films rarely divert from the Hollywood norm in terms of cinematography, while genre films – such as spoof comedies, horror films, and war narratives – are also abundant.

Regardless of their genre, Costa Rican productions often echo Paul Schroeder's contention (2012, 91) that the constructed nature of cinema reflects the constructed nature of social relationships, and several scholars have noted references to the nation in recent Costa Rican film. Carolina

Sanabria states (2011b, 19) that the history of national self-referentiality in Costa Rican film can be traced to the first film made – *El Retorno* – while Amanda Alfaro asserts (2011, 52) that the construction of a national imaginary as a fixed and homogeneous concept is also firmly rooted in Costa Rican cinema. Moreover, Nestor García Canclini points out that:

> the transnationalization of culture brought about by the communications technologies, their reach, and their efficacy are better appreciated as part of the recomposition of urban cultures, along with the migrations and tourism that soften national borders and redefine the concepts of nation, people, and identity. (García Canclini, 1995, 10)

Film, then, plays a part in the reconceptualization of the nation in the eyes of its citizens while also self-consciously playing with existing notions of national identity, especially when it comes to considering the external versus internal image or brand of a country. The predominant idea of Costa Rica as a site for tourism is often contested in national film.

Indeed, within Costa Rican cinema, the national setting is always clear, with idiomatic language a core feature of *tico* film. Esteban Ramírez argues (2014) that national productions are popular for this very reason: Costa Ricans are not used to seeing people like them speaking how they speak on the big screen. As Cortés states, paraphrasing Cuban director Julio García Espinosa, 'Es … común decir que un país sin cine es un país invisible y las pantallas cinematográficas son el espejo de la sociedad' (M. L. Cortés, 2002, 5), and it could certainly be argued that Costa Rica's directors attempt to reflect their version of a national reality within their films. What is especially apparent in these productions is their concentration on the juxtaposition of the tourist image and the 'everyday reality' of those living in the cities of the Central Valley and the fluid nature of identity compared with the ways in which this was explored in the protest literature of the 1970s. These filmic reflections on the nation serve to highlight the changing nature of identity within the country, counterpointing the influence of the increasingly globalized world with the traditional national image of the *tico*.

Intersections at the *Tico* Centre:
Esteban Ramírez's *Gestación* (2009)

Alongside other prolific Costa Rican directors such as Miguel Gómez and Hernán Jiménez, Esteban Ramírez is one of the most widely recognized founders of twenty-first-century Costa Rican film. Having spent most of his childhood in Costa Rica, he chose to remain in the country to go to university and begin his career as a film-maker, unlike many other national directors of his generation. His father was a member of the *Centro de cine* in the 1970s and was one of many directors to make state-funded documentaries at the time. Witnessing these developments in the national film industry first hand, Ramírez saw the opportunities available to him in the country differently from his peers, and went on to study for a degree in Communication at the Universidad de Costa Rica. Although he was yet to pick up a camera, upon leaving university Ramírez felt that he did have the necessary theoretical skills and filmic equipment – via the university and his father – to start making films. His first fiction production, the short film *Rehabilitación concluida*, was followed by *Once rosas*, another short, which won the prize for Best Fiction at the *Muestra de Cine y Video Costarricense*, as the *Costa Rica Festival Internacional de Cine* was then known. *Once rosas*, which cost $70,000, was his first production to be filmed in 35 mm and to win acclaim internationally, being selected to be shown at film festivals in Moscow, São Paulo, Havana, Lima, and Los Angeles. These early experiences of success gave Ramírez the confidence he needed to go on to make his own feature productions, and he notes that witnessing the renaissance of Costa Rican film-making in the twenty-first century encouraged him to step into the career of director full-time.

The possibility of making a film and seeing it released in national cinemas had been made real by Ramírez's predecessors, and as such he took steps towards this with his first feature production in 2004. *Caribe* (2004) was the first Costa Rican feature film to win international acclaim, while *Gestación*, his second film, made in 2009, became the longest-showing Costa Rican film in history with a record number of spectators watching it across national cinemas. Testament to its popularity, it won nine international prizes for direction and acting, including that of Best Director at the *Festival Internacional de Cine de Bogotá*. It has also aired widely on television both in the Americas and in Spain, becoming the first Central American film to be shown on HBO to North American audiences. Moreover, the leading actress, Adriana Álvarez, who plays Jessie, won the Best Actress award at the *Festival de Trieste*, Italy and the *Festival de la chimenea de Villa Verde*, in Spain (M. L. Cortés, 2011b). Ramírez's more recent picture, *Presos* (2015), also attracted large audiences and has achieved international recognition like no other – it is the first and, to date, only Costa Rican film to be made available on subscription-based streaming platform Netflix. Ramírez is proud of his film career, but claims that *Gestación* was, for him, a more complete picture than *Caribe*, and that he felt much closer to the production itself because of the themes contained within it, and the filming location of San José – where he lives (Ramírez, 2014).

He also acknowledges the criticism aimed at the film, which he puts down to the main narrative plot attempting to tackle a very controversial topic in Costa Rica: teenage pregnancy and abortion. He believes that the polemic nature of the plot made it more difficult to win sponsorship and support for the production, meaning that it was made on a lower budget than other Costa Rican films of the time. This did not cause him to abandon the narrative, however, and he is a firm believer that the most important part of film-making is striking a balance between the film's entertainment value and educational or moral standpoint. He notes:

> no me veo haciendo una película de puro entrenamiento. Quiero decir cosas importantes. Y en el caso de *Gestación* ... el embarazo bajó, es cierto que el embarazo bajó con la película, y bajó más cuando se puso en la televisión ya que muchas más personas la vieron. La gente quedó asustada un poquito, tuvo un impacto alto. (Ramírez, 2014)

The educational value Ramírez desired for his film has, according to the director, been seen in the country as he proudly states that teenage pregnancy decreased in the country after *Gestación* was screened (Ramírez, 2014). Whatever the reasons for *Gestación*'s success among audiences – if not always among critics – it became one of the first Costa Rican productions to make a net profit. Although Ramírez himself contends that a cinema industry does not exist in the country and cannot form until films regularly start making enough money for directors to consider it their sole source of income, it seems that with *Gestación* he gained an insight into the possibilities that the national market could offer him and his compatriots.

Gestación, as the title suggests, revolves around a pregnancy. Teo and Jessie – teenagers from different social backgrounds – meet at the mall one day, begin a relationship, and have one, awkward, sexual encounter. When Jessie finds out she is pregnant she chooses to keep the baby owing to the dangers of an illegal abortion, but she is soon ostracized by the nuns at her Catholic school and forced to attend lessons alone. When her friends begin a protest about her treatment, however, Jessie takes her case to court, winning the right to finish her schooling. According to Ramírez, this portion of the script was based on a true story which served as inspiration for the entire narrative (Ramírez, 2014). The finale of *Gestación* is entirely fictional, however, and it sees Teo studying at university while Jessie works while studying; although it is made clear that they are no longer in a relationship, they share the burden of care for their child.

The central narrative within *Gestación* surrounds teenage love and an unplanned pregnancy, both of which engender a coming-of-age-too-soon storyline to which viewers across cultures and borders can relate. The setting up of youth culture, gender, and youth sexuality as a space of 'Otherness' opposed to the *tico* norm in twenty-first-century Costa Rica is examined in detail in *Gestación* and it has been considered shocking by some national viewers. Perhaps Ramírez is correct when he contends (2014) that in countries where sex education is on the curriculum and abortion is legal this film may seem less dramatic. Ramírez's film also serves to undercut the tourist image of Costa Rica, and it considers San José as a teenage city, unsure of where its future lies but unable to return to its modest childhood past. A national viewer will recognize themselves and their surroundings everywhere in this film, and the habitual elements of daily life take centre stage. The fact that the entire narrative is bound up in the geographic *tico* centre also means that it opens a debate around the traditional spaces of opposition to *tiquicidad*, as the film forms a dialogue around the existence of class hierarchy, as well as poverty and gender inequality in a patriarchal society.

Youth Culture and the Teenage City

While the title suggests that the core narrative of *Gestación* surrounds teenage pregnancy, it is perhaps more firmly centred around the construction of the teenage experience on screen. This is a phenomenon that has been explored in detail by film scholars, as the youth film or coming-of-age experience are popular narratives and motifs. Indeed, Alexandra Seibel and Timothy Shary state that 'stories of youth after childhood are quite compelling, since the coming-of-age process is familiar to all cultures and classes of peoples' (2007, 2), and this chapter argues that despite the many local trappings of the narrative and cinematography Ramírez has made a transnational picture with *Gestación*. The three protagonists – Jessie, Teo, and Alba, Jessie's best friend – are all exploring the space of transgressive youth culture, and the tension between childhood and adulthood is highlighted by the setting up of multiply placed identities and associations. Jessie and Alba talk about their school work, moan about their parents, and gossip about the girls in their class. At the same time, Alba talks to Jessie about the boys she has had sex with, teasing Jessie that she is 'la monja del cole' as she is still a virgin. Moreover, when Jessie and Teo do have sex, they do not have the experience to know what to do, nor the language to describe it. The encounter is awkward, and contraception is not mentioned. When Jessie tells Alba about it the next day, she describes it as 'lindo', to which Alba mockingly replies, 'lindo mi abuelita tejiendo', demonstrating the lack of vocabulary Jessie has to explain her feelings. This again chimes with global youth films, as described by Seibel and Shary, who state that 'adolescence and puberty are times of intense sexual development for young people ... global cinema offers a wide range of experiences that youth encounter during that development' (2007, 4), thus firmly placing this film among other, global, productions that attempt to showcase a sense of 'youthhood' and growing up on screen.

The complexities of youth are also made apparent, as, despite their naivety around sex, Teo hangs around with older friends, drinking and partying, and when Jessie falls pregnant, she says that she will undertake the responsibilities which go along with this. These attempts at maturity and the first tentative steps into adulthood come unstuck, however, as the teenagers are frequently seen as children who still need protecting. This generational divide is also a common motif of youth film, and Daniela Berghahn states that 'coming-of-age films are by definition concerned with identity formation and ... the family, as well as the peer group, function as the two most significant poles in this process' (2010, 241). Indeed, Teo fights with his mother, claiming that she cannot understand him, storming off to his bedroom and slamming the door at every opportunity. Similarly, Jessie's and Teo's mothers decide how they will proceed after the pregnancy is revealed. For all their perceived and desired independence, then, the teenagers are still desperately in need of the care and guidance offered to them by their parents, and the education of both their teachers and wider society.

This in-between stage is a common experience for all teens in this film and is, of course, often the centre of the adventure present in coming-of-age narratives. According to Berghahn (2010), coming-of-age films are all about transitions, and it is this move from adolescence to early adulthood that is considered in detail in *Gestación*. Of North American films, Berghahn states that this 'transition typically occurs as a result of a formative experience, such as falling in love, the first sexual encounter, the separation from or death of a loved one, or a rite of passage, such as a test of courage or graduation' (2010, 240). This theme of transition is developed in *Gestación* as it is coupled with a sense of unreal expectation about life that slowly unravels as the plot continues and the teenagers grow closer to adulthood. *Gestación* displays this liminal age-zone which Teo and Jessie inhabit as a space of both disillusionment and rebellion against social norms which is, in this way, a space of hybridity. Indeed, their desperation to be independent is framed by their contradictory naivety and the trappings of their childhoods throughout the film. When Teo initially approaches Jessie, buying her the blue blouse she had been looking at in a shop moments before, the pair seem to imagine that their relationship will last forever. But when we are shown this same item hanging outside Jessie's home – rain pouring down on it – after they have broken up just months later, it is clear that this teenage romance did not last the course of their final year of school, let alone a lifetime. Teo also tells Jessie of his dream of becoming an actor, which is not only entirely against his parents' wishes but also a desire towards which he never takes decisive steps. Jessie, meanwhile, is desperate to study engineering at university and, clearly, she still hopes she will achieve this even after becoming pregnant, saying: 'tenemos que prepararnos y sacar nuestras carreras'.

Through this *Bildungsroman* element of the film and the interactions of the teenagers with their wider communities, Ramírez brings up the issue of youth sexuality as a direct infringement of Costa Rican values, also raising questions about how sex should be taught and dealt with in societies where the subject remains taboo within families and in education. A search for sexual identity is a common, transnational theme dealt with in coming-of-age films and Padva argues that 'youth films often feature such themes as painful adolescence, confrontation with the older generation, the contrast between socialization and selfhood, erotic pubescence, confusing infatuation, and the formation of sexual identity' (2004, 355). Despite this commonality of sexual exploration as a key experience of youthhood, with the the Catholic Church such an elevated a symbol of *tiquicidad* it is clear that Teo and Jessie's decision to have sex sets them in direct conflict with hegemonic norms. As proof of the power of the Church, Jessie is exiled from acceptable society because she has sex outside marriage and Ramírez's suggestion throughout the film is that the roots of these values are found in the teachings of the Catholic Church which permeate everyday life in the country and determine social norms. Indeed, the Church's doctrine is set up to be undermined at several points in the film. Jessie's mother constantly plays Catholic radio stations in the house and she leaves Bible verses written on Post-it notes on the fridge for Jessie. When she realizes her daughter is pregnant, the verse plays a passive-aggressive role with its double meaning from the Bible and in the parallels of their lives: '¿de nada te sirvió ver lo que he sufrido?'. Moreover, Catholic teachings about sin, guilt, and pregnancy are also unquestioningly adhered to by the protagonists. When Teo states that an abortion would be best for the two of them, Jessie responds 'ya no somos dos', demonstrating that the prevalent rhetoric in the country states that the baby is already a person before it is born. Moreover, Teo has also assumed the idea that marriage is the solution to the problem of Jessie's pregnancy, suggesting that if they get married their happy ending will be complete.

Given the dominance of the Catholic Church's ideals in Costa Rican society, the director has made Jessie into a highly sympathetic character in order to make her more palatable to a national audience. Unlike Alba, she has not had sex before, and even though she does have sex with Teo once, she refuses to again. Moreover, while her friends drink and go to parties, she chooses to stay at home, studying and taking care of her young brother. Moreover, in placing Jessie in a Catholic school run by nuns, Ramírez is able to clearly demonstrate and subvert the Church's teachings without openly critiquing them within the script. It is apparent in *Gestación* that the indoctrination of religious-cum-social beliefs begins in education, as each day the nuns begin lessons by declaring, 'Jesús viva', to which the girls must reply, 'Que muera el pecado'. When the nuns discover that Jessie is pregnant, their reaction is severe as they isolate her during school hours, explaining that 'Una manzana podrida puede pudrir a los demás'. In this way, the hegemonic force of the Catholic Church (which acts as what Gramsci terms an 'Ideological State Apparatus', or 'Deputy' of the State, exercising the state's wishes through ideology) exiles Jessie from mainstream society.

The questioning of the Catholic Church in this way also plays into wider contemporary social concerns, as the separation of church and state – and consequently the church and education – has been a topic of debate in Costa Rica in recent years. Although the future of the *estado laico* is yet to be decided upon, it is a topic with which contemporary audiences in the country will be familiar, and it would seem that Ramírez uses this film to pronounce his own judgement on the issue. He has said (Ramírez, 2015) that because of a lack of education many parents have no idea how to speak to their children about sex, as it is a topic considered to be taboo within the family. This is hinted at in *Gestación* as Jessie's mother asks her, '¿Por qué no me contaste?' To which her daughter replies, 'Por la misma razón por la cual que vos no me pudiste preguntarme a mí'. Despite being portrayed as very close on-screen, it is clear that this is not a topic open for discussion within the family unit.

The film also shows that due to a lack of sexual education, several myths about sex and procreation prevail, suggesting that unwanted pregnancies are rife for just this reason. Perhaps not wishing to court controversy, Ramírez deals with this subject implicitly in *Gestación*. Indeed, Sor María, the headmistress of the school, gives a speech which is highly ironic, given the context of the film, as she states:

> El tema de la sexualidad es un asunto de principios. Y en eso los escritos de Dios son muy claros. Es un mito que la ignorancia sexual sea la que produce embarazos adolescentes, enfermedades de transmisión sexual. Los jóvenes nunca han tenido tanta información sexual como hoy en día, y es justamente hoy cuando peor están. El preservativo en manos de un joven adolescente es una invitación gratuita e invitada a la

promiscuidad y ese es el problema, esa es la consecuencia de la pérdida de valores en la familia y en la sociedad.

This argument against sexual education and contraception has already been undermined in the viewer's eyes, however, as Jessie and Teo did not even think about using contraception when they had sex. Teo even exclaimed that it was impossible for Jessie to be pregnant as they had only had sex once, shouting: 'Es imposible. Nada más lo hicimos una vez. No puede ser'. These misinformed ideas abound among other teenagers at their schools, and as such undermine Sor María's speech. In this way Ramírez indirectly demonstrates his support of the implementation of sexual education in the country.

This focus on youth and sexuality exists within many other Latin American films, and of Lucrecia Martel's *La niña santa* (Argentina, 2004) Deborah Martin states that the director conjures up 'that other sensorium that we have all inhabited: childhood, a place which exists beyond adult culture but which simultaneously inhabits it' (2011, 71), a statement that holds true for Ramírez's film. It is also reminiscent of other teenage-focused films, such as Alfonso Cuarón's *Y tu mamá también* (Mexico, 2001), and both films showcase a specific national setting which mirrors the teenage experience. Andrea Noble writes of *Y tu mamá también* that 'the film is full of visual details of the incidental and the everyday' (2005, 144), and in *Gestación* it is also through habitual routines that the themes of the film are explored and a new world vision which turns away from grand narratives is showcased. The city of San José is seen to be mirroring the protagonists' journey, and here it is portrayed as a physical space which is also in transition from a teenage to adult state whereby the *tico* norm must keep up with a new generation's changing perceptions of nationhood. Ramírez has noted of *Gestación* that it has 'un sabor local muy fuerte, ya del centro del país. San José es un personaje más' (2014), showing just how important the national – *tico* – centre of the country is to the narrative. He goes on to contend that 'nunca hemos visto a San José en la pantalla grande, fue bonita. La ciudad era como un lugar de encuentro que me ayudó también a retratar San José y el lenguaje' (Ramírez, 2014). These portraits of the capital are frequently painted for the national and international viewer, with a Costa Rican Central Valley audience able to recognize the sights and landmarks familiar to them.

Before the viewer is even shown the first shot, the noise of the city is amplified. When the shot catches up with the sound, typical scenes of traffic, houses, and shops surrounded by mountains are shown. Even the first words spoken, 'Qué despelote', are audible as the viewer gazes out onto the cityscape, giving the impression that it is the city which is a mess, not the girl at Jessie and Alba's school about whom they are speaking. Moreover, the film moves all over San José from the Mall San Pedro, La Sabana Park, and the *Mercado Central* to Sabanilla and Pavas, and depictions of the gritty, urban city abound. These cityscapes are used as frequent interludes and are filmed using wide-lens panoramic shots to highlight the intensity of the urban landscape. Ramírez is careful to include shots of the more picturesque side of the city too, as Jessie and Alba often sit outside in La Sabana park among the trees and lakes. When Jessie and Teo go out in the evening, they wander through downtown San José, eating in the central market, which twinkles with fairy lights set out for Christmas. The fact that the film is bookended with shots of the capital can be no coincidence either, and Ramírez certainly sets the entire narrative up around the cultural traits of San José and its *tico* inhabitants – who are portrayed as synonymous with Costa Ricans as a whole population. Indeed, the fact that the camera does not leave the capital city is telling, demonstrating that national identity in the twenty-first century is seen as city- and Central Valley-centric.

It is not just the physical qualities of the city which Ramírez strives to portray on screen, however, but the *tico* norm too. He asserts that:

> la temática es el país, pero esos detalles – en *Gestación* hay un montón de detalles – ... como esta forma de comer, de vestir, de ser, son importantísimos que se proyecten ... esa convicción es totalmente necesario que cada país tenga la posibilidad de verse en la pantalla. (Ramírez, 2014)

Film scholar Bértold Salas Murillo also appears to have longed to see his nation on the big screen, as he points out that '*Gestación* mostró a los de la primera década del siglo XXI una patria reconocible, con gentes que hablan, actúan y padecen como cualquier vecino' (2011, 46), while Walter Conejo adds that 'somos un país sin memoria histórica y Esteban Ramírez ha comenzado a construirla' (2011, 89). One of the many ways in which Ramírez does this, giving his film the *tico* stamp, is through the use of *costarrique-ñismos*, which pervade the dialogue. While the notion of the *tico* encompasses much more than an idiolect, using *costarriqueñismos* – a whole dictionary of which has been produced (Quesada Pacheco, 2007) – is just one of the ways in which the *tico* identity has created a rhetoric of exceptionalism and demarcated its national identity as different from other Central American nations. Indeed, words like 'mae' (mate/dude), 'chiva' (cool), or 'voy jalado' (I'm in a rush) are frequently dropped into the script. In this way, a national audience is forced to connect with the film, possibly also producing a wry smile as the dialogue turns to football, with Jessie chanting, 'oye, oye, oye, oye, monstruo, monstruo' at Teo as her team – Deportivo Saprissa – has just beaten his – Club Sport Herediano; references which would be lost on the majority of international viewers. This prompts Salas Murillo to contend that the film was so popular nationally as it shows:

> la presentación de un lenguaje y una cotidianidad muy propios de la juventud costarricense en los primeros años del siglo XXI: la jerga juvenil, sus costumbres, inquietudes y aspiraciones, e incluso la alusión a equipos de fútbol como el Deportivo Saprissa y el Club Sport Herediano. (Salas Murillo, 2011, 47)

Ramírez also includes scenes from everyday life which would be highly recognizable to a national audience, such as Jessie eating *pinto con huevo* – the national dish – for breakfast, the sharing of *tamales* at Christmas, Jessie eating *Churchills* after school, or Teo calling 'upe' before entering Jessie's house. Moreover, he uses one non-professional actor – the homeless man who lives on a patch of land next door to Jessie – to showcase yet another real facet of life in the capital. This comfort zone of the local is subverted, however, by the central narrative of the film – the transgression of *tico* values and *Gestación*'s central metaphor: illegitimacy.

The Margins of the City

While *Gestación* paints a picture of the dominant centre of the country, then, it also sets out to discuss the place of those existing on the periphery of the *tico* norm. This marginality permeates the core plot and the lives of the protagonists, and it can be seen in both the class differences which separate Jessie and Teo and the unequal gendered roles to which they must adhere. These tensions lead Salas Murillo to suggest that the film poses the questions '¿De qué se ufanan los costarricenses?, ¿cómo se comporta una mujer?, ¿cómo se quieren un hombre y una mujer?, ¿cómo es posible quererse más allá de las clases sociales?' (2011, 45). Youth and sexuality are not the only spaces of opposition to the *tico* norm set out in *Gestación*, then, and in a society which has historically portrayed itself as classless this film shows Costa Rica actually to be deeply divided by social hierarchies.

The dichotomy of rich and poor in San José is depicted both visually and within the narrative: Jessie lives in a small house with a corrugated iron roof which stands in a graffiti-strewn neighbourhood filled with temporary shacks (Figure 1). She shares a cramped bedroom with her brother, has to use a friend's mobile phone to contact Teo, and takes the bus marked 'Pavas' so that those local to San José will know she comes from a poor neighbourhood. This is cemented as Jessie cannot buy any of the clothes she browses as she wanders through the mall with Alba, and her mother reminds her that she has a scholarship to go to the Catholic school that she

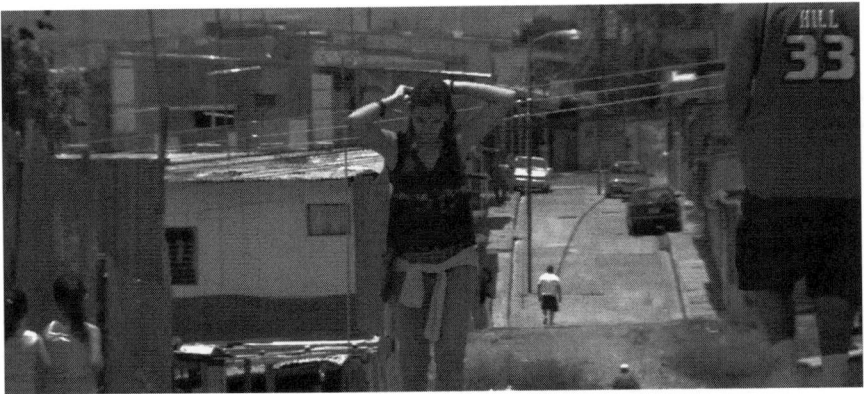

Figure I Jessie walks around Pavas in *Gestación* (Dir. Esteban Ramírez, 2009, Cintel)

now attends. Teo, on the other hand, lives in a large house in Sabanilla – a quiet, residential community – with shining polished floors, all the latest technology, and a maid to keep it clean. He has a television in his bedroom, a mobile phone, and attends a large, bilingual private school set behind locked gates, complete with sports stadium, private school buses, and other teenagers from wealthy households. When Jessie visits his house, Teo shows her photos of his trips to Argentina and the USA, while Jessie, who can only dream of leaving the country, tells her mother, 'cuando esté ingeniera y gane plata te prometo que vamos de viaje juntas', demonstrating that seeing the world is something these women can only dream about while stuck behind the bars of their home which frame many of the shots of the pair.

While the class divide is clearly portrayed to the viewer in the differences between the living conditions of Teo and Jessie, when the pair's mothers meet, this disparity is even more marked. Jessie's mother wears unfashionable work clothes, while Teo's is dressed elegantly and wears pearls. Ramírez chooses not just to demonstrate the material differences existing between these two extremes of rich and poor, however, and the film goes on to deal with the social implications of this class difference too, demonstrating that even the characters themselves do not believe they live in a classless society. When Teo's mother finds out about the relationship, for example, she says, '¿no te has dado cuenta que ustedes son de mundos distintos?' and it is the damaging influence of this notion on the lives of the two young people which is highlighted in *Gestación*. While Jessie must fight to go to university and dreams of having a professional career, this path has been mapped out for Teo for a long time. Through their hybrid love affair which crosses the acceptable *tico* boundaries of class and sex, the ramifications of their transgressions shed light on the social divide:

the rich have opportunities which the poor do not, and they take them for granted. Moreover, when Jessie tells Teo she is pregnant, she does not consider having an abortion as she would never be able to afford one or even find a doctor to perform it. Teo and his family have connections, however, and he is quickly able to find a doctor who will help. The cost is 120,000 *colones* – roughly US$220 – a sum that Jessie would never be able to come across but which Teo finds easily.

The film also details the ways in which social bias works against poorer members of society. As Jessie has only known hardship throughout her life, it is clear that she has had to take on far more responsibility than Teo; about the pregnancy, she states, 'Estoy dispuesta a afrontar todo lo que viene con esto', while he runs away. She is, however, judged unfairly by Teo's mother, who says that she is sure that Jessie had slept with other men and demands a paternity test. While Jessie is labelled as promiscuous, then, Teo is referred to as 'irresponsable'. It is Jessie's mother's reaction to this slight that is perhaps most surprising of all, however, as she reacts with humility – or perhaps servility – rather than anger, stating, 'señora está en todo su derecho'. This is reminiscent of Fanon's concept of the internalization of stereotypes – no matter how damaging they may be to the individual – the perpetuation of which help to maintain social constructs as normative behaviour. Jessie's mother believes herself to be of less value than Teo's mother by virtue of their social standing, and as such acts out in opposition to her best interests.

In *Gestación*, it is not just class divides which discriminate, as marginalization based on class works alongside patriarchal culture in the film to demonstrate the intersectionality of discrimination too. As such, the film calls into question the role of women in a society that teaches that child-rearing and the domestic spheres are the spaces which women should – and must – inhabit. Jessie's entire life has been permeated by a *machista* culture, and the viewer sees that she has gone on to repeat the pattern started by her grandmother of having a child young and perhaps being unable to carry on in education because of this. Jessie's father left her mother who now works full time as well as doing everything around the house – she has taken on the hybrid role of the traditional parental figures: both father as monetary provider and mother as caregiver. Jessie has been expected to aid her in the domestic running of the household as well, preparing her for the normative woman's role in life.

Gendered roles function according to stereotype in Teo's family too: his father works away from home, taking part in public life, while his mother never leaves the confines of her lavish house. Moreover, although she rules the domestic, private space of her home, her social position also allows her to hire a maid to do the housework. The nuclear family is prized in Costa

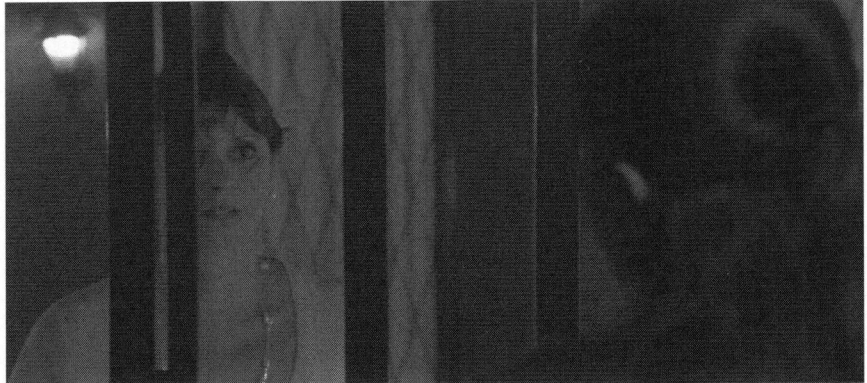

Figure 2 Jessie's mother stands outside the bars of Teo's mother's house in *Gestación*
(Dir. Esteban Ramírez, 2009, Cintel)

Rica, with traditional gendered roles adhered to as the norm. As Jessie's mother breaks with convention and is forced to work, as well as being from a lower social class to Teo's mother, the privileged woman forces her to the periphery both verbally and physically. Not only does she demonize Jessie for getting pregnant, but their meeting takes place in *her* neighbourhood and begins through the bars which encase her house as she refuses to open the door – 'Othering' Jessie and her mother, who are made into visible outsiders in this scene (Figure 2). The male characters do not escape criticism either, though, as Teo tells Jessie that, as his Dad works in another country, he has not seen him for three years. The family unit which looks perfect from the outside, then, has begun to crumble from within. The negative consequences of gendered stereotyping for men is also hinted at, as Teo is frequently jeered at school and called 'playito' and 'maricón' when he states that he does not want to ask out another girl.

The female body is also scrutinized in Ramírez's film as both the creator of new life but also as a burden for women and a site of responsibility. Jessie's reaction to her pregnancy is one of resignation; she never stops to question how and why it happened, instead accepting it as part of being a woman just as her mother and grandmother also had to. As such, she assumes full responsibility for it, saying, 'para mí es muy duro, y ahora quiero estar sola ... yo sé cómo va a ser mi vida cuando tenga este bebé'. Although Jessie sees this as the natural burden that she, as a woman, must bear, the thought of studying and having the career she had hoped for while also being a mother is not initially a possibility for her. Teo, on the other hand, demonstrates disbelief when he finds out about the pregnancy, stating, 'es imposible' and 'me cago en la puta pinche mierda', showing a lack of responsibility on his part. As Carmen Naranjo points out (1989), motherhood has traditionally been the responsibility of women in Costa Rica and it has historically held them back from receiving an education or playing a part in public life. This is made clear in *Gestación* as the viewer is shown scenes of Jessie vomiting at school while enduring whispers and stares, as well as being forced to take her classes privately, away from her peers. These shots are counterpointed immediately within the sequence by shots of Teo continuing his everyday life as normal – going to school during the week, drinking and going to parties at the weekend. This privileged situation is not only due to his class background but also his place in society as a boy, which Gateward and Pomerance describe, in film, as an 'inheritor of privilege and command' (2002, 2). Indeed, it is clear that the young protagonist Teo takes on and assumes this role, using it to his advantage – a luxury that Jessie is not afforded. This gendered discourse is constructed as the *tico* norm throughout the film, and it is especially prevalent in Jessie's education. One of the nuns at her school states, 'Las muchachas tienen que ser finas' when speaking to some pupils. The catcalling of Jessie and Alba by much older men as they talk by the side of the road goes unnoticed and largely unchallenged, though, demonstrating that while women must be well-behaved, men are not judged by the same standards.

In *Gestación*, then, the relationship between women and the screen is not about the to-be-looked-at-ness of the protagonists, but instead it calls into question the representation of the very different roles assigned to women and men in Costa Rica. This is not rural, 'traditional' Costa Rica, either, but the urban – and apparently progressive and liberal – San José, in which gendered stereotypes – as seen in *Retratico* – are considered to have started to move on from patriarchal norms. What *Gestación* makes clear, however, is that the rigidity of gendered stereotypes cannot be considered in isolation, as it is gender's intersection with class that really shapes attitudes towards Jessie and her mother. As Crenshaw asserts, groups that have traditionally been marginalized by society have often found 'strength, community, and intellectual development' (1991, 1242) in the notion of identity politics. Taking violence against women as an example of a feminist cause, she goes on to note, however, that the 'ellison in identity politics is problematic, fundamentally because the violence that many women experience is often shaped by other dimensions of their identity, such as race and class' (1242). Although these two female characters in the film do not suffer as a result of physical violence, they certainly endure the negative social consequences of being poor, female, and from a non-traditional family set-up. Jessie's mother is contrasted with Teo's mother frequently in the film, and she always comes across as caring and hardworking – telling Jessie off for coming home late – while Teo is often left to fend for himself. Despite this favourable comparison in the eyes of the viewer, Teo's mother still shows the poorer family little respect. As Teresa de Lauretis has argued (1987, 9), all identities are intersectional and so several sets of realities must overlap on film as well, just as class and gender interact to create two female characters marginalized by another female character here.

Gestación's narrative sets up the *tico* norm and its 'Other', demonstrating the extent to which traditional stereotypes of woman, man, class position, and sexual conduct have been internalized. While San José is consistently seen as the *tico* centre, standing in for the whole nation, it is also seen to mirror the hybrid space of in-betweenness inhabited by its protagonists, as it is surrounded by both tradition and modernity. As such, although the geographic norm is left unquestioned in this film, the typical tourist image of Costa Rica is undermined. The other norm which is set up and undone by Ramírez is that of the all-pervading rhetoric of the Catholic Church, which is depicted as dogmatic and discriminatory. The educational message of the film is clear: sex education should be taken away from the auspices of the Catholic Church as its message is harmful for the future of the nation. This film also considers other oppositionalities to the *tico* norm and it delves into issues of youth culture and sexuality, depicting these as spaces of 'Otherness'. In *Gestación*, no matter what Teo and Jessie do – or want to do – they are constantly held back or admonished by the boundaries of *tiquicidad*. Moreover, while the dominance of the Central Valley is never questioned, the lives of some of those existing at the margins of the *tico* centre of Costa Rica are explored as myths and stereotypes around class and gender are questioned. Indeed, when watching this film it is impossible for the viewer to conclude that twenty-first-century Costa Rica is still that egalitarian, classless society that the history books portray (Biesanz et al., 1999, 6), nor is it depicted as a society which treats men and women equally. The notion of intersectional identities is at the fore in *Gestación* and this reminds the viewer that although some gendered rights are now seen as the norm – women receiving a university education, for example – many people remain disenfranchised because they experience multiple marginal identities.

With *Gestación*, then, Ramírez makes a film which is transnational in its core *Bildungsroman* plot, but which also shares some truths about the conceptions of *tico* society that the national audience may find uncomfortable, prompting the Costa Rican public to rethink their views on social norms and stereotypes. Bhabha has argued (1994, 8) that globalization can lead to the creation of new imagined communities based around specific borderless issues, and *Gestación* is an example of this sentiment. While it challenges many internal and external norms and images of the country – thus questioning the tourist image so prevalent in Costa Rica's imaginary – it also demonstrates the passage of time, the impact of globalization, and the rhetoric of multiply positioned identities when compared with literature of the 1970s. Indeed, many internal stereotypes appear to be beginning to be openly questioned in this film, mainly in terms of the role of religious-centred gender norms, while at the same time the internal 'Others', such as those living at the geographic margins, people of colour, and the LGBTQ+ community, remain entirely invisible in this portrayal of the city.

Trans Spaces in San José: Jurgen Ureña's *Abrázame como antes* (2016)

Considering San José from a very different angle to *Gestación*, Jurgen Ureña's second feature-length production, *Abrázame como antes* (2016), can certainly be considered ground-breaking not just within the panorama of Costa Rican cinema but also within Latin American film-making. I refer to this as a 'trans' film in terms of the non-specificity of setting (which positions it within a transnational context, setting itself in stark contrast to Ramírez's picture) as well as in relation to the transgender women that the camera follows through three nights of their lives, thus queering the space of San José both visually and thematically.[3] In these respects, the film is entirely opposite to Ramírez's, where the city of San José, its location as a Costa Rican film, and its showcasing of *tiquicidad* are all at the very heart of the film. Although both films take place in the capital and *tico* centre, then, the setting in this film is entirely unrecognizable from Ramírez's production. Moreover, where *Gestación* challenges some religious, gendered, and class-based norms, it also strives to make its subversion acceptable for a national audience socialized according to *tico* ideals. *Abrázame como antes,* on the other hand, stands from the very beginning on the side of the 'Other', disregarding any normative or prejudiced standpoints around gender and sexuality by consistently challenging them.

The director, Jurgen Ureña, is a film-maker who also works in the Department of Communication at the Universidad Veritas in San José and as a journalist for the *Áncora* cultural supplement of the newspaper *La nación*. He has made several short films as well as one previous feature, *Muñecas rusas*, which was released in 2014. While he is perhaps Costa Rica's most experimental director when it comes to form – *Muñecas rusas* is a minimalist, labyrinthine tale which blurs the lines between the narrative and metanarrative that, according to

3 For more on the idea of trans as being inherently radical, transgressive, and transnational, see Lim, 2007.

critic William Venegas, had national audiences leaving the cinema (2014) – Ureña appears to have struck a conciliatory tone in *Abrázame como antes*. Although the use of colour and non-traditional camerawork is striking, the viewer is also drawn into a carefully conceived and crafted narrative. The fact that the film won the award for 'Best Central American Film' at the *Costa Rica Festival Internacional de Cine*, where it premiered in December 2016, attests to its jury- and audience-pleasing potential.

Abrázame como antes, so named after a line from the Spanish version of Jeane Manson's 1979 *Avant de Nous Dire Adieu, Porque el amor se va*, which is sung in its entirety by one of the protagonists at a nightclub in the film, offers a glimpse and an insight into the lives of three transgender women who work as prostitutes in central San José. Verónica (Jimena Franco), the central character, hangs around urban areas after dark with her companions, Greta (Natalia Porras) and Thalaya (Thalaya). Having been picked up by a couple of men cruising for sex, the car Verónica and Natalia are in with their unseen clients suddenly jolts, and Verónica soon realizes a young homeless boy has been hit and injured. As he tries to limp away, Verónica decides to lose her clients and help the boy instead. As he refuses to let her call an ambulance, she insists on taking him to the apartment she shares with Greta, where she discovers his name (Tato), wraps his broken ankle in bandages, and proceeds to lock him in the house in order to look after him until he recovers. The central plot line revolves around the lives of these women, demonstrating Verónica's desire to share the maternal love that she so desperately seeks but which was not forthcoming from her own mother, by whom she was abandoned. While the film does not overtly centre on questions of gender or sexuality, it rather observes and enters the space inhabited by these women who live outside the gendered constraints put in place by *tico* society but who pay the price for their subversion: life at the margins of that society.

While the film exists in a physical and ideological space which inhabits the periphery of *tiquicidad* in terms of both San José's night-time world and hegemonic conceptions of gender and sexuality, it is also exemplary, and perhaps unique, in its treatment of its transgender protagonists. Loosely based on the Tatiana Lobo short story 'Candelaria al azar' (1990), Ureña initially made two short films on this subject before *Abrázame como antes* was shot. Eventually doing away with what he felt were stereotypes of transgender women, and in which the women were played by cis men, he embarked on a process of focus groups which eventually led him to the casting of non-professional actresses – transgender prostitutes from San José themselves – who in turn helped Ureña in his quest for a nuanced representation. Indeed, the actress who plays Greta, Natalia Porras, has said of Ureña and this film 'Costa Rica may not have given me a country, but this movie did' (Betarcourt, 2016). This chapter therefore explores ideas of the counterhegemoni≞ depiction of San José, nationhood, gender, and sexuality in this film, considering the processes involved in the making of it to be revolutionary acts.

Queering San José

When considering the tropes of Costa Rican national identity, it is clear that several of these are torn apart by Ureña's film. In a similar way to *Gestación*, *Abrázame como antes* clearly distances itself from the tourist image of the nation, with no coastlines, jungles, or even any landscapes in sight. While this film is clearly located in a city, only viewers with a good knowledge of San José would recognize it as it is not exhibited in the same way as in Ramírez's film and nor does it attempt to validate the capital as picturesque. The panoramic shots and city vistas that Ramírez is so fond of are notably absent in Ureña's picture, and instead we see an urban, gritty city centre which barely sees the light of day; perhaps the most visually striking decision is the fact that the world outside Verónica's apartment is only seen in the dead of night. With reference to the film *Tres Marías* (Francisco González, 2010), María Lourdes Cortés has pointed out that San José is a city of two halves – day and night – and that at night 'la marginalidad la ha poblado. Una ciudad tomada por jóvenes, delincuentes, prostitutas, y travestis' (2016, 72). While in this film the 'travestis' are actually transgender women, this 'Other' side of the city which comes out at night is apparent in *Abrázame como antes* too. The fact that people and activities that would traditionally be seen as the unsavoury underbelly of society are not only brought to light but also presented in both a light-hearted and sympathetic manner certainly situates this film as a deliberate antithesis to *tico* norms. Indeed, as Cortés also states: 'uno de los principales logros de Ureña es presentar a seres que, justamente, se quedan fuera del pura vida' (2016, 227), and this sentiment certainly applies to this film as it breaks entirely from the light, bright tourist image. This film is also very much located in the sphere of the transnational, demonstrating that queer cinema does not act according to the maxims of national borders or societies.

Furthermore, owing to the fact that the film is shot either in interior spaces or outside, with the location shots taking place at night, the lack of specificity of location means this narrative could be taking place anywhere (Figure 3). There are no mentions of Costa Rica, no flags, no major touristic locations to link the film visually to its country of origin. Indeed, while the accent and ways of speaking will be noticeably Costa Rican to a local audience, an international viewer – especially one watching via subtitles – may well be

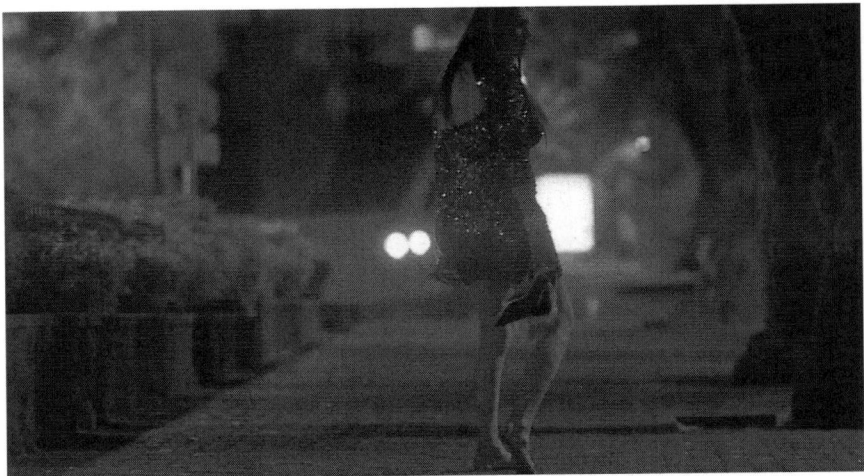

Figure 3 Verónica and San José are only shown at night or in shadow in *Abrázame como antes* (Dir. Jurgen Ureña, 2016, Mina Films)

none the wiser as to the provenance of the film. The transnational quality of the narrative also establishes this film as inhabiting what Jack Halberstam terms a queer time and space, which exist 'in opposition to the institutions of family, heterosexuality, and reproduction. They ... develop according to other logics of location, movement, and identification' (2005, 1). Within this definition, it is clear that the protagonists of the film live outside the established and socially accepted boundaries of the *tico* world, as they remain indoors during the day and outdoors at night, living in dark spaces with little interaction with societal norms. This use of darkness to frame the cinematography of the film indicates that these characters are made to live outside the limits of everyday society. Moreover, as depicted by Halberstam's definition of a queer space, they inhabit a world where the family is not the paradigmatic mother–father–children set up; Verónica has taken Greta into her home and under her wing, just as she does with Tato, cooking for them and fussing around them, acting as a mother might. These are not her biological children; however, the film portrays them as a family all the same.

Traditional, Catholic – and *tico* – ideas of gender and sexuality are therefore disrupted by the fact that these women, who take great care and attention to style their make-up, hair, and clothes according to accepted norms of female beauty, also have penises and sleep with men for money. Indeed, Halberstam goes on to discuss the power of the transgender look, of which she asserts, 'we can locate a transgender look, a mode of seeing and being seen that is not simply at odds with binary gender but that is a part of a reorientation of the body in space and time' (107). The implications of being seen as a transgender woman in Costa Rican society are huge – this film is one of the only ways in which many people will really see these women at all, and it carries with it the inherent visual and repetitive nature of cinema itself as it can be watched, paused, and re-watched. The affective power of this transgender look – which is all about seeing the narrative through trans rather than cis eyes – is also made a focus of Ureña's film through the getting-ready scenes. These shots, where the protagonists put on their make-up, do each other's hair, and get dressed allow them to share an important daily activity with the viewer as well as sharing their hopes and fears on screen. These scenes use extended shots and close-ups to imbue them with a sense of realism and make the audience feel as though they are both part of the conversation as well as possibly part of the solution. The numerous close-ups used in these scenes also serve to create this affective link between the viewer and the protagonists – when they laugh, we also laugh; when they are thoughtful, we are encouraged to think too. Through the harnessing of the transgender look and the space it creates and appropriates in this film, we clearly see that the very concepts of sex, gender, and sexuality are undone and subverted. Within this queer space in the film, Verónica, Natalia, and Thalaya are able to live outside the restrictive constructs of *tico* society in terms of breaking the normative and imposed trajectory of biological sex → gender → sexual attraction as laid out by Butler (Blumenfeld and Breen, 2005, 10–17). They are transgender women with breasts and penises, who ascribe to the female gender and some tropes that go with this – albeit while others are broken – and who are sexually attracted to men. This rupture with prescribed gender roles, then, is something integral to both the film itself and to the on-screen representation of transgender people who have been invisibilized in Costa Rican film, and society, up until this point, as well as comprising a powerful critique of the imposition of the hegemonic and destructive gender codes upheld by *tico* ideals.

Existing scholarship on the representation of trans characters in film often converges around the idea that on-screen portrayals of the trans community are either steeped in negative association or entrenched in stereotype. Indeed, Melissa Rigney argues that transgender roles tend either to encompass psychotic, disturbed, abnormal, or dangerous characters or to provide a melodramatic sense of comic relief (2008, 181–2). What these tropes have in common, then, is that the trans character is always 'Othered' within the central narrative of the film and/or within mainstream discourse itself (Rigney, 2008, 181–2). Indeed, Rigney asserts that the view that biological sex is fixed at birth and that it is no less than a psychosis to wish to change this is thereby perpetuated in films which include trans characters (182). Furthermore, in Gustavo Subero's 2008 investigation into Latin American films that deal in trans themes or characters, his assessment of the lack of screen time or the way the characters are depicted is cutting. He notes that:

> although all the protagonists identify as homosexual and even self-identify as females, their incursion into crossdressing responds more to a necessity to offer a laughable and/or entertaining version of femininity as part of an onstage performance. Therefore, these subjects perform a performance of gender – that is, their performance of femaleness is read by the people around them as the satirized imitation of womanliness from a man who does not see himself as a women (regardless of his sexual orientation) – thus their crossdressing does not have the ultimate intention of externalizing an inner-felt gender identity. (Subero, 2008, 175)

With this contention Subero highlights several problematic areas which exist within the context of trans films in Latin America. First, in adherence with Rigney's contention, while homosexuality is given some element of nuance, the idea of being transvestite or transgender is only manifest in the idea of 'cross-dressing' as entertainment. It is not treated as a serious identity, but an incursion into a world of performance and satire for the male gaze. This, of course, therefore negates the very real lives existing beyond transvestitism whereby being a woman is not a choice or a flirtation, it is not 'dressing up' for a night of performance, rather it is an everyday, lived reality. Subero argues that these realities are not depicted so as 'to avoid the alienation of such [Latin American] audiences' (161) as 'the directors have decided against depicting such bodily transgressions' (161). It seems that just like in Costa Rica the hegemonic view of gender identity in the nations of Latin America considered by Subero also conforms to patriarchal and Catholic norms that suggest: (a) biological sex is fixed and unchangeable, and that (b) biological men should be masculine and attracted to women, while biological women should be feminine and attracted to men.

As discussed by Rigney, fixed notions of gender identity are not restricted solely to Latin American films, and I would argue that even when trans identities are depicted in a positive light on film it is the journey to being recognized as transgender – which is likely to involve societal and familial rejection – which takes centre stage in many narratives. Films such as Vicente Aranda's *Cambio de sexo* (1976, Spain), Alain Berliner's *Ma vie en rose* (1997, Belgium), Kimberly Peirce's *Boys Don't Cry* (1999, USA), and Tim Hooper's *The Danish Girl* (2015, UK) all span different national and chronological contexts, and yet they share a common trans theme: the realization, transformation, and subsequent struggle for recognition due to a non-conformist gender identity. While the trauma of being rejected by family members and peers, and the difficulties in recognizing and identifying as trans, are immensely important issues which have been addressed by these films, few narratives have set themselves at a point beyond this initial stage of transformation. This is what makes Ureña's film so interesting: not only is it putting transgender characters at the centre stage of a narrative from a different perspective to many films that have gone before it, but it is doing so from Costa Rica, a nation with fixed ideas about gender and one in which film-makers still rarely dare to speak of an existent film industry.

Representing the 'Other'

While Ureña freely admits that before making this film he had no insight into the trans community in Costa Rica, he has made laborious and deliberate efforts to present a valuable and nuanced portrayal in this film. Writing or attempting to represent characters with very different identities – especially those which are marginalized by mainstream society – can be fraught with difficulty. Trying to elicit a new understanding from audiences that ends up patronizing the 'Other' or creating affective bonds with central characters through stereotyping or falling into the trap of typecasting or cultural appropriation are all-too-common pitfalls. In his quest to avoid these, Ureña embarked on a painstaking and lengthy learning and creation process when making his film, and, along the way, has demonstrated the ethical possibilities for film-making when thinking responsibly about marginalized stories from a hegemonic – in this case *tico*centric – point of view. After envisioning Lobo's short story, 'Candelaria al azar', as a script, and gaining the author's permission to make it into a film, Ureña proceeded to make two short films based on the story in 2010 and 2011. One, *Paso en falso*, had a traditional narrative and cinematography, while the other, *Los inadaptados*, experimented with form and style. Ureña refers to these as his architect sketches, the drafts that he needed in order to work out what the final picture should look like (A. Quesada, 2017).

The director has noted of the first short, 'al fin y al cabo, teníamos a un hombre vestido de mujer, y esa era una visión un poco básica y superficial de lo que significaba una persona trans en todas sus manifestaciones' (A. Quesada, 2017). Such self-awareness and self-critique have clearly shaped the final product in innumerable ways, as Ureña's next decision proved crucial to the final outcome: he contacted the NGO Transvida, a charity which works with trans people in San José, and was able to put together a focus group involving 15 trans women, some of whom were working as prostitutes, to gain feedback about his portrayal of the trans community in the film. Of this critical session, Ureña states, 'ellas me confirmaron lo que más o menos intuía, que se trataba de una caricatura, hasta un poco ofensivo' (A. Quesada, 2017). Ureña learned that his cis male protagonist dressed in women's clothes could never fully represent these women, and that his narrative was marred by stereotypes which led to two-dimensional characterization. Taking these comments on board, he came up with a drastic proposal: he would offer them a free course in acting, and they would offer him creative workshops where they told him about their lives and revealed their personalities so he could use these in the film (A. Quesada, 2017).

These mutual-learning workshops went on for six months, by the end of which, of the 13 women that had begun the training, only three were left. These three were Jimena Franco, Natalia Porras, and Thalaya, who went on to be the protagonists of the film. The use of focus groups and mutual exchange in the creation of a filmic narrative is certainly innovative when it comes to making films which represent marginalized groups to which one does not belong, and it brings to mind Spivak's contention that subalternity, when considered as a space of hybridity, can facilitate the exchange of ideas without the hierarchy which is often present when margin and centre meet. She writes:

> it's much more than just strategic inclusion ... It seems to me that finding the subaltern is not so hard, but actually entering into a responsibility structure with the subaltern, with responses flowing both ways: learning to learn without this quick-fix frenzy of doing good with an implicit assumption of cultural supremacy which is legitimized by unexamined romanticization, that's the hard part. (Landry and Maclean, 1996, 293)

That Ureña did not force his vision of the film onto the transgender women of his focus group, and that he saw the workshops as a space of mutual exchange, demonstrates the positive and beneficial nature of embracing hybridized subalternity in the film-making process.

Moreover, as *Remezcla*'s Manuel Betancourt remarks, the fact that Ureña went beyond this and actually cast trans actresses to play his protagonists is groundbreaking on a global scale:

> If the project was going to be an authentic look at these characters, he needed a trans actress in the leading role. At a time when both Hollywood and indie productions in the U.S. continue to cast cis-gender actors to play trans roles (that is, casting male-identified and male-born actors to play trans women, as Eddie Redmayne did in *The Danish Girl* and Jared Leto did in *Dallas Buyers Club*), Ureña's decision looks all the more radical. (Betancourt, 2016)

While the use of non-professional actors to play themselves or people like them is nothing new, and was a standard technique in the Italian neorealist movement, the entire process behind the creation of *Abrázame como antes* works together to produce a film which deliberately seeks nuanced character portrayals. Indeed, Ureña has stated that he did not want to be morbid, moralizing, or melodramatic in this film (A. Quesada, 2017), and nor did he want to elicit sadness or sympathy from the viewer (Anon., 2017). Rather, considering the psychotic–comic dichotomy of trans representation in films that have gone before, as detailed by Rigney, then, we see characters who are not depicted as abnormal or dangerous but quite the opposite. They are friendly, kind, funny, witty, caring, and yet they can also misjudge situations, get jealous, and argue. Verónica shows Tato and Greta great tenderness; she wraps Tato's broken leg in a bandage, procures him crutches, buys him new clothes, and tells him everything will be OK; she puts in Greta's hair extensions, makes her food, and advises her about man trouble.

While there are humorous occurrences in the film, these are not melodramatic outbursts. Rather, they involve dry wit, sarcasm, and self-deprecation, which are affective qualities that help the viewer access and identify with the characters. For example, after Verónica has consulted a tarot card reader – a pagan and exotic activity for Catholic Costa Rica – she mocks herself, saying, 'Fui a ver una de esas brujas locas, peor que yo, y me dijo lo mismo que yo digo a las strippers de la noche ... mujer me cobró 20'. Although she does not laugh while discussing this anecdote, a viewer that does not believe in superstition will understand her annoyance and offer a wry smile to accompany her regret. Moreover, Verónica's way of delivering friendly slights is also a source of humour for the viewer. When she enters Thalaya's room and looks at photos her friend has commissioned, she remarks, '¿En estas fotos es usted? Qué cantidad de Photoshop', just loud enough for the viewer to hear. When she tells Thalaya she was gorgeous the previous evening, just like now, Thalaya, who has a nylon head wrap in place of her usual wig and who is busy putting on make-up, responds, laughing, '¡Atrevida! Espérese a que termine. Una capita más ... ¡o dos!'. The fact that these characters show real depth of human emotion and are able to laugh at themselves is therefore one way in which Ureña creates complex protagonists to whom he reasonably expects the audience to relate.

While the use of non-professional actresses, transgender protagonists, and the showcasing of a depth of personality traits are therefore used by Ureña to nuance his film, he is also careful to craft a plot which centres around the everyday lives of characters who are no longer on the journey of gender discovery or struggling to accept their gender identities. Rather, these women have passed this phase in their lives and the viewer is offered an insight into the routines, thoughts, and feelings of post-transition normality. Indeed, although visually evident to the viewer, the fact that the protagonists are transgender women is only overtly mentioned once in the film, ten minutes before the end, thereby ensuring it is not a point on which the central narrative hangs. Interestingly, the brief dialogue in which it is mentioned serves to play down their being transgender, thereby normalizing it rather than highlighting it. This scene occurs when Tato, who has now been living in the apartment with Verónica and Greta for a couple of days, sleeps with Greta. Afterwards, this character – who has very few lines in the film – begins the following dialogue:

> TATO: ¿Usted, por qué es así?
> GRETA: ¿Así cómo?
> TATO: Así como una chica, pero ...
> GRETA: ¿Pero con pipi? ¿Por qué? ¿No le gusta? ... Y usted, ¿por qué es así? ¿Hmm?
> TATO: ¿Así cómo?
> GRETA: Así tan callado, tan extraño.

This fleeting mention of the mechanics of Greta's transgender body – described here as a girl with a willy – demonstrates Tato's curiosity but also Greta's disinterest in this subject; the dialogue makes it clear that she has other things on her mind, being transgender is no longer her only concern as it may once have been. Moreover, she turns the question back on Tato, asking him why he is the way he is – so quiet and strange. In this way the scripting makes Ureña's agenda clear: that all the characters in the film, just as in society, are unique and individual; that they have been born a certain way requires no further explanation, thus normalizing the fluidity of gender concepts rather than reinforcing strict ideas of masculinity and femininity associated with *tico* norms.

While *Abrázame como antes* does not diminish the fact that the protagonists are transgender, or that they work as prostitutes, it works to ensure that the viewer understands that they are not *only* trans women, but that they also have individual personalities, problems, complexities, and talents that go beyond purely gender or sexual identity. Although Ki Namaste reads Butler's ideas on queer theory as excluding trans people based on the criticism of performance which, Namaste argues (1996, 198), limits trans identities within the remit of queer theory, in this film I would contend that habitus and performance can actually be considered to be actively working to destabilize gender categories. While on the surface it seems that the protagonists mimic hegemonic practices associated with femininity – creating a certain look with long hair, shaved legs, lots of make-up, high heels, and tight dresses – they are actually also underlining the instability of the idea of what constitutes a 'real woman', demonstrating that such a category cannot really exist.

Indeed, through a careful depiction of their everyday lives and habits, the audience is presented a new perspective on the 'Other' that lives alongside, but separately from, mainstream *tico* society, and thus sees that perhaps the characters' daily concerns are not so different from their own. Much of the film is shot using a handheld camera, which gives it a documentary quality. As Verónica cooks at the stove, prays the rosary by a picture of her mother, or hammers the heel of her shoe into place, the viewer takes on the perspective of voyeur, gazing into the personal space of the apartment. Even when looking at the women from afar on the streets of San José, the proximity of the camera to the ground, the fact that the women regularly have their backs to the camera, and the extra diegetic sound which can be too loud at times to hear what the protagonists say, all add to the sense that what the spectator is viewing is real rather than staged or scripted. This allows the viewer to think about the incoherence of the mainstream *tico* idea that these women – who are both transgender and prostitutes – are somehow different from the rest of society as they have many of the same habits as anyone else. That gender is merely a performance which anyone can put on and own is made clear in their daily rituals, which include dressing, styling their hair, and putting on make-up. Rather than the negative connotations surrounding Butler's concept of performance as reinforcing gender categories, then, these women actually disrupt fixed gender norms and draw strength from both the processes involved in the stylized performance of gender and their lived embodiment of their own gender identities.

The film's narrative maintains these ideas throughout, and at every turn coheres in order to question the *tico* norm. The central narrative focuses on Verónica's quasi-maternal instincts which lead her to take in Tato, just as she took in Greta in the past, in order to protect him from the outside world and give him stability. In this way, the film complicates concepts of gender and maternity. Ureña states that he cast Franco as Verónica because she is 'un personaje maternal' and Franco has a careful way of moving which he associates with his idea of what a mother is (A. Quesada, 2017). He goes on to state that 'sentí que Jimena era ideal justamente por eso, es una persona con muchas calidades que uno podría asociar con una madre. La paciencia, la comprensión estaban en ella como persona' (A. Quesada, 2017). Although there can be no intrinsic traits associated with every mother, and despite the fact that Ureña appears to reify what he thinks a mother should be, he makes the point with this film that the revered position of woman as mother is not dependent on sex or gender identity.

While Verónica cannot physically carry and give birth to a child, she feels the desire to provide, to protect, and to fuss over others, perhaps more vulnerable than herself. She insists on shopping and cooking for Tato and Greta, looking after the apartment, and caring for them. It is made clear that part of this desire has been provoked by her own maternal abandonment, and as such *Abrázame como antes* both in theme and title refers us to a primordial longing to be taken care of and to take care of others. This is not seen as the preserve of man or woman, but a human urge. Just as in Pedro Almodóvar's *Volver* (2006) whereby the song from which the title is derived is sung by a daughter to her thought-to-be-dead mother, in this film the song, although sung by Thalaya, resonates with Verónica, forcing her to face her longing for a maternal relationship. Unlike in *Volver*, where mother and daughter are reunited and then reconciled, in this film Verónica accepts that she must forget her mother (which she eventually does by putting away the photo she had of her surrounded by candles in a shrine-like set up), just as her mother has forgotten her, and instead be a mother-figure to others. These instincts are presented as natural for Verónica, just as they are often associated with being a natural part of motherhood – despite this too being a social construct. When Thalaya tuts at Verónica 'Vos y tus rollos', rolling her eyes when she is told that Verónica has taken Tato in, Verónica replies 'Yo siempre he sido así', thus indicating that qualities and characteristics traditionally only associated with biological women can certainly cross multiple gender categories.

The other protagonists also have personalities and interests that exist outside their trans identities, thus disrupting the norms of other trans narratives. Thalaya, for example, loves to perform, and yet when she sings on stage it is not a melodramatic or camped up performance akin to those Subero analyses (2008) in other Latin American films. While Namaste has argued that 'drag is about performance, while the homoerotic is about identity' (1996, 187), in this film Thalaya is neither in 'drag', nor is she performing to attract sexual attention. Rather, she dresses as she always does, showing off a talent for singing as well as for languages as she sings fluently in Italian and Spanish (Figure 4). The song conveys emotion, and her audience – both within the film as well as its viewers – are captivated by her, thus subverting the trend of trans film depicting issues and concerns solely relevant to trans people. Greta also demonstrates preoccupations and interests outside gender identity. She is passionate about drawing – both in the film and in real life – and Natalia Porras, the actress, notes that she was grateful to Ureña for allowing her artwork to be shown on screen. The pencil drawings fill Greta's dimly lit room and the sketchpad is the first thing she turns to when she wakes up in the morning after lighting a cigarette.

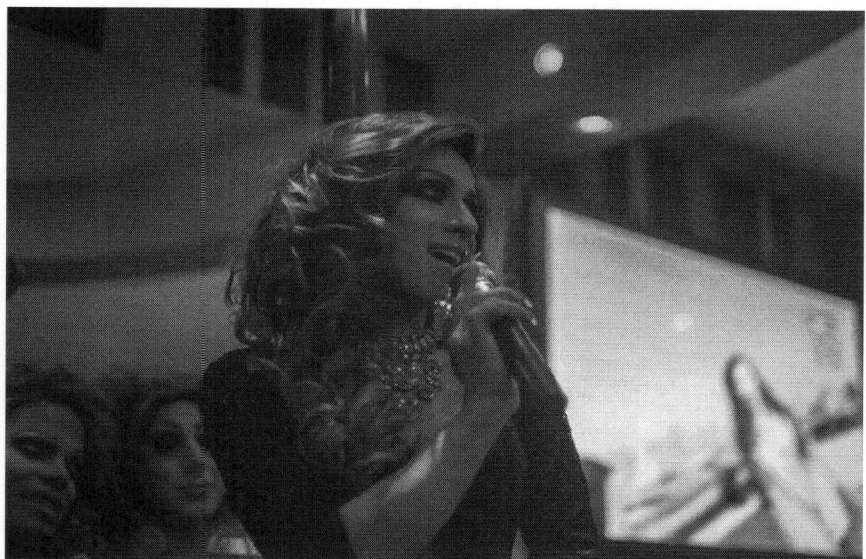

Figure 4 Thalaya sings the title track in a nightclub in *Abrázame como antes* (Dir. Jurgen Ureña, 2016, Mina Films)

Moreover, Greta spends the film preoccupied with the fact that one of her clients is attracted to, and being attracted by, another woman. Although he lavishes Greta with gifts and goes to the club where Thalaya performs with her, Greta's rival spends the night trying to lure him away. After a heavy night of drinking, upon spotting the rival in the park Greta runs over to fight her, pushing her into a pond before chasing her away and laughing, calling her names. Human emotions and passions which transcend gender boundaries – such as creativity and jealousy – form many of the subplots contained within the film, thereby exposing the redundancy of these categories. These categories are also implicitly ridiculed by the protagonists as they refer to each other affectionately as 'mujer' and 'chiquilla', but who call their adversaries 'playos'. While they consider themselves to be women, they do not show solidarity with other transgender characters by also recognizing them as women when insulting them. Moreover, despite identifying as women, they also refer to their male clients as gay, thus blurring the boundaries of gay and straight, man and woman, and calling into question the validity of these rigid oppositions, showing us their redundancy and the true, multiply placed nature of gender and sexed identities.

Despite this radical examination of transgender lives which demonstrates a total upheaval of accepted gendered and sexual norms and thus constitutes a striking example of counterhegemonic production for *tico* society, Subero's words of warning must still be taken into account. He contends that in Latin America there exists:

> a kind of heteronormative filmic fear to depict the fluidity of sexuality beyond the biologically oriented binary man–woman. I suggest that Latin American audiences do not respond positively to transvestic images (i.e., the cinematic acknowledgment of transvestism) because they transgress the fixity of gender roles within heteronormativity. (Subero, 2008, 159)

Although the film won the most prestigious national prize at the *Festival Internacional de Cine* in Costa Rica, Poe Lang notes (2017) that as the film was being premiered someone walked out of the cinema. Indeed, Quesada states, when interviewing Ureña, that 'a pesar de que sí ha habido un cambio importante, el mundo de los transexuales ha sido un tema tabú en Costa Rica por mucho tiempo' (2017). The fact that he describes the protagonists as transsexuals, rather than transgender – as we find out from Greta that she has not had reassignment surgery – is also perhaps telling. Not only does Ureña contend that this is 'un tema que usualmente metemos debajo de la alfombra de la sociedad' (A. Quesada, 2017), but he is also very honest, going on to state that 'Si yo me ubico como era antes de hacer esta película, cuando caminaba por Barrio Amón y veía a estas chicas transgénero prostituirse, mi capacidad de conocer y valorar ese mundo era nula' (A. Quesada, 2017).

While Ureña clearly has an open mind when it comes to learning about the 'Other' in *tico* society, it is also evident in the film, however implicitly, that the rest of *tico* society is not as ready to accept gender and sexual difference into their idea of the nation. Jimena Franco makes this damning statement:

> you live here, and it starts with family when they don't accept gays, when they reject their sons and they're caught up with 'el que dirán,' and throw them out on the street. And the street is waiting for them. It's a trap almost. From there you're not far from alcohol, drugs, prostitution. Of course, what's missing in this country are opportunities. And for us in the trans community, we have nothing. Not even the slightest chance at a low-paying job. It's such that we don't even have a name: what's on our ID is a man's name, not our own. (Betancourt, 2016)

Meanwhile, Natalia Porras points out that she was denied an education and humiliated as a child for being trans (Betancourt, 2016). This, the exclusion of internal 'Others', is still clearly visible and raw in the real lives of these trans women, and the ignorance surrounding their lives and struggles is ever-present in society. It is important, then, that this film does not exoticize nor romanticize the lives of the women it presents on screen, but nor does it portray them as victims, there to be patronized by those that oppress them for their viewing pleasure.

Abrázame como antes certainly attempts to revalorize the lives of these women without reducing them to their trans bodies and identities – as well as deliberately setting out not to elicit a sense of sympathy from the viewer – and yet it is clear that these women have been rejected from mainstream society. Not only must these women inhabit the night, that alternative and transgressive side of San José, but they are also shown to have been cast out of society. Other than the men that solicit them, and the other outsiders – such as the tarot card reader – the transgender women reside together, having little contact with the rest of society. Although Verónica must buy her groceries and clothes from somewhere, the camera does not follow her into the outside world, perhaps so as not to show the viewer the treatment she may receive outside the home. This transgender community is clearly a small but tight-knit group which must help and look out for each other. While putting in Greta's hair extensions, Verónica talks about their meeting and her subsequent rescuing of Greta, stating, 'Yo soy tu ángel, usted es mi ángel'. This idea of having to save those who do not conform to fixed gender roles demonstrates the harmful nature of the *tico* norm for those who identify outside it.

Moreover, this rupture with society is also indicated by the absence of certain characters, as well as by those who are depicted on screen. Although the viewer is often confronted with the big picture of Verónica's mother that she keeps almost as a shrine, with Catholic icons and candles lit around it, we are told that this mother has abandoned Verónica. No other family members or friends are mentioned as playing a part in any of these women's lives. It is also made clear, just as Franco states when interviewed, that there are no jobs for transgender people in Costa Rica. Indeed, Thalaya advises Verónica, 'No dejés la calle porque eso es lo que nos deja plata. Para esto nacimos'. Despite the fact that Verónica is clearly tired and disillusioned by this life, then, she does not have any alternative in order to live in the country. The cinematography also serves to demonstrate how these women are 'Othered' by society, through the use of blocking shots and extra diegetic sound, which visually and audibly denotes their marginalization and estrangement. In the apartment, the camera is often half-hidden below or behind an item of furniture, and thus the viewer takes up the position of spying on the women as though they are a rare and dangerous species. Whenever they are outside, the external noises of traffic and birdsong are overpowering, often so loud that the dialogue takes on secondary importance. The outside world is constantly attempting to hide these women and their presence in society; so when Natalia Porras states that 'Costa Rica may not have given me a country, but this movie did' (Betancourt, 2016), this pronouncement takes on a renewed significance.

Abrázame como antes presents us, therefore, with a truly revolutionary piece within the panorama of both Costa Rican and Latin American – and potentially even global – cinema. Its showcasing of a transnational space, a queer space, inhabited by transgender women is bold in an overtly and, at times, aggressively patriarchal, Catholic, and patriotic country. More than this, however, the director's conception of the 'Other', which he seeks to portray, and the evolution of the film-making process, also demonstrate a bold move towards an ethical and hybrid way of conceiving of film itself, considering it as a mutual learning process as well as an exercise in visual storytelling. That the film depicts a nuanced portrayal of the trans women it films is unquestionable, and although *Abrázame como antes* is aware of *tico* societal norms around gender categories and sexual rigidity, it openly rejects these in favour of a fluid approach, as suggested by Butler. Although Ureña's film, just like Duncan's, Naranjo's, and Chase's literary works before him, attempts to counterbalance and undermine the *tico* norm, then, we see that conceptions of national *tico* identity are still prevalent well into the twenty-first century. The fact that narratives such as these continue to be told, however, demonstrates the enduring desire on the part of some within Costa Rica to break with the strict boundaries of *tico* identity and ideals. Indeed, *Abrázame como antes* demonstrates the soft and affective power of film, as it shows us the fragility of these social norms through the ease of their undoing, as well as their harmful nature as they work against the characters with whom the audience is made to sympathize.

Undercutting Norms at the Periphery: Paz Fábrega's *Agua fría de mar* (2009)

While both *Gestación* and *Abrázame como antes* share their city-centric approach to showcasing and challenging conceptions of national identity in Costa Rica, Paz Fábrega's first feature film is set at the geographic periphery on the country's Pacific coast. Although *Agua fría de mar* received more acclaim internationally than in her home country, Fábrega is certainly among the most prominent directors in Costa Rica and this film was shown at festivals across the world, winning the Tiger Award at the Rotterdam film festival. While released onto the festival circuit in 2009, it was not made public in Costa Rica until 2011 due to the fact that, in Fábrega's words, 'El tipo de cine que hago no es para un público masivo' (Fábrega, 2015). Indeed, the type of cinema popular within Costa Rica tends to be big-budget Hollywood productions, with only one national film – *Maikol Yordan de Viaje Perdido*[4] – outstripping these at the local box office, and *Agua fría de mar* and Fábrega's more recent *Viaje* (2015) certainly lean towards an art-house aesthetic and narrative. Despite quite negative receptions from local audiences to both her films, however, I argue that this refusal to conform to popular film-making practices is an important part of what makes *Agua fría de mar* a counterhegemonic production. Creating a space for a new world vision which showcases the everyday habits and emotions of its protagonists through unsettling cinematography goes some way to deconstructing the image of the nation as a happy and carefree space and Costa Rica's coastline as a site of uncomplicated touristic pleasure. Instead, as will be seen, Fábrega creates an uncanny sentiment in the spectator. Moreover, she also uses her debut feature to inscribe women and a female consciousness onto the patriarchal society seen within the film, as well as exposing the myth of the country as classless and subverting the idealization of the family unit.

At times a slow-paced and haunting narrative, *Agua fría de mar* tells the story of a young couple – Mariana and Rodrigo – who arrive at a beach on Costa Rica's Bahía Ballena for a New Year break. Here, they meet Karina, a seven-year-old girl, who tells them she has run away because her family has been killed and she is living with her uncle who abuses her. Although the audience is unsure as to the veracity of her story at this point, Mariana is deeply moved by the girl's account. From this point onwards, the film narrates the parallels between the emotional lives of these two protagonists as Karina goes back to her family who are staying on the beach while Mariana and her fiancé go to stay in a hotel above it. While Mariana grows increasingly despondent and withdrawn in the foreign-owned hotel on the cliff, with Rodrigo frequently away trying to sell his family's plot of land to a North American buyer, Karina does everything she can to get her parents'

---

4 It is estimated that half a million people watched the film in its first week and in total the film was seen by 770,000 in cinemas alone (17 per cent of the Costa Rican population) (M. L. Cortés, 2016, 17). In the six weeks it enjoyed at the box office, Gómez's production took US$3 million in sales. For a film made for only US$200,000, this is by far the largest profit made by any Costa Rica film and it outstripped its Hollywood competitors in the country during this period (Murillo, 2014). As with all Gómez's films, his recipe for success is rooted in the *tico* characteristics on show which can be seen in the actors and locations, as well as the language and jokes woven into each narrative. Gómez is clear about how he likes to make films: they must be profitable, and the only way of making a profit in Costa Rica seems to be to make films cheaply, almost exclusively for a local audience, and hope that this patriotic appeal brings in sales.

attention, having been grounded for running away. Apparently fed up after several days of isolation – even though her friends have now joined her – Mariana walks down the steep cliff full of vegetation and onto the beach where several families have made vehicles and tents into makeshift holiday homes. Stopping outside Karina's family's lorry, she falls and injures herself, prompting Karina's parents to insist on driving her to the nearest hospital with Karina on board. While speaking to Karina's mother when waiting for the doctor, Mariana finds out that Karina lied to her about her family situation, and she returns to her hotel in silence amidst firework displays and parties. Once there, she chooses to bypass her friends and instead goes directly to her room and closes the shutters. In the final scene, Karina, arriving at the beach with her parents to find barbecues, music, and parties in full swing, wanders alone towards the sea.

Counterhegemonic Narratives and the 'Uncanny'

While Fábrega has long been one of the chief critics of the over-representation of Hollywood films in Costa Rican cinemas as well as of the lack of art-house films shown in the country, this has not deterred her from undercutting these norms. Indeed, she states that audiences want Costa Rican films that are 'como las otras películas en cartelera, que sean lo más parecidas posibles a las gringas pero acá' (Fábrega, 2011) and that 'el tipo de cine que me interesa prácticamente no existe aquí. No sólo no llega, no se valora, se ve como un cine marginal ... siento que el cine está atrapado en una tiranía de la historia' (Fábrega, 2015). Despite the often negative viewing figures and reviews of her films among Costa Rican audiences, her contention that the type of film she makes is seen as a marginal genre is reminiscent of Laura Mulvey's argument that 'the alternative cinema [non-Hollywood] provides a space for cinema to be born which is radical in both a political and an aesthetic sense and challenges the basic assumptions of the mainstream film' (1985, 805). This signifies that consciously making films that exist as a counterpoint to a Hollywood aesthetic can actually create an alternative space for a country's film industry, and I argue that Fábrega as a director has opened up a national space for other radical films, such as *Abrázame como antes*, to be made. In the post-digital era, with film-making increasing in Costa Rica, which in turn allows for a plethora of new voices to be heard, Fábrega is certainly using film to create a counterhegemonic aesthetic and narrative where the incidental and the emotional take centre stage.

While there is a cohesive narrative that focuses in on Mariana and Karina's experiences over a few days of their holidays in Bahía Ballena in the film, critics such as José Solís have contended that too many open-ended plot lines are incorporated into it, thus creating an unintentional void within the narrative (Solís, 2010). The film certainly does not adhere to a typical 'order–disorder–order restored' narrative arc and yet I argue that what actually frustrates Solís about the film is that it does not match up to his expectations of what a national production in Costa Rica should be due to its lack of overtly 'national' elements. Although Fábrega centres all her work in and around Costa Rican landscapes, people, and realities, she also purposely undercuts the image of the nation created in tourist and patriotic media. Although still employing certain normative national identifiers – such as the use of *costarriqueñismos* which pepper the dialogue, location filming, and non-professional actors – she also invites the viewer to appreciate the subtleties of the mise-en-scène and be drawn into the affective mood created by her screenplay, which is transnational in its nature, perhaps explaining the film's success at international film festivals. Indeed, Fábrega defends her narrative choices and argues that the core theme of the film depicts the process of realization that as individuals we are alone in the world and responsible for our own actions and happiness (Fábrega, 2015) – a far cry from the discourse that being born in Costa Rica automatically qualifies citizens for happiness.

In terms of the unintentional void noted by Solís, Fábrega claims that her intention with *Agua fría de mar* was to divert attention constantly from one potential plot to another, never letting any of them take over the narrative as a whole, while also showcasing the protagonists' different reactions to certain uncomfortable discoveries (Tabernero, 2011). We can see this as several aspects of the protagonists' storylines are left hanging and the audience remains questioning whether Karina has been sexually abused or just makes up stories for attention, whether Mariana is recovering from a past trauma that makes her wet the bed or – and at the heart of the film – whether it is actually the eerie coastline which is making both characters fall into their own personal abyss. This aspect of plotlessness signals a new world vision where the habitual and everyday are set up in opposition to grand narratives and stylized norms apparent in high-ticketing productions. In this film, the viewer finds their gaze frequently redirected and pointed towards new possibilities, while Karina's desperation for attention and Mariana's introspective retreat reflect the traumatic transition they are both undergoing. As part of this transition, there is an uncanny focus on the merging of Mariana and Karina's experiences and attitudes as well as a clear fascination with habitus and the quotidian. Indeed, entire scenes depict apparently uneventful occurrences, such as Mariana's friends arriving at the hotel, or Karina's family clearing away their food after lunch and talking about the beach. These are filmed as long takes with a static camera, conferring a feeling of both realism and stagnation on the viewer as we are invited to watch and experience the minutiae of those on screen in real time. This conscious rejection of an overtly national or grand narrative in favour of the portrayal of more habitual issues and everyday situations could be a consequence of the digital turn, as wider access to film-making makes room for 'smaller' concerns to come to the fore. This points towards the exploration of a peripheral vision which Hart contends (2015, 8) forms a core part of the new space of post-digital turn cinema in nations which had previously existed at the periphery of the global cinematic industry. For Fábrega and Costa Rica, this focus on the everyday and, often, the boredom associated with it also serves to signal a sense of disillusionment which is anathema to the 'Happiest Country in the World' image promoted, upheld, and lauded by *tico* identity.

This idea is furthered by the ongoing suggestion of an unnatural or uncanny occurrence as Mariana and Karina's feelings continue to mirror each other. Sigmund Freud's essay on the concept of the 'uncanny' (1919, 1) perhaps continues to be the best-known work on the topic, even nearly a century after its publication, and he describes this idea as something that produces dread but that is not necessarily fearful. In this film, the protagonists feel trapped by their surroundings, despite having a large group of friends and family around them, and towards the end of the film they both deal with their emotions in the same way – by physically distancing themselves from others. Indeed, displaying this sense of dread, Mariana leaves a conversation among her friends and the North American buyer of Rodrigo's land and wanders down the cliff towards the beach. Meanwhile, also alone and unnoticed, Karina has run away from the other children and plays by herself in a cove. Both seem to want to experience adventure while remaining hidden from the world, and the hidden camera spying on others' lives – as if it tries to ascertain who and what 'normal' should be – is an important part in the atmospheric construction of the film which does not portray fear, but an unease which also pervades the cinematography. The camera – sometimes following one of the protagonists' gazes and sometimes wandering on the beach – is often placed behind an object to create a blocking shot, where dialogue can be followed without being seen (Figure 5). The spectator's point of view is therefore often voyeuristic, and we are forced to gaze on others from among the long grass, under water in the sea, behind rocks on the beach, behind a car windscreen looking out onto a conversation taking place outside the car, or under the cover of darkness. This idea of having to spy on others to try to uncover norms after feeling abnormal demonstrates how these 'normative' ideals – that Karina and Mariana should enjoy time with family and friends and be happy on their beach holiday – pervade the protagonists' mindsets and

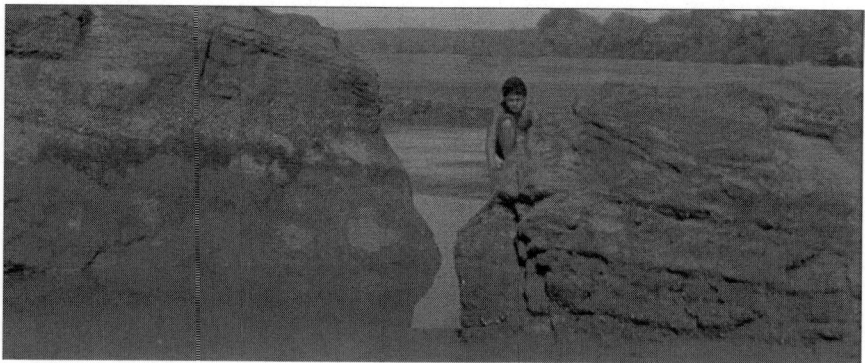

Figure 5 One of many blocking shots giving the perspective of spying in *Agua fría de mar* (Dir. Paz Fábrega, 2009, Temporal)

daily lives. This can also connect to the journey that both Mariana and Karina find themselves on which is a type of 'coming-of-age' story, described by Berghahn as one which 'provide[s] them with a variety of experiences, essential for the adolescent's maturation and emancipation' after which 'the protagonist would eventually return home, where he would assume his role and position in society' (2010, 240). It appears to be this role in society and this role in the world that both characters are attempting to find by going through a personal trauma and spying on others to see how they live.

This creation of an unsettling atmosphere is enhanced through the use of eyeline match and disjointed cuts. The eyeline match allows the viewer to gaze upon the world from the protagonists' points of view, and Karina frequently watches other people's lives play out in front of her while she cannot be seen, just as Mariana watches Karina's family clearing away the dinner table from behind a tree on the beach, remaining hidden herself. According to Freud, an author of fiction 'creates a kind of uncertainty in us ... by not letting us know ... whether [s]he is taking us into the real world or into a purely fantastical creation of his [her] own creation' (1919, 7). This use of everyday and mundane tasks being spied on by the protagonists and by us as viewers therefore adds to this idea of the uncanny, not quite letting us know what is real and what is fantastic. Moreover, when considering certain scenes through Karina's gaze, the shots are sometimes blurred or disjointed, such as when she watches the boys playing with fire on the beach. This points towards the blurring of the line between reality and fiction in her head as well as being suggestive of her own journey of losing trust in those around her. This blurring of lines and inability to understand their semi-articulated feelings is enhanced when Mariana and Karina are forced together alongside Karina's family as they take her to the local hospital.

Their mutual silence and brief glances towards each other when the other is not looking stand in opposition to the other characters that surround them who are warm and chatty. When they both arrive back from the hospital to their respective New Year's Eve parties, their mutual disillusionment continues and they both run away, further highlighting the unease felt by the viewer and undercutting the happy and carefree nature of the festivities seen on screen.

This subverting of national images and ideals is further highlighted when considering the role played by nature and the unnatural in the film. Although it is not an autobiographical piece, Fábrega drew on her own experiences of travelling to the Pacific coast at a time in her life where she felt pressured to try to fit into social norms, and she asserts that the landscapes associated with this coastline – which play a central role in this film – are able to embody this feeling of uselessness and dejection that both Mariana and Karina face (Fábrega, 2015). They often serve to heighten the tension within the narrative too, as the convergence of the feelings and experiences of the protagonists steadily increases. Again, this is a technique pointed out by Freud as common in creating an uncanny sensation in the spectator as the transferring of mental processes or the identification with another person is seen as uncanny (1919, 9). Indeed, Freud suggests that 'by doubling, dividing and interchanging the self' this unnatural sense of unease is created, as well as through 'the constant recurrence of similar situations, a same face, or character-trait' (1919, 9). In *Agua fría de mar* this begins with the sense of boredom that appears to threaten to overwhelm both protagonists. Mariana is stuck in the hotel on the cliffs with no one around and nowhere to go, while Karina is grounded for running away and is stuck inside the truck while her family goes on a trip. Although both stare out past the camera as we watch them, as though watching a prisoner, their reactions to this situation differ. While Karina escapes, running out onto the beach and finding a poisonous snake which she forces to bite her so she can fall ill and garner attention, Mariana withdraws into herself. When Rodrigo comes back that evening she is on the bed, crying, and when he asks what is wrong, she replies: 'No hago nada. Siento inútil. No hago nada. Estoy ostinada [bored]'. Again, this pronouncement recalls Freud's notion of the uncanny which can also form from 'a sense of helplessness sometimes experienced in dreams' (1919, 10), and perhaps it is no wonder that during much of the film Mariana is seen asleep during the day, waking up disorientated and confused.

This unsettling turn of events appears strange to the spectator when Mariana had previously cheerfully explained her job as a microbiologist to Karina, leading the audience to question this sudden change in attitude. Indeed, it points towards the cause of Mariana's unease as being her presence

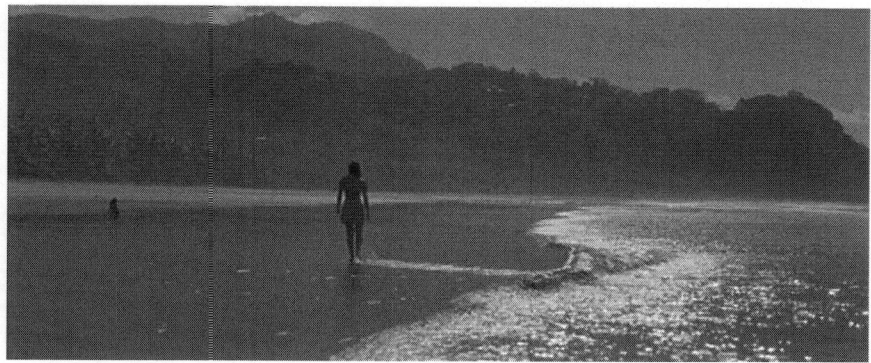

Figure 6 The sea gives the impression of pushing Mariana and Karina towards each other in *Agua fría de mar* (Dir. Paz Fábrega, 2009, Temporal)

at the geographic, wild, margins of the nation, turning the picture-postcard image of the Pacific coast on its head. This sense of nature as ruling human emotion is heightened when the camera films Mariana and Karina's second meeting on a deserted beach. Despite the idyllic white sand, clear water, and verdant rainforest framing the image, the camera is a distant observer, not daring to get too close to the woman and child. On screen, it is clear to see Mariana chasing after a retreating Karina, and yet all the viewer can hear is the sea roaring aggressively towards them as though pushing them together (Figure 6). Although they are shouting, no dialogue can be heard, again demonstrating the power of nature that trumps human actions.

By situating *Agua fría de mar* at the coast and in a rural landscape, the film also plays with notions of what it is to be *tico*, who the *tico* is performing for, and the relationship of the dominant centre – where the protagonists are from – with the geographic margins. As Francisco-J. Hernández Adrián has pointed out (2015), land and seascapes are important characteristics of Latin American film, which he contends are used to exoticize countries in the eyes of an international audience, performing a version of the nation or region that the tourist gaze expects to see. Although Sanabria asserts (2011b, 21) that the film plays with pauses and long scenic shots in order to reflect the tourist image of the country, I would argue that Fábrega actually sets up this image at certain points in order to deconstruct it. The title of the film hints at this, as although the country is associated with its beaches, the fact that this sea water is cold does not quite fit its idyllic connotations. Moreover, as the opening credits roll, before any images have been shown, the viewer can hear the sea lapping gently on the shore. The opening shots, however, show people living in tents, looking out unenthusiastically over the beach where children play, all cast in sepia. While Costa Rica's visibility as a tourist

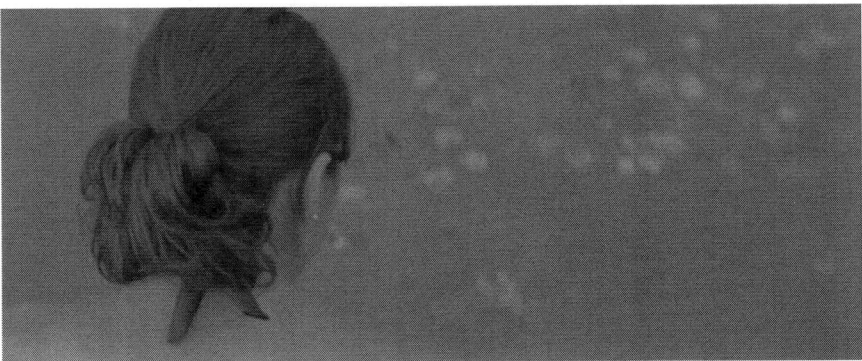

Figure 7 The green swimming pool full of decomposing vegetation in *Agua fría de mar* (Dir. Paz Fábrega, 2009, Temporal)

destination has been recognizable for some time, then, this scene sets up the disruption of the perfect, idealistic tourist image by forcing the viewer to see a picture with which they are familiar through a defamiliarized lens. The fact that the two protagonists, while on holiday in such a beautiful location, can be so disillusioned with life, further undermines the image of the country as a tropical, happy haven.

It is this very use of nature and backdrop that has been praised by international film festivals, with the Rotterdam committee stating that 'la película transporta al espectador en un viaje extraordinario por la naturaleza que interactúa de manera mágica con los seres humanos' (Anon., 2011). However, this magical way that nature and humans interact in the film is perceived to be something rotting as opposed to a positive sensation, thus adding to the unease that encompasses this would-be tourist haven in which the film is located. While seen through the characters' withdrawal from those around them and their spiralling into inertia, this can also be seen as physically reflected in the setting of many scenes. The decomposing swimming pool that Mariana swims in is green and full of rotting vegetation (Figure 7), reminiscent of Lucrecia Martel's *La ciénaga* (2001), where it also confers a feeling of stagnation on the narrative and characters. The child protagonist as verging on monstrous or uncanny is, according to Deborah Martin (2011, 645), also a component of some of Martel's films. Moreover, the jungle through which Mariana must climb to reach the beach is pictured as hostile, with trees and plants towering above her and animal noises the only audible sound, while when Mariana does eventually make it to the beach and see Karina's family, she falls down a hole in the sand and sprains her ankle.

Both the power and majesty of nature are therefore depicted in this film, but the question of who owns nature as well as ideas of how tourism affects a nation also come into play. Rodrigo and Mariana have taken this trip to Bahía Ballena in order to sell off Rodrigo's family's piece of land. Bob, a North American, is an interested buyer, and he explains to Rodrigo that he came to Costa Rica – where he now lives – to get away from snow in the USA. He mentions that rain does not bother him, and that he likes the greenery of this side of the country more than the drier climate in the north, demonstrating that he has bought into the tourist image of the country as a natural habitat for tourists to enjoy – he does not even consider living where the majority of Costa Ricans do, in the Central Valley. When the pair arrive at the piece of land, Rodrigo begins his sales pitch in which he explains that his grandfather came from the local area, but that his father moved to San José to work, and the family has stayed there. Tabernero puts this thread of the narrative down to the whims of the young who only think in the moment. I would contend, however, that in considering the issue of land ownership and wealthy foreign groups living in Costa Rica, Fábrega opens a debate around the country's ideas around national sovereignty, demonstrating how much national land is actually eaten up by foreigners. Due to the *tico* notion that 'real life' in the twenty-first century, or at least political, economic, and social life, all takes place in the Central Valley, the outlying land of which they are so proud when it comes to selling the country to tourists is actually being taken over by North Americans.

Indeed, it seems as though it is these wealthy tourists who are realizing the capitalist potential of the country, and utilizing it for their own benefit. As one of Rodrigo's friends remarks, 'Tener una propiedad ... en varios años se hace mucho mejor', when talking about the selling off of properties on the coast. It is clear that tourist expansion is ongoing, but that Costa Ricans themselves will not profit from it. Bob, for example, is planning 'A small hotel, a boutique hotel. Ten bedrooms, but very exclusive. We're very excited about it ... we like the seasons around here ... it's wonderful all year round ... we like working with the government down here. The local municipality is very good permitwise'. The 'exclusive' clientele he hopes to attract will not be Costa Ricans – and it certainly will not be those Costa Ricans staying in tents on the beach – and, just like Bob, it is also implied that they will not consider it necessary to speak Spanish or deal with the *tico* centre while they are in the country. This juxtaposition therefore constructs a veiled critique of different holiday cultures based on wealth. Moreover, while Rodrigo's friend notes that people come to Costa Rica from outside because 'eso es lo que le gusta a la gente, el contacto con la naturaleza, respirar el aire puro', he also states that, unfortunately, Costa Rican landowners 'vende barato ... porque no hay plata', demonstrating that the real money being made in tourism is not helping local economies at the periphery.

Undercutting the *Tico* Norm: Women, Class, and Imperfect Families

Despite the relative 'plotlessness' of the narrative itself, it is the comparisons between Mariana and Karina that become the focus of the film, and in featuring solely female protagonists Fábrega uses her work to inscribe women into the nation's consciousness as well as into Costa Rica's film industry itself. However, while her use of nature and the slow pace of the film's narrative won favour further afield, it was these aspects of *Agua fría de mar* which were criticized within Costa Rica, with Carolina Sanabria writing that in the film 'las intenciones intimistas se confunden con abundancia de silencios, con exceso de laconismo, lo que deriva en una construcción débil, poco delineada de personajes' (2011a, 21). However, it is exactly this contention – that there is a lack of character development –which I would question in Sanabria's analysis, as the viewer leaves the film feeling far more intimately acquainted with Mariana and Karina than is either of their families – something which relatively few Costa Rican films offer when it comes to female protagonists. It is not just the fact that the viewer has more access to both characters than their families do, but it is the use of camerawork that creates unsettling parallels between the two that serves to aid the creation of an affective bond between them and the audience too. Throughout the film, the camera moves in on both their faces, offering emotive close-ups as they stare upon something the viewer cannot see, inviting us to connect with them and to try to understand their feelings. The camera focuses on one of their faces before immediately cutting to that of the other as they both share the same expression, creating the unsettling effect of the doppelgänger (Freud, 1919, 9–10). The use of close-up in this way suggests to the audience that at any given time Mariana and Karina share a feeling, be it boredom or frustration, as well as inviting us to connect with the characters. Although they do not share the same space, the manner in which the camera records their eyes staring past the lens before cutting to the other implies that they are looking at, towards, or for each other, further highlighting the uncanny symmetry that has been created between them in the eyes of the audience. While they are not connected within the narrative, then, within the cinematography the protagonists remain inextricably linked in the viewer's mind and allow us an intimacy with this woman and girl at different stages of their lives.

Despite more recent films such as *Abrázame como antes, Nina y Laura* (Alejo Crisóstomo, 2015), and *Atrás hay relámpagos* (Julio Hernández Cordón, 2016) dealing in female protagonists, Fábrega was one of the first Costa Rican directors to make this step,[5] and as such her treatment of gender, although

---

5 Maureen Jiménez's *Mujeres apasionadas* (2003) also has female-only protagonists.

subtle, proves interesting. Although Tabernero suggests that what both Mariana and Karina go through is 'profundamente feminina' – as Karina realizes that the first man she loves – her father – cannot always rescue her, while Mariana sees that the last man she is to love – Rodrigo, her fiancé – can also not be responsible for her happiness – I argue that this is not the case in the film and suggests an overly simplistic and patriarchal reading. Indeed, the causes of both characters' discontent are far more complex than this assertion and Fábrega herself states that this realization of being alone is a crisis point that can happen to anyone, at any time, demonstrating the universal possibilities of this emotion and experience that she wanted to portray.

What I argue we do see in the film, from a gendered point of view, however, are the ways in which patriarchal society continues to pervade everyday life and negatively affects women in the film. Rodrigo, although at times caring and understanding – such as when Mariana wets the bed – still plays the dominant, active male role highlighted by Laura Mulvey (1985, 814) whereby Mariana is the passive image that the man can decide to save – or not. Mariana may be given the agency to be the author of her own destiny within the narrative, but practically speaking she is bound by him, demonstrating Mulvey's contention that she is 'bound by a symbolic order in which man can live out his phantasies and obsessions through linguistic command by imposing them on the silent image of the woman still tied to her place as bearer of meaning, not maker of meaning' (1985, 804). Indeed, Rodrigo leaves her alone during the day to conduct his business appointments – selling his grandfather's land which was passed down the patriarchal lineage to him to make money from – and she has no way to leave the empty, stagnating hotel. Finding herself isolated and clearly affected by both her surroundings and her meeting with Karina, her disillusionment and despondency increase.

Moreover, it is clear that Rodrigo insists on being the holder of the aforementioned linguistic command which Mariana must follow at all times. After speaking to his father on the phone, Mariana tells Rodrigo she would like to phone her mother. He retorts that they will spend hours 'hablando paja' [talking rubbish] and that – because her mother is so used to her calling and worries when she does not – it is good for her to get used to them not speaking all the time. Mariana again takes his word as law and even when her mother phones her, she repeats Rodrigo's words back to her, having assumed and internalized them as her own thoughts. Despite narrating that Mariana has a good job in San José as a bio-scientist, Rodrigo and Karina's father are the only characters seen as actively working in the film. While Rodrigo sells his land to another man, or gathers with his male friends to talk economics as the women play in the swimming pool, Karina's father provides for his family and drives to the hospital. Karina's mother, on the other hand, makes food and cleans the makeshift house. The times that gender roles are subverted within this traditional familial relationship, when Karina's father shows his daughter a lot of affection, are immediately cast as suspicious by the viewer who associate the act with potential child abuse. While women are portrayed as complex beings who do have the power to choose their own paths – as the crises experienced by Mariana and Karina demonstrate – many gendered roles also appear to be adhered to in this film which opens a dialogue on the changing nature of the traditional, patriarchal society and the longevity of the power of the internalization of stereotypes.

Another *tico* myth that is challenged in the film is that of a classless society, and the cultural distinction between different social groups is laid bare in the film. This emphasis on the class divide within the country was a conscious decision in the making of the film as, in Fábrega's own words, 'Costa Rica es un país bastante pequeñito pero bastante cerrado por grupos sociales, que pasa bastante en Latinoamérica en general' (Tabernero, 2011). In the narrative, Mariana and Rodrigo are set up as an upper-middle-class couple and both hail from San José and have professional careers. The fact that their state-of-the-art four-wheel drive is brand new is also highlighted, as Karina states that she does not like the new-car smell of it when she gets in. Moreover, the couple stay in an expensive, foreign-owned hotel on top of a cliff, which looks down directly onto the beach where the poorer families in their lorries, tents, and trailers are staying. Mariana also acts awkwardly when she meets the cleaner in the hotel, muttering a muted 'hola', before waiting in silence for her to vacate the room. Karina, on the other hand, is shown several times as sleeping in the same bed as her parents and brothers, highlighting the fact that they cannot afford a hotel. Her father's lorry is branded 'carnes la inmaculada' on one side, implying that he has a blue-collar profession either as butcher or lorry driver. This notion of closed social groups also comes to the fore as Mariana and Karina do not know how to act around each other. Indeed, as Karina's manipulative character develops, the audience wonders if she told Mariana the story about her family dying and being abused to garner sympathy and possibly even adoption from the wealthy *tica*. Mariana also feels embarrassed and impotent when faced with Karina, as she asks Rodrigo what people do when they hear about situations of abuse; when he states he does not know, she seems paralysed and does nothing. Moreover, when she eventually escapes the hotel and walks down the cliff to the beach, she gazes on the life of those poorer than her in a voyeuristic manner, hiding herself behind a tree when Karina's father spots her.

Although this relationship between social classes is seen as an awkward one in which the crossing of social barriers is not the norm, the 'rich' are not portrayed as living better lives than the 'poor' in this film. The expensive hotel, perched on a cliff, is isolated and shabby, and its green swimming pool is host to rotting vegetation. It does not even have a pathway down to the clean, natural beach below, which Mariana's friend says has beautiful coral reefs. The negative consequences of isolating oneself from other social classes is also highlighted when Mariana comes face to face with Karina's family when she does make it down to the beach. The viewer has earlier seen the strength of community spirit among those living in the tent and lorry accommodation, as the families socialize together and share food and necessities among themselves. As soon as Mariana falls down the hole in the sand, spraining her ankle, Karina's parents rush to her aid and drive her a long way to the nearest hospital on the night of New Year's Eve. Karina's mother even gives her a T-shirt to wear and lets her keep it. In contrast to Mariana's silent and often sullen character – she does not thank the family for their help – Karina's mother speaks of how happy she is with her life and family, reflecting that being married is 'muy bonito' and that her wedding day was the happiest of her life. Back on the beach, the New Year celebrations are a communal affair, with shared food, drink, dancing, and music. Although the working-class families are perhaps portrayed in a stereotypical light – they are happy with the simplicity of their lives and speak about superficial matters – they are certainly favourably compared to Mariana's complexities and introspection, which come across at times as arrogance and self-absorption.

Another taboo that this film broaches – and perhaps the most sensitive of all – is that of the unhappy family as existing in the nation. Despite the rhetoric of the world's happiest country and, within that, the importance of the family as a microcosm of the nation, as discussed in Chapter 1, the family as we see it here demonstrates an unsettling relationship between adults and children that stands in stark contrast to the paradisiacal setting. The opening shots show a very young boy and girl, dressed in swimming shorts and a bikini, lying asleep on a rug on the beach, resting on each other in an adult position and not moving. Later on, these same children are buried from the neck down in the sand and appear as no more than floating heads (Figure 8). According to Freud (1919, 5), the uncanny manifests as objects which may or may not be alive, or are inanimate, such as waxwork figures, or dolls. The positioning, mise-en-scène, and framing of this shot connects with this idea of an uncanny image which, in this case, does not show children as we would expect them to look.

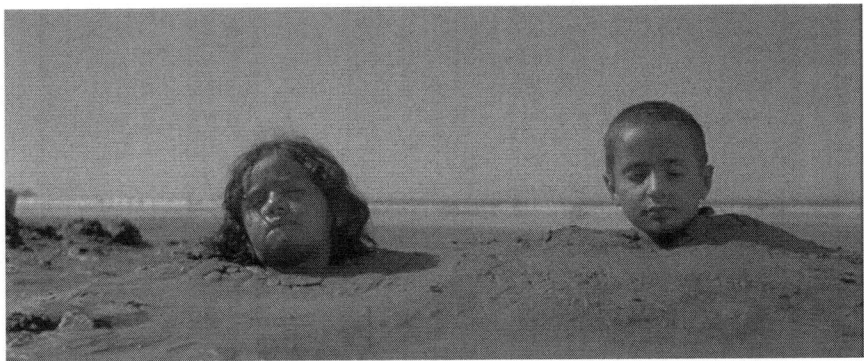

Figure 8 The children buried in the sand create a sense of the uncanny in *Agua fría de mar* (Dir. Paz Fábrega, 2009, Temporal)

Moreover, the naive and innocent beliefs often attributed to children, such as their parents always being good, or animals as creatures that should always be trusted and protected, are turned on their heads, and again these show the uncanny nature of infantile fears coming to pass (Freud, 1919, 9). In *Agua fría de mar*, the animosity that Karina's mother feels towards her daughter is palpable and she frequently punishes her, while heaping praise and affection on her younger brothers. At the same time, the 'serpientes marinas' that come out of the sea and onto the beach writhe in a fascinating manner creating beautiful patterns on the sand. When the children gather round an adult working on the beach who picks one up, however, he warns them that the small snakes contain venom that can kill almost instantly. Later on, it is one of these snakes that has been found dead with which Karina tries to inject herself with venom to make herself ill to gain the attention she has missed while being grounded. This film, therefore, demonstrates that children can and do have much more agency than adults realize: in *Agua fría de mar* they build a network of tunnels, make up harmful stories, run away, and form adult-like communities.

Furthermore, the children in this film are also framed as having a peculiar relationship with sexuality, and this is seen most overtly when Karina tells Mariana that her uncle kisses her on the mouth using his tongue and promises to marry her when she is older. This sense of unease carries on throughout the narrative as – even though the theme of child abuse is never actually realized – it is deliberately kept ambiguous as to whether or not Karina has told the truth. In the opening scenes, the camera is set low on the sand and the viewer watches Karina building sandcastles. When her construction is washed away, a man runs over to her, picks her up, and carries her out into the water, diving with her into the waves and holding onto her tightly. Although it is clear that they are laughing, the only sound that can be heard is the mix of waves and wind chimes, which lend this interaction an eerie aesthetic, especially since it is shot in the half-light of dusk. Moreover, when Karina and the man arrive back at the family truck, night has fallen and it is completely dark. The mother asks what they have been doing all this time, and it is this unanswered question that the audience wonders about too. As they both get changed for dinner, Karina and the man look troubled, and she watches him covertly as he dresses, mimicking his movements and touching her hand to her lips. It has been remarked that in North American films 'domestic confinement is central to the paternalistic socialization of girls. Developing a sense of independence and finding a place of one's own is certainly an important aspect of the maturation process' (Gateward and Pomerance, 2002, 17), and it is clear that to some extent this film is a coming-of-age drama for Karina, especially as it seems to represent her finding her place in her family as well as in society.

Fábrega's contention that childhood is akin to the labyrinths that the children in this film find themselves tunnelling through and creating (Tabernero, 2011) is therefore reflected in the relationships between family members, as Karina is seen to crave the attention she gets from her father from everyone else too, attempting to manipulate those who do not show it to her. The disquiet felt at the beginning of the film around the relationship between Karina and her father is never explained, and although Mariana eventually finds out that the man is Karina's father – not her uncle as she had been led to believe – and that she seemingly enjoys his company, some viewers have still expressed disquiet at their closeness (Fábrega, 2015). Again, this is reminiscent of Martel's films, in particular *La niña santa* (2004), whereby the child protagonist is always looking and not looked at, as well as always desiring, thus giving her an uncanny edge (Martin, 2011, 64–5). Although the director meant for this element of the narrative to be just one of the many misdirections in the film, joining other threads of plot which are never followed through to a conclusion, it clearly leaves the spectator questioning the purpose of this incident. The potential storyline of child abuse is seen again when Mariana and Rodrigo take a nap when arriving at the hotel and, upon waking, it becomes apparent that Mariana has wet herself. It is clearly not the first time this has happened, but the issue is neither explored further by the characters nor is it resolved. This incident suggests the theme of child abuse once more, however, as the possibility of Karina's disclosure to Mariana as releasing a past trauma for her is left lingering; this is a feeling described by Freud as an 'emotional affect' which has been 'transformed by repression into morbid anxiety' (1919, 13), which only goes to highlight further the sense of dread and unease that will pervade the film's narrative and aesthetic.

In *Agua fría de mar*, then, Fábrega has made a film which is positioned outside the *tico* mainstream geographically, thematically, and conceptually. The overriding ideology of plotlessness sets the film up in opposition to both Hollywood and *tico* norms, as the habitual and the everyday are showcased here rather than the monumental. Set on a distant coastline far away from the dominant cultural centre of San José and the Central Valley but still using protagonists from the *tico* centre, the film calls into question the interplay between dominant and peripheral ideals as well as the relationship between Costa Rican land and foreign tourism. Thematically, the film also explores the social class and gender differences that exist among the country's inhabitants, and the potentially harmful nature of the rigid implementation of these. It is also a marginal film from a cinematographic point of view, as Fábrega's use of blocking shots and dark, unsettling mise-en-scène are uncommon in the type of cinema usually shown in Costa Rica, as well as standing in sharp contrast to the tourist version, or the exoticized appeal, of the country's coastline. The postcolonial power formation of dominant centre and marginalized periphery is clearly demarcated within the film and this forces the viewer to consider *tico* constructs of social norms and to question them. This occurs both thematically and stylistically through the visual motifs of plotlessness which showcase an all-pervasive sense of unease and disillusionment throughout the film, despite the contentions of the American tourists that Costa Rica is the happiest and most beautiful country on earth.

Constructing the Margins: Representing Limón
in Patricia Velásquez's *Dos aguas* (2014)

Despite some Costa Rican films such as *Agua fría de mar* or Miguel Gómez's *Maikol Yordan de viaje perdido* being set in rural or coastal areas, as of 2017, only two productions have been made about – and in – the largely Afro-Costa Rican province of Limón. Esteban Ramírez's feature film *Caribe* (2004) was one of few cinematic ventures in the first decade of the twenty-first century, and it depicts a tropical, exotic, romanticized vision of Limón where foreigners and *mestizos* rule both the town and the narrative. None of the protagonists is Afro-Costa Rican – and very few even have speaking parts – thus throwing up several questions around the whitewashing of the actual local population in the film.[6] In contrast, the only other film to be made in

6 For more on this, see Harvey-Kattou, 2018.

Limón, to date – Patricia Velásquez's 2015 production *Dos aguas* – puts the Afro-Costa Rican population of the coastal town of Puerto Viejo at the very centre of the narrative and it firmly locates itself as a *limonense* film, ending with a dedication from the director and her partner Oscar Herrera, who co-wrote the script, 'a nuestro amado Caribe'. Both Velásquez and Herrera are from the Central Valley, and although Velásquez lived for some time in Limón and subsequently spent two years there while making the film, just as in Ureña's *Abrázame como antes*, the question of portraying a marginalized group – an 'Other' – on screen raises ethical issues around representation. In a similar way to Ureña, Velásquez appears aware of the problematic nature of this film and as such she also demonstrates a community-led approach in the conception and making of it in her attempt to depict the reality of the Costa Rican Caribbean. The result is that there are few trappings of the *tico* in this film, and although there are panoramic shots of beaches and jungles, which play to the tourist gaze, there is little else recognizably *tico* which an audience unfamiliar with the area would connect with either the Central Valley or the tourist images associated with Costa Rica.

Velásquez herself trained in Costa Rica, studying communication at the University of Costa Rica. Like Ramírez, then, she is one of the few directors of her generation not to have studied film-making abroad. Having begun her career working for various NGOs in child and sex workers' rights before becoming a journalist, her semi-ethnographic approach to her first venture into film-making is perhaps unsurprising, as is the topic of the film itself: a town's younger generations slowly becoming enthralled to drugs owing to socioeconomic problems and state discrimination (Salas, 2015). The film centres on the Brown family, focusing on their youngest son Nató and the struggles of his older brother Jefferson to make money. Jefferson wants Nató to be given the chance he never had – to go to a football academy – and decides to turn to the local drug gang to earn the money to make this dream come true. That it is his, and not Nató's dream, does not seem to matter, and when he is assaulted by the gang, eventually stealing money from Señor Bazim – a local French tourist-cum-resident – to pay them back, Nató, with the help of his best friend Klane, decides to step in to help. The two waters in the film's title refer to a point off the Caribbean coast where two currents converge, trapping debris in their midst, and it is this location which has become a common point where drug smugglers unload their cargo when chased by police in order to pick it up later. It is a journey to *dos aguas* that Nató and Klane undertake, and yet despite not finding the eponymous two waters they do discover the body of the missing Señor Bazim, who drowned – or perhaps drowned himself – in the Caribbean Sea some days previously.

This melancholic production combines beautiful photography, a haunting soundtrack, and a meagre script with ethnographic and journalistic elements. Jumping between underwater shots of powerful waves or Señor Bazim's feet slowly walking out to sea and helicopter pilots looking for drug smugglers, then on to the Brown family's mealtimes, sat at the table, praying over their food, the film mixes genres and aesthetics to tell a sparse story. Its reception has been mixed and, like other productions which would more readily be classed as art-house than Hollywood, it received a more positive reception from international festivals than local audiences. Premiering at the *Festival Internacional de Cine de Panamá* in April 2015, it has also been screened at festivals in Texas, Colombia, Mexico, and Miami, and it won the *Centroamérica Construye* award from the ICARO Festival, also in 2015. Alongside this international recognition, due to it being the only national production to include Afro-Costa Ricans on screen, it was also declared an item of public interest by the Costa Rican Ministry of Culture and Youth. The importance of this film, then, lies more in what it attempts rather than what it achieves, and as the only national production to visibilize the Afro-Costa Rican population in Costa Rican cinema, Velásquez is clear about her aims for the film. She has said that 'Esta película presenta de un modo muy sutil, casi como un subtexto, la realidad de un pueblo abatido por la coyuntura política y social, que arrastra los vestigios de una sociedad racista' (*Dos aguas* website). It is these ideas that permeate the film, and the representation of the Caribbean province, its marginalized position in the national context, and the 'Otherness' of Afro-Costa Ricans from the *tico* norm, even in as multicultural a place as Limón, take centre stage. At the same time, despite Velásquez's contention that 'un tema fuerte es que el filme habla sobre la población afrodescendiente y algo que me daba terror es que se percibiera como una película racista' (Báez, 2015), there do exist elements of this film which exoticize the location, and others that attempt to make the characters and their lives more palatable for a *tico* audience.

A *Josefina* in Limón

Despite living in the Central Valley, Velásquez has also spent time in Limón and visits frequently. In an interview, she explains why she chose to make a film about the region:

El Caribe de Costa Rica es una región que llevo en el corazón y que conozco bastante bien. Quería hacer una película que retratara a la gente del Caribe, que es trabajadora, pero vive en condiciones muy limitadas. Por otra parte para mí es de los lugares más bellos que tiene el país, y es un lugar muy especial, donde no importan el color de la piel o la nacionalidad. Mucho de la historia que escribimos Oscar Herrera y yo surge a partir de nuestra experiencia en el Caribe y de historias que nos iban contando. Aurora Gámez, quien es hotelera en la zona, fue fundamental en la elaboración del guión. Muchos relatos que nos contó están allí, incluso la incluimos en la película como uno de los personajes. (Magro, 2015)

Her motivation for writing about the Caribbean was, then, purposely counterhegemonic. Recognizing that Limón and its Afro-Costa Rican inhabitants are marginalized not just by *tico* ideology but also in terms of government investment, her aim with this film was to revalorize the region and its people in the eyes of the nation, giving a voice to *limonenses* within the panorama of Costa Rican – and Central American – cinema. Although having experienced life in Limón and having carried out research there, Velásquez, in a similar way to Ureña, also took great care to make the film as 'authentic' as possible in order to realize an accurate portrayal of a marginalized group to which she does not belong.

Conscious of the fact that not only was she not part of the community that the film represents, but that she is part of the dominant cultural group of the *tico* while her film sets out to depict the marginalized culture of Afro-Costa Ricans, she and Herrera conceived of the film-making process as a community project, rather than their own piece of work. Beginning by travelling to Puerto Viejo, they spent two years gathering stories and opinions on what the film's narrative should focus on, followed by casting sessions with local people. Of this method, the director argues that 'prácticamente todo el pueblo de Puerto Viejo está involucrado de una forma u otra en la película', ensuring that the idea of the film as a community project came to fruition. Moreover, in using solely non-professional actors, all of whom come from and live in Puerto Viejo, Velásquez aimed for an authenticity to her production that would not have been possible otherwise. Although this came with a cost – film critic William Venegas wrote (2015) a scathing review of the acting of all the characters other than César Maurel who plays Señor Bazim – it also results in a film which attempts to distance itself from stereotypes and demonstrate how people really live in the area. This has led one critic to argue that, contrary to Venegas' reservations, 'El resultado es una película que busca romper con las ideas preconcebidas y la visión más turística, para mostrar un Caribe real y pulsante' (Báez, 2015).

It was not just in the use of non-professional actors that Velásquez focused on local people and knowledge, but in the conception of the narrative and lack of scripting too. Spivak's contention that to understand the margins better one must inhabit them while entering into a dialogue of mutual learning has also been a big part of Velásquez's approach to this film, just as it was for Ureña's *Abrázame como antes*. Deciding which plots and subplots to include in the script – drug trafficking and gangs; a depressed tourist who swims to his death; prostitution, theft, and assault; family values – came after consultation with members of the community, including hotel owner Aurora Gámez, who plays herself in the film (Domínguez, 2015). While the exact nature of the stories told in *Dos aguas* are fictional, then, they are based on real occurrences woven together into a loose narrative. Part of the lack of a driving central plot line was also down to the choice not to have a formal script for the actors. The director explains: 'nunca se les entregó el guión y cada escena se trabajó con improvisaciones ... sin necesariamente hiciera referencia al guión' (Magro, 2015). This is reminiscent of Fábrega's *Agua fría de mar*, which also uses a lack of plot-driven narrative to stand in opposition to the hegemonic norms of both film-making and society.

This choice to forego a script is certainly innovative, but Velásquez contends that her actors had undergone little training in memorizing lines and that, more importantly, unscripted dialogues would allow them to use the words, phrases, and gestures that came naturally to them. While employing a neo-realist technique by using non-professional actors, then, a big part of the decision was also ethical; as Velásquez comments: 'sabíamos que no hablábamos como la gente del Caribe y menos aún como los niños, no queríamos que quedara artificial ... el guión es construcción de los actores' (Báez, 2015). Just like Ureña, then, Velásquez in this film was determined to enter into this hybrid space in order to learn from the people she chose to record. Despite the many potential pitfalls in representing an 'Other' on screen, then, it would appear that many people from Limón felt the film was successful in its aim to portray the reality of living in the province. As Yamileth Angulo says of one cinemagoer from Limón after the film's premiere in Panamá: 'Lo tocó profundamente, pues conoce bien la realidad de la provincia' (2015).

While Velásquez chose to use real people, speech, and places (the whole film was shot on location in Puerto Viejo) for largely ethical reasons, the themes in the film were also carefully considered so as to avoid or undercut stereotypes. Of the initial idea for the film, the director notes that it stemmed from a conversation she had with Herrera 'sobre nuestro querido Caribe y sus pocas opciones, resultado de una economía deprimida, que se mueve cada vez más a partir del narcotráfico. Una realidad que está allí, cruda e imparable' (*Dos aguas* website). Despite the response received from the community that drug trafficking is a growing issue in the province, the fact that Limón suffers from the negative associations of drugs and crime in the *tico*'s conception of it could certainly make the perpetuation of this issue problematic in the film. Aware of this pitfall, the inclusion of this theme has been mitigated by Velásquez in certain ways in order to avoid essentializing the whole province as subject to drug traffickers. Velásquez contends that:

> No queríamos hacer una película ni de balazos ni de pandilleros ni nada de eso, sino más bien de cómo afecta a una familia normal. Es decir, no es una familia desintegrada, ni con problemas, traumas psicológicos o desintegración. La película está contada desde la visión de un niño de 12 años que se da cuenta de que su hermano está involucrado en este mundo, sin saber muy claramente cómo. En realidad nunca vemos la violencia, las pandillas o la droga, lo que vemos son las consecuencias. (Báez, 2015)

The end result is true to Velásquez's vision, and the fact that there is no graphic violence in the film, and that only the result of violence (the assault on Jefferson and on the boys' parents which leaves them tied up in their own home) rather than the act itself is shown on screen, certainly goes some way to painting Puerto Viejo as a place of safety where the existence of one gang does not mean all the inhabitants are complicit in the drug trade. Indeed, the gang's presence is only brought onto the screen twice: the first time in a long shot as they wave guns and climb into a car, their faces too distant to be seen; the second instance occurs at night where they drive away from the Brown's home under the cover of darkness. The impersonal shooting of these scenes demonstrates the director's commitment to ensuring it is the 'good' family and not the 'bad' drug traffickers who are the focus of the audience's attention. Moreover, Velásquez is clear that in this film she wished to demonstrate that people from stable, loving homes can just as easily get involved in the drug trade in Limón as those from a stereotypical broken home and poor environment because of the lack of investment in the province. It is Jefferson who succumbs to the desire to make money to improve his family's situation, especially that of his brother Nató, and yet he is more afraid of letting his father down than of the consequences of not paying back the gang. After he is assaulted by them he exclaims, 'Mi tata no se puede dar cuenta de esto y además las policías lo que van a hacer es enredar las cosas'. In this way the film sets out to subvert the negative – and racist – stereotypes which exist of Limón in the *tico* imaginary, including broken families, lazy people, and the dominance of the drug trade.

When *ticos* refer to Limón, then, it is often as though it exists for them as a separate country. It is perhaps a place for holidays and tourism, somewhere to experience Afro-Caribbean culture, music, and food, but it is also a place where the peace-loving *tico* must be careful due to violent images perpetuated about the province. However, the positive facet of *limonense* culture which, alongside its natural habitat, has been absorbed by the *tico* centre is its love of football – the national sport – and creation of professional footballers. Although there are few Afro-Costa Ricans accepted by the mainstream, football stars like Paulo Wanchope in the 1990s and early 2000s and Joel Campbell in the 2010s have been cheered by the *ticos* for the *selección* throughout their careers – reminiscent of Spivak's assertion that the centre occasionally welcomes the margin in order to gain from this itself. In the film these associations continue, and we see the sport as intrinsically connected to Limón. The buildings in the film are seen to be simple, wooden constructions, and yet the football stadium in which Nató trains is huge and modern, boasting rows of seats, neatly cut grass, and impressive training facilities, clearly demonstrating that the central government has indeed invested in this aspect of Limón since it benefits the country as a whole. The irony, of course, is that would-be footballers in the film, which include Jefferson and Nató, cannot afford the training sessions, camps, or the equipment – such as boots – needed to continue playing. This ironic twist is pushed even further when Nató confesses to Klane, 'No le diga a mi hermano, pero no me gusta tanto el fútbol'. The inclusion of this aside in the film first encourages the viewer to feel the pointlessness of Jefferson's situation ever more acutely as he only becomes involved with the gang in order to put Nató through a training camp. Secondly, it also serves to undercut the stereotype that all Afro-Costa Ricans – and indeed all black people – should be good at, and passionate about, sport, which is one of the only areas in which the centre selectively allows this group to excel in public life.[7]

It is this theme of the Caribbean region and its Afro-Costa Rican population as both an 'Other' and a marginalized group within the nation that this film also explores from several points of view. In her attempt to portray a realistic version of Puerto Viejo on screen, Velásquez places paramount importance on the everyday and habitual encounters among family and friends. She has said that: '*Dos aguas* es también un retrato del Caribe, de su gente, de sus rincones y sus anhelos, allí están representadas las costumbres, los rituales, los amaneceres, las noches tranquilas interrumpidas por los congos y los grillos' (Salas, 2015). It is clear, then, that Bourdieu's concept of social habitus – or the set of underlying rules which govern our everyday lives and which, in turn, are perpetuated and become the 'norm' (1977, 73–80) – is depicted in this film through the showcasing of the small details of the lives of the characters. Within this paradigm, then, *Dos aguas* shows us how families and friends interact in

---

7 For more on this, see Gane-McCalla, 2011.

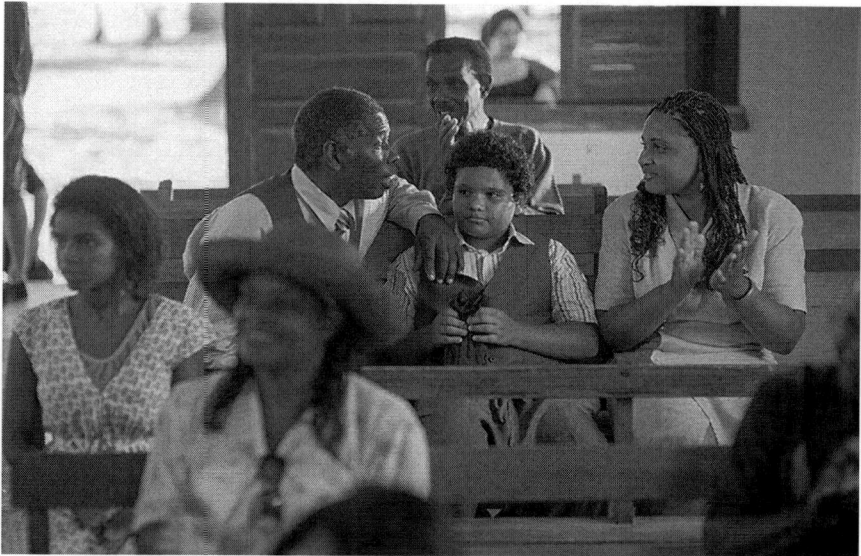

Figure 9 The family at the local *limonense* Pentecostal church in *Dos aguas* (Dir. Patricia Velásquez, 2014, Tiempo Líquido)

Puerto Viejo, how people speak, their religious and community customs, as well as the ideologies which underpin habitus.

What is noteworthy when considering the role of identity and habitus in this film is that skin colour plays a much smaller part in the *limonense* construction of ethnic identity than it may, for example, in Europe or the USA. The brothers Jefferson and Nató are lighter in skin tone than some who would self-define as *mestizo*, and yet they clearly identify as Afro-Costa Ricans. Stuart Hall defines (1996) his concept of ethnicity as encompassing several elements of identity, arguing that all identities are plural and have multiple influences. In this film, Afro-Costa Rican ethnicity is therefore not just about skin colour, but it is seen to include a variety of cultural elements: the mixing of English, Patois, and Spanish, the Protestant religion, and the sense of the community as the wider family and all these facets are showcased through habitus. The language of the film is a pertinent example of this, as the brothers speak Spanish among themselves and with friends, occasionally even using *tico* slang such as 'mae', and yet they speak and are spoken to in a mixture of English, Spanish, and Patois by their parents at home, with Mr Brown generally addressing them in English but lapsing into faultless Spanish at times too. This reminds us of Dorothy Mosby's contention (2003, x) that Afro-Costa Ricans, since the 1970s, have been a bicultural community, mixing cultures and languages to form a new, hybrid identity. This can also be seen as the family attend a Pentecostal church service (Figure 9), which is entirely in English, and as such the history of this region is displayed in these everyday occurrences in the film. Moreover, the community is portrayed as close-knit and independent. This is seen when Nató meets his father after his fishing expedition ends and is tasked with taking fish to Señor Bazim, or when the Frenchman goes missing and Mr Brown is the first person to be called, immediately organizing a community search party. It is striking that, despite the fact a man is missing and a suitcase of money has been stolen from him, no police are involved in either investigation. Instead, the community stands alone to solve its own problems with no help from central government.

Indeed, the fact that Limón has been economically, socially, and ideologically marginalized within Costa Rica is apparent in the film. While this point is made subtly, through the showcasing of habitus, Velásquez is conscious of the region's history and the part it plays in shaping its identity today. She asserts that 'Limón ... fue siempre una zona marginada ... la población negra del país no fue considerada ciudadana ni siquiera, y aún hoy día es una zona que la gente del país no visita tanto, pues tienen muchos prejuicios sobre ella' (Magro, 2015). These prejudices have to do with poverty and crime, and these are two aspects that the director does not shy away from in this picture. We see Mr Brown, who does everything possible to provide for and support his family, go out on a small, rickety fishing boat in clothes with holes in to bring in a meagre catch of just a few fish, some of which he gives away to Señor Bazim. He is not the only one to turn to fishing in order to survive, and in the film several people – young and old, in boats and on the shore – are seen to take their rods to the sea. The fact that Puerto Viejo also has a good tourist trade, and restaurants, hotels, hostels, and souvenir stands are common to see in the town, is not shown in this film. I argue that Velásquez has chosen not to show this aspect of Puerto Viejo in order to accentuate the curtailed possibilities for legal economic progress there. While the tourist trade will provide for some, it is clearly not enough work for all, especially as the only hotel we are shown in the film is not run by a local.

The fact that illegal trade in the form of drug trafficking is a stereotype associated with Limón is also discussed in the film. Velásquez argues that 'cada vez que sale una noticia de Limón, tiene que ver con violencia, tiene que ver con tráfico, es una situación que está pasando y es innegable, pero también hay un montón de prejuicios al respecto que caen sobre la población afrodescendiente' (Báez, 2015). While it is made clear in the film that there is a problem with the illegal drug trade and drug trafficking, it is not shown to have infiltrated the whole town or to form a central part of life; in this way, the 'good' in the community wins out over the faceless 'bad' of the drug gang. María Lourdes Cortés argues that in *Dos aguas* 'El edén se fractura. Con la droga se corrompe la armonía que permeaba la vida rural, la infancia del protagonista y la estabilidad familiar' (2016, 50). This statement is certainly true as the first scene in the film shows Nató and Jefferson on the local bus together, with Nató complaining to Jefferson that the bus gets stopped at the same police check every day. Jefferson then explains to his brother that this is necessary to check for drugs. The fact that Nató was unaware of this shows in part his naivety (and this is yet another film that discusses youth culture and has a coming-of-age storyline), but also the film's agenda, which is to show that while drugs may be an issue in Limón, it is not at the centre of the community. Indeed, before Jefferson became involved with the gang, Nató had not witnessed violence nor did he know about the gangs in the town. Although Cortés also argues (50) that the film's ending demonstrates both Nató's and the country's broken future, the idea that Limón is not considered to be a part of the wider country is also made clear in the film, and thus I contend that *Dos aguas* actually demands action from the central government and the *tico* majority to invest in the province and to examine the prejudices that surround it.

The major contradiction seen in the film – and in the town itself – with regard to its position in the nation's imaginary, however, is the complication of this prevailing negative view of Limón standing alongside the fact that the province is also seen as a tourist attraction that serves the purposes of the external-facing nation-image of Costa Rica. We see shots of tourists playing on the beach, carefree and happy, and yet the inhabitants of the town are only shown using the beach as a cut through as they go to school or work, or as their site of work as they stand and fish or launch their boats. Moreover, when Nató and Klane bring the fish to Señor Bazim at the hotel, in the background, tourists descend from the hotel steps straight into a tour bus, demonstrating that the sterilized way in which they experience Limón is very different from the experiences of the people living there, who only ride bikes or walk. Moreover, the external shots of the house in which the Brown family live are paradisiacal: the small but clean structure is framed by lush vegetation; it looks out over palm trees onto a deserted, wild beach. While this is a location that tourists would pay a lot to stay in, the audience is given this view after the family has argued about not having enough money to send Nató to a football camp, despite both parents working. The fact that tourism does not generate enough income for local families to live from is therefore highlighted in this scene.

The rupturing of this tourist image continues in the cinematographic choices made in the film, as the shots oscillate between news-report-style

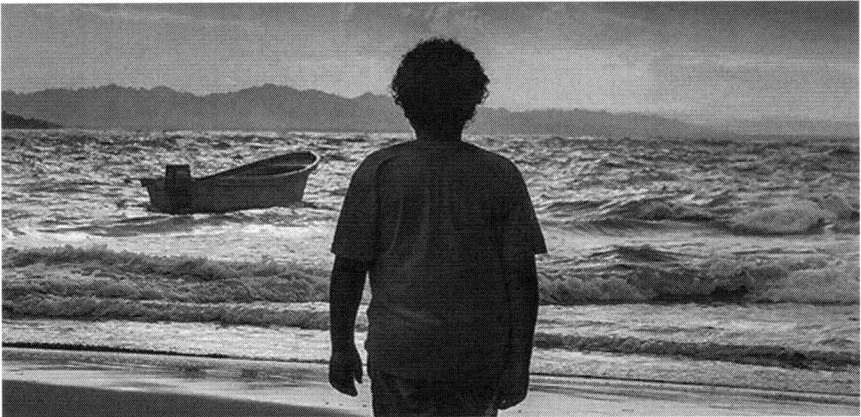

Figure 10 Nató looks over the dangerous sea which has swept away Señor Bazim in *Dos aguas* (Dir. Patricia Velásquez, 2014, Tiempo Líquido)

realism and beautifully crafted long shots that reflect the multiply placed identity of Limón itself. In two scenes which are shot from a helicopter there is no music, the only sounds that can be heard are the rotor blades, and the handheld camera is shaky as it searches the sea below for drug traffickers. These scenes are immediately counterpointed by carefully photographed and framed long shots, which bring to the screen the natural beauty of the region against a soft, musical backdrop. These two very different styles are disjointed and do jar the viewing experience, and yet they demonstrate the two contradictory associations the *tico* centre has with Limón: drug trafficking and a tropical paradise. Even this paradise is lost, however, as the sea is made into a character itself, becoming a threatening, dangerous, or unyielding force against which the town regularly loses. Fishing catches are scarce, and the sea is never filmed in sunlight which renders it blue or turquoise but under a sky which transforms it into grey, overpowering waves. The sound of the sea whenever the action takes places in it or on the beach is almost deafening, and when Klane steals away from his broken home to seek solace sitting on the prow of a rowing boat it seems that the sea will give him no respite from violence. Moreover, it is this grey watery power that takes the life of Señor Bazim, and in the last scenes of the film the viewer is shown his body being mercilessly pulled under and turned over, holding him down. The sea, which is a key part of Limón as a place for both drug trafficking and tourism, is therefore seen to be dangerous in this film, undercutting the tourist image and the idea of Costa Rica's coastlines as peaceful, safe havens, much like in *Agua fría de mar*. The natural waters of these two films contain a dreadful power, unleashing it on unsuspecting citizens (Figure 10).

Consuming Limón from the *Tico* Centre

Despite Velásquez being aware of the potential pitfalls of representing a province and a community of which she is not a part, there are certainly some aspects of the film which jar when thinking about the idea of representation. As noted, the blurring of the boundary in the film's aesthetic between ethnography and fiction as well as the lack of scripted dialogue dislocates the film's core narrative. This leaves the viewer to watch the film as more of a sensory experience rather than sympathizing with the characters and storylines; hence many of the subtle messages contained within the film might easily be lost. While there are elements of the tourist image of Limón that Velásquez tries to subvert, there are also certain elements of the film which play on the tropical and the exotic, and one look at the official *Dos aguas* website, which shows vibrant beaches and Caribbean colours, demonstrates this. Indeed, although Velásquez argues that the people and the reality of the province are meant to be at the forefront of this film, one critic argues that 'La expresiva fotografía de Gustavo Brenes le ha dado a la Naturaleza un papel más que protagónico: dentro de su belleza exuberante, profusa o ubérrima, esa Naturaleza es aplastante: es caribeña' (Venegas, 2015). In this review, Venegas demonstrates how the film has been consumed by a member of the *tico* centre: the Caribbean is associated with natural beauty, not its people. Perhaps some of this tropical exaltation stems from Velásquez's own experiences and perceptions of the province, as she describes 'El Caribe sur de Costa Rica, un lugar exuberante, que le estalla a uno en los ojos, lleno de riquezas' (*Dos aguas* website). This overbearing natural world is certainly showcased in the film, and from the opening shots of rivers, swamps, overgrown vegetation, thick forests, and pristine beaches, the image of Limón as a paradise for the tourist gaze is set up. The panoramic long-takes included in the film are always of nature, and the majority of scenes shot outdoors heighten the extra diegetic sounds of the rainforest or of the sea.

This tropicalization of the Caribbean, of course, plays into colonial discourses of a foreignness which is at once awe-inspiring and frightening; the places, the landscapes, the people are certainly 'Other' in Limón in this film. Indeed, it also plays into the vision of the *tico* centre's view of Limón, so while *Dos aguas* is counterhegemonic in terms of giving a platform to Limón within the panorama of national cinema, it also reinforces the tropical association of the province. Writing about Mexican cinema, Andrea Noble points out (2005, 130–4) that the core issue with film-making about an already marginalized group is the risk of 'Othering' them even further by exoticizing them, and she contends that this is particularly prevalent in ethnographic films. On the *Dos aguas* website, Velásquez writes that the film is about 'la gente fuerte del Caribe, que aprende temprano a sobrevivir entre las culebras y la lluvia imparable, pero que a la vez es incansable porque tienen el privilegio de vivir en uno de los lugares más hermosos'. That she views the population of Limón in this way is certainly problematic. Learning to live in one's home country in dangerous conditions should not be praised; rather, the lack of infrastructure that makes it easy for people there to live safely should be critiqued. Moreover, the history of the Afro-Costa Rican population's arrival and subsequent enforced stay in Limón has certainly not been a privileged one. Forced to work in extremely poor conditions, for little and sometimes no pay, not to be recognized legally by their country, and to continue to suffer socioeconomic hardship and racist abuse is certainly no privilege.

While *Dos aguas* attempts to show several positive elements of life in Puerto Viejo, some scenes further marginalize the population in the *tico*'s eyes. When Nató and Klane ride their bikes to Nató's house, calypso music plays and they ride on a narrow road through a jungle where there are no cars, just bikes and boats as modes of transport. Señor Bazim hides out here, walking from his hotel room through the jungle every day to swim in the sea by a deserted beach. In one scene he pauses to look up at a sloth, which slowly makes its way from tree to tree. The camera lingers on the sloth, paralleling his slow pace and his journey among the trees with that of the Frenchman. This association with the exotic is part of Said's concept (1995) of the Orient, and seeing the 'Other' as exotic further marginalizes and colonizes, or orientalizes them, in Said's words. The province of Limón and its Afro-Costa Rican population are therefore praised in this film for their perseverance and survival in the face of economic and geographic limitations, and Velásquez has stated: 'Yo espero que sobre todo en Costa Rica la gente pueda cambiar su percepción del Caribe y analizarla en todas sus dimensiones' (Magro, 2015). Without a critique of these limitations, however, the mobilizing message of the film – or how Velásquez wants to use it as soft power – is lost.

Another way in which the film unsuccessfully seeks to use this soft power to change *tico* perceptions is in the simplistic nature of its characters, which are made more palatable for a *tico* audience in order for them to be more readily accepted by the mainstream. Although some facets of *limonense* life which stand in contrast to the *tico* identity are highlighted, others are adhered to in a rigid manner. Velásquez even alludes to this as she was determined to show that people from stable families could be affected by the drug trade. The pillar of this stable family is Mr Brown. He is shown to be a community leader who works hard for his family. He sits down to eat with his wife and children every day, insists they go to church, and pray over their meals; he is caring, generous, and servile. Jefferson only gets involved with the gang because of his deep desire to help his brother achieve what he believes to be his dream, and Nató is shown to be unlike his friend Klane who spends his time flirting with girls – instead, the audience hears that he spends time on his schoolwork and gets excellent grades. The parallels between the Browns and the ideal *tico* family also apply to gendered roles, however, and it is certainly a patriarchal family where the mother has little agency. In fact, throughout the film, women play a minor role. Although Doris Brown works in the hotel, it is frowned upon by the family when she does not come home in time for dinner. When the family discuss the training camp for Nató, the camera sits so that Mr Brown cannot be seen, and yet his voice is the only one that matters when he says they cannot afford it. As Jefferson, enraged, storms out of the room, Doris shouts: 'Diay Jefferson, no le falta respeto a su papá', demonstrating the importance placed on his role as patriarchal head of the family.

The film also represents other facets of the characters and their lives as being in line with *tico* norms. For example, Klane's mother is a prostitute with several young children – another stereotype of Limón – and the drug gang, which is always armed, violently assaults the Brown family. These incidents may serve the opposite of their purpose, and, rather than causing the *tico* to be ashamed of the treatment of Afro-Costa Ricans by the rest of the country, reassure them that their perception of them was, in fact, correct. Moreover, the role of the European man and the *mestiza* woman as white saviours is also perpetuated in this film, further playing into this existing filmic complex. This trope involves a white character from a dominant group either welcome a person of colour into their midst or go to a hostile environment in order to save them (Hughey, 2014). The character of Señor Bazim plays no other real function in the film, and the subplot around his stay in the country and his family whom he constantly asserts will come to join him is troubling. When Nató says he needs money for football training, it is Señor Bazim who immediately offers him some errand work for which he can pay him. It also appears that the town thinks highly of Señor Bazim, with Mr Brown stating that he helped everyone in the town and Nató believing that he would help Jefferson out of his debt. It is then Jefferson who steals into his room – the blocking shots as he hides among the bushes alerting the audience to his unethical mission – and takes his money; a young black boy turned to a life of crime, stealing from a reputable white, European man. The other saviour of the town is the only person to offer employment away from fishing and drugs – Aurora Gámez, the owner of the hotel. Gámez plays herself in the film and Almonds and Corals is her actual hotel. She describes herself as having been 'searching for a magical spot in the Caribbean, travelling by motorcycle and on foot' and that when she 'awoke in an illuminated tropical forest of breathtaking beauty' she felt compelled to buy the land and build her business there. It is clear that Gámez consumed the fantasy of the Caribbean and that she has the privilege to buy land, own her own business, and prosper there. Just as the railroad and UFC communities were structured with white overseers and black workers, this is how the hotel is set up in the film, as all her members of staff are Afro-Costa Rican.

Differentiating *Dos aguas* from other films set at the geographic margins of Costa Rica – such as Gómez's *Maikol Yordan de viaje perdido* – it is clear that the director has purposely sought to ethically represent and revalorize the province at the centre of the film. While blurring the boundaries between an ethnographic documentary and a fictional story – in both the narrative and the aesthetic of the film – she has succeeded in creating a picture of Limón that both *limonenses* and *ticos* would recognize. However, owing to the lack of core narrative and the employment of some tropicalization and colonial tropes, the film at once subverts certain elements of the *tico* norm only to reaffirm them in other ways.

While literature from the sociological revolution of 1970s Costa Rica stood in purposeful and direct opposition to the *tico* norms of ethnic, geographic, gendered, and sexual belonging, then, film from the digital revolution of twenty-first-century Costa Rica is seen to showcase a wider complexity of national considerations in terms of identity. Some of the monumental concerns of identity politics have shifted, and a wider, more nuanced set of issues which often centre on the everyday and the habitual have come to the fore in a bid to represent a 'national reality'. The consideration of Costa Rica's tourist image which stands in contrast to the lives of people in the Central Valley and in those rural and coastal tourist areas is apparent in all these productions, with the idealized vision of Costa Rica almost always subverted. As *Gestación* and *Abrázame como antes* showcase, San José is an urban landscape full of diverse individuals and experiences, while *Dos aguas* and *Agua fría de mar* undercut the notion of the idyllic coastline at every turn, and these images work against the *tico* norm of a peaceful, happy nation. However, in other ways, it would appear that little has changed since Isaac Felipe Azofeifa wrote, almost 50 years ago:

> Más de la mitad de la población del país vive encerrada en el refugio amable de la Meseta. Cuando el costarricense habla de su tierra está pensando en la que va del volcán Irazú a los cerros del Aguacate; del volcán Poas a los cerros de Bustamente. Aquí, junto con la capital del

país, a sólo 15 o 20 kilómetros de las demás, se agrupan las cuatro provincias. Las tres restantes, periféricas, no cuentan. El costarricense las visita como turista y los políticos también. (Azofeifa, 1971, 319)

Indeed, although the idea of geographic identity is also under scrutiny in all these films – and the panorama of Costa Rican cinema shows this to be a central question in how the nation is represented – we still see that 'real life' is portrayed as taking place in the Central Valley, while the periphery, even in its revalorization, is depicted as a site where tensions arise due to this normative assumption.

These films also discuss several spaces of 'Otherness' familiar to the counterhegemonic production which challenges *tico* ideals, such as gender and sexuality, youth culture, and the narrative choice of a certain plotlessness which stands in filmic opposition to the dominance of Hollywood discourse. These more traditional subversions of the *tico* norm at times also underline its dominance: while in cases such as *Gestación* and *Abrázame como antes* the rigidity of gendered roles are undermined, *Dos aguas* adheres to them unquestioningly while *Agua fría de mar* undoes them in some ways but demonstrates their reinforcement in certain cases, perhaps underlining the traditional nature of the geographic margins. Moreover, although *Abrázame como antes* and *Dos aguas* portray the sexual and ethnic 'Other' in order to give them a visible space in the nation's cinematic history, it is clear from these films that these groups remain very much 'Othered' by mainstream ideologies. Indeed, the invisibility of these 'Others' in nearly every other Costa Rican production of the twenty-first century to date signifies a lack of their acceptance into the mainstream; they are only included in films which focus on their difference. The *tico* norm is therefore set up as white, patriarchal, heteronormative, and Central Valley-centric – mirroring the traditional, dominant ideals which were scrutinized by literature in the 1970s. At the same time, these films also attempt to showcase a new – and nuanced – world-view of the everyday in Costa Rica. While the habits depicted in these films often demonstrate the prevalence of the *tico* ideology, then, they also hint at its slow unravelling which they in turn hope to influence through the soft power of cinema.

Some Concluding Remarks

As in so much of the world, normative and hegemonic concepts of what constitutes a national identity in Costa Rica have long been white supremacist, patriarchal, and heteronormative. In this particular case, the patriotic pride in the nation's mythical beginnings and the all-consuming fervour to mark the country out as exceptional, especially in comparison with its neighbours, have been brought together in the term *tico*. The *tico* is exclusionary and exclusive, putting the motherland above all else, and it also engenders harmful falsehoods. In this book I have argued that the colonial lens through which many modern nations continue to view the world and themselves has permeated Costa Rica, causing a divide between those included in the imagined community of the citizenry and those internal 'Others' who exist but are not welcomed as a real or valued part of the nation. The case studies under scrutiny prove the coexistence of these hegemonic ideals and their counternarratives in the same national space, thus demonstrating the fallacy of the aforementioned fixed idea of a national identity. In the ever more globalized world of the twenty-first century, the rise of new technology, new media, and global trade has led to a steady breaking down of boundaries – both within nations and the national borders themselves – and as such the very concept of rigid identities continues to be reinforced by those who oppose this trend while also being challenged by others.

Within Costa Rica, it is soft power which has been used to question these normative behaviours which privilege certain groups over others rather than violent or coercive means – perhaps in part due to the foundation of one of its core national values of peace. An analysis of the sociological revolution of the 1970s demonstrates that literature was used as a device for change and subversion, with ethnic, gendered, and sexual identity politics becoming the foundations for this type of protest. Using critiques of the ways in which norms are interpellated, internalized, mimicked, and then outwardly performed, these authors have colluded in exposing the very fabric of the nation as based on myths and legends which continue to do harm over a century after their conception. While twenty-first-century film attempts to showcase a more nuanced version of an 'everyday reality' for many Costa Ricans, it can be seen that as some try to hold on to ideals of tradition, others attempt to uncover a hidden reality, representing those excluded from the 'official' discourse. The use of habitus and the incidental details depicted in these films builds a new world vision which at once creates a visual community while also exposing many of the flaws in dominant narratives of national identity. Despite showing that many spaces of 'Otherness' remain present today, these films also demonstrate that opposition has gained traction which in turn has led to changes not only in social rhetoric but also in the protection and recognition offered to marginalized groups by law. The soft power of these creative works of opposition to hegemonic norms demonstrates that these media can be used with the aim of instigating a change in habitus and behaviour which will, in turn, begin to change these very norms as society evolves.

Who or What Counts as *Tico*?

This question is of primary importance in framing the debate around Costa Rican nationhood. The 'traditional' or 'ideal' Costa Rican has been narrated by historical and educational books as well as folklore and family tradition, and continues to play a role in the contemporary nation both within and outside its borders. While internally these values of patriotism, peace, hard work, and education are lauded, the nation's internationally prevalent external image highlights a commitment to nature and peace, while also showcasing the country as progressive and Eurocentric enough to feel safe, but exotic enough to become a major tourist destination. It is these underlying assumptions and values which have defined the *tico* identity, and within this the divide between the use of terminology such as *tico* and *costarricense* is seen to be based on geographic belonging, ethnicity and gendered and sexual behaviours, beliefs, and orientations. Those whose geographic belonging and cultural traditions are not based around the Central Valley do not always believe they are *ticos* in the eyes of the country, nor do those identifying outside the remit of the 'white' and 'mestizo' boxes presented to them on the census. Moreover, those actively working against a patriarchal, heteronormative, and Catholic culture more generally may discount themselves from aligning with the term *tico*, explaining that its connotations are too rigid and too exclusive.

Although the texts analysed in previous chapters have as their primary purpose the desire to challenge the rigidity of the *tico* identity in some way, the boundaries and foundations of it have still been narrated. In terms of the dominant construction of whiteness and the geographic constraints of the Central Valley, Quince Duncan demonstrates the normativity of Eurocentric discourses of racism and prejudice in *Los cuatro espejos*. His central character has internalized hegemonic assumptions about the superiority of the white, Eurocentric *tico* and the inferiority of Afro-Costa Ricans and the geographic periphery. As such, Charles McForbes acts according to habit and inserts himself into the customs of San José, even to the point of adopting racism and prejudice against other Afro-Costa Ricans. Patricia Velásquez's *Dos aguas* demonstrates the continuing 'Otherness' of both Limón and its population through a portrayal of its linguistic, visual, and socioeconomic difference. Although both these works aim to revalorize the Afro-Costa Rican community, the film still slips into the exoticizing narratives often associated with the Caribbean region. In a similar way, Esteban Ramírez's *Gestación* and Paz Fábrega's *Agua fría de mar* also showcase normative values of geographic belonging. Not only is San José displayed as the whole of Costa Rica in the former and as the centre of commerce and Costa Rican life – as opposed to North American tourism – in the latter, but people of colour do not enter the frame, portraying the capital as an ethnically homogeneous area on screen and underlining the norm of whiteness. Moreover, when Fábrega or Velásquez take the camera away from the Central Valley, the tensions existing between the centre and periphery are made clear.

Despite the continuing need for the feminist movement in Costa Rica, unlike the ethnic and geographic discourses of 'Otherness' surrounding the *tico*, texts from the 1970s and the 2010s do demonstrate a changing trend in gendered expectations and stereotypes. Carmen Naranjo's short stories *Simbiosis del encuentro* and *A los payasos todos los quieren* demonstrate her vision of a society heavily entrenched in disparate – and prejudicial – gendered roles, where women have internalized their place in the private sphere while men occupy public spaces. Moreover, the child narrator in *Payasos* offers a clear depiction of the ways in which stereotypes are engendered in childhood, depicting the performativity of one's gender as starting from an early age. The pressure to conform to gendered roles is also highlighted by Naranjo as negative consequences befall her characters when they subvert these norms. Alfonso Chase also uses his short story *El hilo del viento* to depict the male role in patriarchal society, demonstrating the violent consequences for Luis Esteban when he refuses to ascribe to accepted tropes of masculinity.

The film media from the twenty-first century under consideration do demonstrate a shift – in some regards – in how gendered roles are positioned in contemporary *tico* society, however. In *Gestación*, women work in public spaces and have narrative agency: Jessie decides to keep her baby and she and her mother both end the film as independent, working women providing for their families. Moreover, in this film, gendered expectations are rigid, but discrimination is also shown to be intersectional as the marginalization of the female characters is also dependent on their wealth and class. In *Abrázame como antes*, on the other hand, Ureña puts San José's transgender women on screen for the first time, giving them narrative and visual power in a groundbreaking film which goes beyond stereotypes and prejudicial depictions. Despite their inclusion in Costa Rican cinema, however, their role in society is still seen to be as an 'Other', acting under the cloak of darkness. In both the films set at the geographic margins of the nation, *Agua fría de mar* and *Dos aguas*, it is interesting to note the differing approaches by these two female directors to including women in their narratives. While Fábrega centres her film on a woman and girl, giving them agency within the narrative while still underlining the negative impact patriarchal expectations impose on them, in *Dos Aguas* the women all assume supporting, and supportive, roles traditionally associated with motherly and wifely behaviour.

The way the country interacts with the outside world is also seen to be assumed knowledge and of paramount importance to twenty-first-century Costa Rica, demonstrating the border-crossing possibilities of global media and of twenty-first-century society, while the literature of the 1970s demonstrated more inward-facing concerns. In the latter period, there is an assumed knowledge of Costa Rica's external tourist image as natural and exotic. In setting both *Gestación* and *Abrázame como antes* in San José the directors subvert the images traditionally associated with the country. In *Dos aguas*, on the other hand, the geographic setting of the film does set up the tourist image, as the natural landscape provides the backdrop to the narrative as well as forming a core part of the plot. Here, the normative images of the country involve the sea, beaches, and lush forests as well as a tropical heat which all work together to create the same sense of the discomfort and the possibility of peril as in Chase's work. In *Agua fría de mar*, this backdrop of the famed natural landscapes of the country, which won over international critics, also appears more sinister than welcoming, creating an uncanny atmosphere for the protagonists as the land around them is slowly bought up by North American settlers.

Not only is the *tico* norm narrated in these case studies, then, but it is also shown to be perpetuated through habit and routine. The focal point of Duncan's work depicts his protagonist looking in the mirror, precipitating his identity crisis, while Naranjo's characters' boredom accelerates the sex change in 'Simbiosis'. Chase's portrayal of the *tico* norm is also seen through small details surrounding the everyday life of his protagonists. Despite the fact that all this literature deals in monumental themes, then, it challenges normative behaviour through the articulation and questioning of everyday assumptions – or habitus. In the films analysed, this showcasing of the incidental and the everyday is also highlighted. Although Ramírez's story is based around the grand narrative of teenage pregnancy, the film explores this through scenes of everyday life in a similar way to the other films discussed in Chapter 3. Although in *Dos aguas* sociopolitical tensions and the international drug trade form the core narrative, the story is told via family dinners, conversations between friends, and work and home life. *Abrázame como antes* is full of small details which eschew the possible grand narrative and instead focus the viewer on concerns of motherhood, belonging, and family through an exploration of habitual details such as getting ready to go out, doing hair and make-up, and sharing food. *Agua fría de mar*, moreover, enunciates the tedium of routine as an overtly traumatic experience, and the incidental in this film becomes the eerie, imbuing the narrative with meaning. This concern with the small details and a move away from the monumental is undoubtedly, in part, one of the consequences of the digital turn as the accessibility of film-making and distribution has allowed for a new world vision to be portrayed. In a similar way, the literature of the 1970s has set up normative behaviour in order later to subvert it, forcing the reader to question their own habits and assumptions which perpetuate negative and exclusionary stereotypes, thus demonstrating the need to question habitus in order to challenge these norms.

Challenges to the Norm

The soft power of creative practice can be long-standing, and these works can reflect an existing cultural movement or feeling as well as attempting to start or empower one. Costa Rica's art scene is no different, and the aesthetic and narrative ways in which normative ideals have been challenged has witnessed a shift over time. In literature of the 1970s, norms are set up to be undermined, challenging the reader to mobilize and question their own prejudice or adherence to them. The techniques used are subtle, and include allegory and the use of subtext or code. Films from the twenty-first century, however, showcase the *tico* norm visually, through portrayals of the incidental and the everyday, using language, landscape, food, clothing, and social interactions as comfort zones which are then juxtaposed with a wider social issue, such as complex and non-binary ideals of ethnic, gender, sexual, or geographic belonging.

The many internal 'Others' within the nation continue to be seen as marginalized groups, however, despite the differences in their constructions.

The allegory of the national or a national journey is a common theme, and just as Duncan uses Charles McForbes' life to represent all young Afro-Costa Ricans who made the journey from the periphery – Limón – to the centre – San José – and were faced with the same challenges, Ramírez shows San José to be a teenage city on its way to adulthood through the characters of Jessie and Teo, while Fábrega uses Mariana to demonstrate the consequences a physical and emotional journey can have on young people as well as the power of nature. The ultimate solutions of a reconciling of the past while embracing the future echo throughout these works.

The use of subtext and code is also prevalent within counterhegemonic national narratives. In Naranjo's 'Simbiosis', the fantastic works to cover the feminist undertones, whereas, because of the position of the child narrator in 'Payasos', much of the narrative goes unsaid, leaving the reader to fill in the gaps. In Alfonso Chase's 'La lluvia. El silencio. La música.', the three titular nouns are used as code words throughout the text, signifying the fight between normative society and queer experiences. In 'El hilo del viento', the fantastic is used to depict the physical nature of violent prejudice, using words with a double meaning and a subtext to veil an overt critique of homophobia. Characterization and plot line are also used to demonstrate the negative consequences behind the internalization of norms and the mimicry of them. Duncan's protagonist demonstrates prejudice against other Afro-Costa Ricans as he has internalized and performed the rhetoric of the superiority of one ethnic group over another. Naranjo's characters are also shown to have internalized gender stereotypes in her short stories, and Ana and Manuel continue to perform these even when their physical sexes change, while her child narrator must pretend to be something she is not in order to be accepted by society. Similarly, in Chase's works, his narrator in 'Lluvia' is unable to realize his romantic aims because the type of relationship he wants is not a possibility in *tico* society, while Luis Esteban is brutally killed for his non-normative lifestyle in 'El hilo'. The internalization of norms can also be seen in the character of Jessie's mother in *Gestación* who, despite being a working, single mother, allows herself to be subordinate – if not subservient – to Teo's mother due to their class differences.

It is not just the negative impact of the internalization of the *tico* norm which is showcased throughout much Costa Rican creative production, however, but also the paradigm of employing a negative portrayal of a traditionally positive motif. Within both Naranjo and Chase's works, the child narrators should be setting out on a journey of discovery of the world around them. They begin the stories full of innocent questions, but they are quickly shown to be naive and their innocence is stripped back as they find out they must conform to society's expectations of them in order to be accepted by their families. In a similar way, just as Jessie and Teo should be at the happiest time in their lives – finishing school and beginning adulthood – in Ramírez's *Gestación*, their experience is turned on its head because of their sexual transgression in the eyes of the Catholic Church. Moreover, Nató in *Dos aguas*, is another child protagonist whose innocence is destroyed due to the incursion of wider social issues into his previously peaceful life, and in *Agua fría de mar*, Karina and Mariana, who should be enjoying their summer holidays, are instead pulled into a journey towards a personal abyss.

In light of Costa Rica's internal and external image being so focused on nature, eco-tourism, and the 'exotic', these works also consider the place of physical motifs in comparison with the national identity that they portray. Indeed, in Chase's 'El hilo', the magical forest in which animals and humans live symbiotically is destroyed by the sudden violence perpetrated by the narrator's brothers. Velásquez also compares the two ideals of nature and peace in *Dos aguas*. Through the use of the handheld camera, blocking shots, long shots, and close-ups, Velásquez creates an uneasy atmosphere which is in sharp contrast to the idyllic surroundings of the beach and forest, usually portrayed as tourist havens. Fábrega uses similar techniques to create an uncanny atmosphere around the coastline, with nature itself sometimes acting as a powerful physical force to determine the actions and outcomes of the protagonists. The relationship between tourism and the inhabitants of the margins is also brought to the fore. Within the city, the tourist image is undermined, as in *Los cuatro espejos*, *Gestación*, and *Abrázame como antes* the city is inextricably linked to discrimination. In these depictions, the dominant centre of the country is a gritty place where youth culture abounds, violence lurks, and social discord is prevalent. This city is no exotic haven, and it is far removed from the traditional representations of Costa Rica's tourist image, which is made up of beaches, forests, volcanoes, peace, and tranquillity.

While the concept of the *tico* and all this identity encompasses continues to live on in Costa Rica today, the place of internal 'Others' – those excluded from official rhetoric and pushed to the margins – has begun to shift. While it is clear that this shift towards more liberal and progressive positions on the fluidity of identity first took hold in the 1970s, social and political change has come about much more recently. The declaration of Costa Rica as a multiethnic and pluricultural state in 2014, the election of the first female President in 2010, and the opening of a debate around same-sex marriage, trans lives, and LGBTQ+ protections have been incredibly important moments in the nation – a notable win for campaigners being the right to change the gender and name assigned at birth for trans people as of 2018. More recently, even further steps have been made as Epsy Campbell became the first Afro-Costa Rican to hold the Vice-Presidency of the country and, despite much political upheaval around the ruling, it was made illegal for signatories of the Inter-American Court of Human Rights – Costa Rica included – to ban same-sex marriage. These changes signpost that the rigid conception of national identity, despite its falsehood, which has at once fostered patriotism and, perhaps, peace, has also caused divisions and exclusions, and it is these latter issues which are now being contested. What is also clear is that authors and film-makers will continue to build upon the work of their predecessors, therefore continuing to challenge *tico* norms and ideals in the imagined space of the nation, using their influence as a means of bringing about social change.

As I write this, in 2018, we are seeing a renewed rise of nationalism in many countries across the globe: results, perhaps, of a breaking down of borders caused by the use of new technologies and social media, globalized businesses and trade, and an increase in the movement of people from one nation-state to another, which has begun internationalizing many national spaces. Just like the *tico*, harking back to a reified past appears to provide a safety blanket to citizens of many nations across the globe who are concerned about losing their identity and power; and yet this fixed idea of who should be included and welcomed into the nation – both ideologically and physically – and who should be excluded and forced out is dividing the world into ever smaller segments. Patriotic ideals often lie far from historical accuracy and cannot be seen as immutable, just as Costa Rica's egalitarian, peaceful, Euro-descendent, Catholic paradise that exists in the mind's eye of many *ticos* has never been played out in reality. In the midst of exclusionary ideals, however, there are always those who oppose oppression and stand in the face of epistemic violence, and the soft power of those who write and record contemporary concerns – which will pass on to become the history of the future – is itself a valuable part of the fabric of each nation. Whatever the future holds for the *ticos*, then, it is clear that debates around national identities are here to stay.

Bibliography

Abreu Gómez, Emilio. 1950. *Escritores de Costa Rica* (San José, Costa Rica: Lehmann).

Ahern, Maureen (ed.). 1988. *A Rosario Castellanos Reader* (Austin: University of Texas Press).

Ahluwalia, Pal. 2006. 'Négritude and Nativism', in *The Post-Colonial Studies Reader*, ed. by Bill Ashcroft, Gareth Griffiths, and Helen Tiffin (London: Routledge), pp. 230–2.

Alcoff, Linda. 2006. *Visible Identities: Race, Gender, and the Self* (Oxford: Oxford University Press).

Alfaro Córdoba, Amanda. 2011. 'Comunidades cinematográficas: Las dinámicas de producción que dieron vida a El Camino', in *Revista Comunicación*, 20.2: 52–9.

Althusser, Louis. 1971. *Lenin and Philosophy and Other Essays*, trans. by Ben Brewster (New York and London: Monthly Review Press).

Alvarado, Josué. 2015. 'Película costarricense "Dos Aguas" lanza su primer trailer, a pocos días de su estreno', in *CR Hoy* <https://www.crhoy.com/archivo/pelicula-costarricense-dos-aguas-lanza-su-primer-trailer-a-pocos-dias-de-su-estreno/entretenimiento/> [accessed 16 August 2017].

Alvaray, Luisela. 2008. 'National, Regional, and Global: New Waves of Latin American Cinema', in *Cinema Journal*, 47.3: 48–65.

Alvarenga Venutolo, Patricia. 2012. *Identidades en disputa: Las reinvenciones del género y de la sexualidad en la Costa Rica de la primera mitad del Siglo XX* (Costa Rica: Editorial Universidad de Costa Rica).

Anderson, Benedict. 2006. *Imagined Communities: Reflections on the Origin and Spread of Nationalism*, 2nd edn (London: Verso).

Anderson, Moji. 2004. 'Arguing Over the "Caribbean": Tourism on Costa Rica's Caribbean Coast', in *Caribbean Quarterly*, 51.2: 31–52.

—. 2012. 'Comparison and Connection in the Study of Afro-Latin America', in *African and Black Diaspora*, 5.1: 35–48.

Andrews, George Reid. 2004. *Afro-Latin America: 1800–2000* (Oxford: Oxford University Press).

—. 2008. 'Diaspora Crossings: Afro-Latin America in the Afro-Atlantic', in *Latin American Research Review*, 43.3: 209–24.

—. 2009. 'Afro-Latin America: Five Questions', in *Latin American and Caribbean Ethnic Studies*, 4.2: 191–210.

Angulo, Yamileth. 2015. 'Película costarricense "Dos Aguas" tuvo un intenso estreno en Panamá', in *El mundo* <https://www.elmundo.cr/pelicula-costarricense-dos-aguas-tuvo-un-intenso-estreno-en-panama/> [accessed 16 August 2017].

Anon. 1999. 'Narcotic Drugs: Agreement between the United States of America and Costa Rica', Treaties and Other International Acts Series 13005, Department of State, United States of America <https://www.state.gov/documents/organization/120374.pdf> [accessed 17 August 2015].

—. 2007. 'Personas destacadas: Quince Duncan', in *El Instituto Interamericano de Derechos Humanos* <https://www.iidh.ed.cr/> [accessed 5 April 2013].

—. 2009. 'Ser 'Polo' NO es Tuanis!!', in *Carepicha Blog* <h3dicho.ticoblogger.com> [accessed 3 June 2015].

—. 2011. 'El dilema del cine costarricense', in *Grupo Ronchauita Blog* <http://generacion-rebelde-roncahuita.blogspot.co.uk/2011/03/el-dilema-del-cine-costarricense.html> [accessed 3 June 2015].

—. 2012a. 'El 51% de los costarricenses no lee libros, según encuesta', in *El País de Costa Rica* <www.elpais.cr> [accessed 26 March 2015].

—. 2012b. 'Ficha estadística de Costa Rica', in *Banco Centroamericano de Integración Estadística* <http://www.bcie.org/> [accessed 17 August 2015].

—. 2014. 'Mario Chacón: "Esta película nació para hacerse"', in *DeleFoco* <http://revista.delefoco.com/53-mario-chacn-esta-pelcula-naci-para-hacerse.aspx> [accessed 16 August 2017].

—. 2017. Jurgen Ureña, Director de *Abrázame Como Antes*: 'Hay una profunda necesidad de diálogo', in *Costa Rica cine fest* <http://costaricacinefest.go.cr/articulo/jurgen-Ureña-director-abrazame-antes-hay-profunda-necesidad-dialogo> [accessed 1 February 2017].

Anzaldúa, Gloria. 1987. *Borderlands/La Frontera* (San Francisco, CA: Aunt Lute Books).

Araya, Seidy. 2003. *Seis narradoras de Centroamérica* (Heredia, Costa Rica: Editorial Universidad Nacional).

Arizpe, Lourdes and Carmen Naranjo. 1979. 'Interview with Carmen Naranjo: Women and Latin American Literature', in *Signs*, 5.1: 98–110.

Aronna, Michael, John Beverley, and José Oviedo (eds.). 1995. *The Postmodernism Debate in Latin America* (Durham, NC: Duke University Press).

Ashcroft, Bill, Gareth Griffiths, and Helen Tiffin (eds.). 2006. *The Post-Colonial Studies Reader* (London: Routledge).

Azofeifa, Isaac Felipe. 1971. 'La isla que somos', in *Ensayistas costarricenses*, ed. by Luis Ferrero (San José, Costa Rica: Lehmann).

Báez, Eunice. 2015. 'Película *Dos Aguas*: un retrato del Caribe', in *Revista Perfil* <https://www.revistaperfil.com/vida/cultura/pelicula-dos-aguas-un-retrato-del-caribe/PYPFDBEJXNEA3KMAOITEDQHEUY/story/> [accessed 16 August 2017].

Balderston, Daniel. 1992. *The Latin American Short Story: An Annotated Guide to Anthologies and Criticism* (London: Greenwood Press).

Barnhart, Anne. 2007. *Finding Women Writers of Costa Rica: A Bibliographical Guide to Anthologies of Poetry and Short Stories* (New Orleans, LA: SALALM Secretariat).

Barrionuevo, Claudia. 2017. 'Abrázame como antes', in *La República* <https://www.larepublica.net/noticia/abrazame-como-antes> [accessed 2 February 2017].

Barrow, Sarah. 2007. 'Peruvian Cinema and the Struggle for International Recognition', in *Contemporary Latin American Cinema: Breaking into the Global Market*, ed. by Deborah Shaw (Lanham, MD: Rowman & Littlefield), pp. 173–90.

Basham, Richard. 1976. 'Machismo', in *Frontiers: A Journal of Women Studies*, 1.2: 126–43.

Beasley-Murray, Jon. 2010. *Posthegemony: Political Theory and Latin America* (Minneapolis: University of Minnesota Press).

Beasley-Murray, Jon and Alberto Moreiras. 2001. *The Subaltern Affect* (Oxford: Angelaki).

Bell, John. 1996. *Crisis in Costa Rica: The 1948 Revolution* (Austin: University of Texas Press).

Benson, Jackson J. (ed.). 1975. *The Short Stories of Ernest Hemingway: Critical Essays* (Durham, NC: Duke University Press).

Berghahn, D. 2010. 'Coming of Age in "the Hood": The Diasporic Youth Film and Questions of Genre', in *European Cinema in Motion*, ed. by D. Berghahn and C. Sternberg (London: Palgrave Macmillan), pp. 235–55.

Bermúdez Barrios, Nayibe. 2011. *Latin American Cinemas: Local Views and Transnational Connections* (Calgary, Alberta: University of Calgary Press).

Betancourt, Manuel. 2016. 'Cast of Trans Drama "Abrázame Como Antes" On Why Their Community Desperately Needed This Film', in *Remezcla* <http://remezcla. com/features/film/abrazame-como-antes-interview-costa-rica-film-festival-2016/?utm_content=bufferca227&utm_medium=social&utm_source=twitter. com&utm_campaign=buffer> [accessed 2 February 2017].

Beverley, John. 1999. *Subalternity and Representation: Arguments in Cultural Theory* (Durham, NC: Duke University Press, 1999).

Bhabha, Homi. 1990. *Nation and Narration* (Oxford: Routledge).

—. 1994. *The Location of Culture* (London and New York: Routledge).

—. 2006a. 'Cultural Diversity and Cultural Differences', in *The Post-Colonial Studies Reader*, ed. by Bill Ashcroft, Gareth Griffiths, and Helen Tiffin (London: Routledge), pp. 155–7.

—. 2006b. 'Signs Taken for Wonders', in *The Post-Colonial Studies Reader*, ed. by Bill Ashcroft, Gareth Griffiths, and Helen Tiffin (London: Routledge), pp. 38–43.

Biesanz, Mavis Hiltunen, Karen Zubris Biesanz, and Richard Biesanz. 1999. *The Ticos: Culture and Social Change in Costa Rica* (London: Lynne Rienner Publishers).

Bird, Leonard. 1984. *Costa Rica: The Unarmed Democracy* (London: Sheppard Press).

Blumenfeld, Warren J. and Margaret Sönser Breen (eds.). 2005. *Butler Matters: Judith Butler's Impact on Feminist and Queer Studies* (Aldershot: Ashgate).

Bolaños Esquivel, Bernardo and Guillermo González Campos. 2011. 'La adaptación audiovisual de obras literarias costarricenses: Primeros recuentos para un camino dispar', in *Revista Comunicación*, 20.2: 32–43.

Bonilla, Abelardo. 1981. *Historia de la literatura costarricense*, 4th edn (San José, Costa Rica: Universidad Autónoma de Centroamérica).

Borloz Soto, Virginia. 2007. *Carmen Naranjo, una metáfora viviente* (San José, Costa Rica: Universidad de Costa Rica).

Bourdieu, Philippe. 1977. *Outline of a Theory of Practice* (Cambridge: Cambridge University Press).

Bourgois, Philippe. 1998. 'The Black Diaspora in Costa Rica: Upward Mobility and Ethnic Discrimination', in *Blackness in Latin America and the Caribbean: Social Dynamics and Cultural Transformations, Central America and the Northern South American Lowlands*, ed. by Arlene Torres and Norman E. Whitten (Bloomington: Indiana University Press), pp. 119–32.

Bravo, Judy. 1993. 'Relatos de mujeres: Antología de narradoras de Costa Rica by Linda Berrón', in *Chasqui*, 22.2: 153–4.

Brenes, María José. 2014. 'Cine costarricense busca abrir ventanas para proyectarse al mundo', in *Univisión Noticias* <https://www.univision.com/noticias> [accessed 14 September 2014].

Brenes, Paula. 2015. '¿De qué se trata el plan estratégico para el sector audiovisual?', in *Delefoco* <http://revista.delefoco.com/2403-de-qu-se-trata-el-plan-estratgico-para-el-sector-audiovisual.aspx> [accessed 15 June 2015].

Brenes Quirós, César. 2012. '¿A quiénes seduce el cine?', in *El financiero* <https://www.elfinancierocr.com/negocios/a-quienes-seduce-el-cine/7HYSFBS7FJAUHHIT64BI7CWT5U/story/> [accessed 20 February 2015].

—. 2014. '31 nuevas salas de cine abrirán en Costa Rica durante 2015', in *El financiero* <https://www.elfinancierocr.com/negocios/31-nuevas-salas-de-cine-abriran-en-costa-rica-durante-2015/5M6US54KWZER5HVNL4D2M4DUHA/story/> [accessed 30 March 2015].

Butler, Judith. 1993. 'Critically Queer', in *GLQ: A Journal of Gay and Lesbian Studies*, 1.1: 17–32.

—. 1999. *Gender Trouble: Feminism and the Subversion of Identity* (London: Routledge).

—. 2004. *Undoing Gender* (London: Routledge).

Butler, Judith and Gayatri Chakravorty Spivak. 2007. *Who Sings the Nation-State?* (Oxford: Seagull Books).

Calderón Quesada, Héctor. 2013. 'Las imágenes que el país se merece', in *Delefoco* <http://www.delefoco.com/Default.aspx?action=article-view&id=163> [accessed 5 September 2014].

Carrasco, Candide. 2003. 'Voces gay en la narrativa costarricense', in *Letras*, 1.35: 81–101.

Castillo, Debra. 1992. *Talking Back: Toward a Latin American Feminist Literary Criticism* (Ithaca, NY: Cornell University Press).

Castro Rawson, Margarita. 1971. *El costumbrismo en Costa Rica* (San José, Costa Rica: Imprenta Lehmann).

Castro-Klaren, Sara. 2013. *A Companion to Latin American Literature and Culture* (London: Wiley-Blackwell).

Cavallaro, Dani. 2011. *The World of Angela Carter: A Critical Investigation* (Jefferson, NC: McFarland).

Censo. 2011. 'Quinto Censo Nacional de Población y VI de Vivienda 2011: resultados generales', in *Instituto Nacional de Estadística y Censo* <www.cipacdh.org/pdf/Resultados_Generales_Censo_2011.pdf> [accessed 3 June 2015].

Centro Costarricense de Producción Cinematográfica (CCPC). 2015. *Centro de Cine* website <https://www.centrodecine.go.cr/> [accessed 5 September 2014].

Césaire, Aimé. 1995. 'What Is Négritude to Me', in *African Presence in the Americas*, ed. by Carlos Moore (Trenton, NJ: Africa World Press), pp. 13–20.

Chacón, Albino. 2004. 'El sentido de la literatura de Quince Duncan en la historia cultural de Costa Rica, a propósito de la publicación de sus Cuentos Escogidos', read at Museo Nacional, San José, Costa Rica.

Chanan, Michael. 1997. 'The Changing Geography of Third Cinema', in *Screen Special Latin American Issue*, 38.4: 372–88.

—. 2006. 'Latin American Cinema: From Underdevelopment to Postmodernism', in *Remapping World Cinema: Identity, Culture, and Politics in Film*, ed. by Stephanie Dennison and Song Hwee Lim (London: Wallflower), pp. 38–52.

Chang Vargas, Giselle and Fernando González Vásquez. 1981. *Cultura popular traditional: fundamento de la identidad cultural* (San José, Costa Rica: Editorial Universidad Estatal a Distancia).

Chase, Alfonso. 1975. *Narrativa contemporánea de Costa Rica* (San José, Costa Rica: MCJ Publicaciones).

—. 2011. *Mirar con inocencia*, 2nd edn (San José, Costa Rica: Eduvisión).

Chaverri, Amalia. 2005. 'América Central debe ser nombrada', in *Literaturas centroamericanas hoy: desde la dolorosa cintura de América*, ed. by Karl Kohut and Mackenbach Werner (Madrid: Iberoamericana), pp. 201–18.

Chaves, José Ricardo. 2017. 'Tico no, mejor costarricense', in *La Nación* <https://www.nacion.com/opinion/foros/tico-no-mejor-costarricense/RNI2GYKYO VAOBMIVN36JU36DFY/story/> [accessed 16 August 2017].

Chomsky, Avi. 1994. 'West Indian Workers in Costa Rican Radical and Nationalist Ideology 1900–1950', in *The Americas*, 51.1: 11–40.

—. 1995. 'Afro-Jamaican Traditions and Labor Organizing on United Fruit Company Plantations in Costa Rica, 1910', in *Journal of Social History*, 28.4: 837–55.

—. 1996. *West Indian Workers and the United Fruit Company in Costa Rica, 1870–1940* (Baton Rouge: Louisiana State University Press).

Christian, Michelle. 2013. '"... Latin America Without the Downside": Racial Exceptionalism and Global Tourism in Costa Rica', in *Ethnic and Racial Studies*, 36.10: 1599–618.

Ciplijauskaité, Biruté. 1988. *La novela femenina contemporánea (1970–1985): Hacia una tipología de la narración en primera persona* (Barcelona: Anthropos).

Cixous, Hélène. 1976. 'The Laugh of the Medusa', trans. by Keith Cohen and Paula Cohen, in *Signs*, 1.4: 875–93.

Cohen, Henry. 2000. 'The English Language Folk Tradition of Limón Province, Costa Rica', in *Caribbean Quarterly*, 46.1: 1–23.

Conejo Valverde, Walter. 2011. 'Gestación', in *Revista Comunicación*, 20.2: 88–9.

Conrad, B. K. 2006. 'Neo-Institutionalism, Social Movements, and the Cultural Reproduction of a Mentalité: Promise Keepers Reconstruct the Madonna/Whore Complex', in *Sociological Quarterly*, 47.2: 305–31.

Corrales, Gloriana. 2014. 'Película *Italia 90* abandona las carteleras', in *La Nación* <https://www.nacion.com/viva/cine/pelicula-em-italia-90-em-abandona-las-carteleras/LFRAGQ2ABNGQLLYKLMW654A6BY/story/> [accessed 5 September 2014].

Cortés, Carlos. 2000. 'El fin del mito de la igualdad: Breve panfleto contra el "aprismo" literario: para una sociología de la literatura postsocialdemócrata', in *Literaturas centroamericanas hoy: desde la dolorosa cintura de América*, ed. by Karl Kohut and Mackenbach Werner (Madrid: Iberoamericana), pp. 147–54.

—. 2003. *La invención de Costa Rica y otras invenciones* (San José, Costa Rica: Editorial Costa Rica).

—. 2007. *La gran novela perdida: historia personal de la narrativa costarrisible* (San José, Costa Rica: Ediciones Perro Azul).

Cortés, María Lourdes. 1999. 'El polvo de los sueños: Aproximación a la nueva narrativa costarricense', in *Hispamérica*, 28.83: 81–7.

—. 2002. *El espejo imposible: Un siglo de cine en Costa Rica* (San José, Costa Rica: Farben Grupo Editorial Norma).

—. 2008. *Luz en la pantalla: imágenes para el nuevo siglo* (San José, Costa Rica: Centro Cultural de España).

—. 2011a. 'De El retorno a El regreso', in *La Nación* <https://www.nacion.com/archivo/de-em-el-retorno-em-a-em-el-regreso-em/5FJRK2S5DNHNDAWZW6KGJEGEDI/story/> [accessed 5 September 2014].

—. 2011b. 'El nuevo cine costarricense', in *Revista Comunicación*, 20.2: 4–17.

—. 2014. Personal Interview. 9 October.

—. 2016. *Fabulaciones del nuevo cine costarricense* (San José, Costa Rica: URUK editores).

Cottrol, R. J. 2005. 'From Emancipation to Equality: The Afro-Latin's Unfinished Struggle: Afro-Latin America, 1800–2000 by George Reid Andrews', in *American Quarterly*, 57.2: 573–82.

Creighton, H. 2008. 'How Far is the "Rhetoric of Inclusion; Reality of Exclusion" Argument Applicable to the Relationship of Afro-Latin Americans to the Nation-State?', in *History Compass*, 6.3: 843–54.

Crenshaw, Kimberlé. 1991. 'Mapping the Margins', in *Stanford Law Review*, 43.6: 1241–99.

Cuevas Molina, Rafael. 1999. 'Cultura y educación', in *Costa Rica contemporánea: raíces del estado de la nación*, ed. by Juan Rafael Quesada Camacho (San José, Costa Rica: Editorial de la Universidad de Costa Rica), pp. 241–310.

—. 2003. *Tendencias de la dinámica cultural en Costa Rica en el siglo XX* (San José, Costa Rica: Editorial Universidad de Costa Rica).

Davis, Lisa E. 1984. 'The World of the West Indian Black in Central America: The Recent Works of Quince Duncan', in *Voices from Under: Black Narrative in Latin America and the Caribbean*, ed. by William Luis (London: Greenwood Press), pp. 149–63.

Dennison, Stephanie. 2013. 'Issues in Contemporary Hispanic Filmmaking', in *Contemporary Hispanic Cinema: Interrogating the Transnational in Spanish and Latin American Film*, ed. by Stephanie Dennison (Woodbridge: Tamesis), pp. 1–24.

Derrida, Jacques. 1967. *L'écriture et la différence* (Paris: Seuil).

Díaz, Doriam. 1999. 'Una vida construida de palabras', in *La Nación* <http://wvw.nacion.com/viva/1999/julio/11/portada.html> [accessed 3 March 2015].

Díaz-Azofeifa, Gisella. 2012. 'Paradoxes of Costa Rican Multiculturalism', in *Latin American and Caribbean Ethnic Studies*, 7.2: 137–54.

Dirks, Nicholas B. 2006. 'Colonialism and Culture', in *The Post-Colonial Studies Reader*, ed. by Bill Ashcroft, Gareth Griffiths, and Helen Tiffin (London: Routledge), pp. 57–61.

Dixon, Kwame. 2006. 'Beyond Race and Gender: Recent Works on Afro-Latin America', in *Latin American Research Review*, 41.3: 247–58.

Dobles, Aurelia. 2004. 'Las películas son actos de pasión más que otra cosa', in *La Nación* <http://wvw.nacion.com/ancora/2004/febrero/08/ancora4.html> [accessed 3 June 2015].

Docherty, Thomas. 2013. 'Official Identity and Clandestine Experience', in *Identity and Form in Contemporary Literature*, ed. by Ana María Sánchez-Arce (London: Routledge), pp. 19–37.

Domínguez, Daniel. 2015. 'El drama "Dos aguas": Dos fenómenos dentro de Costa Rica', in *La Prensa* <https://www.prensa.com/cine_y_mas/aguas-fenomenos-dentro-pais_7_4185401422.html> [accessed 16 August 2017].

Donawa, V. 2009. 'Defining and Documenting Afro-Latin America', in *Latin American and Caribbean Ethnic Studies*, 4.3: 351–4.

Duncan, Cynthia. 2010. *Unraveling the Real: The Fantastic in Spanish-American Ficciones* (Philadelphia: Temple University Press).

Duncan, Quince. 1973. *Los cuatro espejos* (San José, Costa Rica: Editorial Costa Rica).

—. 1975. *El negro en la literatura costarricense* (San José, Costa Rica: Editorial Costa Rica).

—. 1986. *Cultura negra y teología* (San José, Costa Rica: Editorial Departamento Ecuménico de Investigaciones).

—. 1987. 'Visión panorámica de la narrativa costarricense', in *Revista Iberoamericana*, 138–9: 79–94.

—. 2001. *Contra el silencio: Afrodescendientes y racismo en el Caribe Continental Hispánico* (San José, Costa Rica: Editorial Universidad Nacional a la Distancia).

—. 2005. 'El Afrorealismo: una dimensión nueva de la literatura latinoamericana', in *Istmo*, 10.

—. 2009. *Génesis y evolución del racismo real-doctrinario Quince Duncan* (San José, Costa Rica: IIDH).

—. 2013. Personal Interview. 10 July.

Duncan, Quince and Carlos Meléndez. 1972. *El negro en Costa Rica* (San José, Costa Rica: Editorial Costa Rica).

Durán Luzio, Juan. 2003. *Senderos de identidad: Diez ensayos sobre literatura costarricense* (San José, Costa Rica: Editorial Costa Rica).

Eagleton, Mary (ed.). 2011. *Feminist Literary Theory: A Reader*, 3rd edn (Oxford: Wiley-Blackwell)

Eagly, Alice and Antonio Mladinic. 1989. 'Gender Stereotypes and Attitudes Towards Women and Men', in *Personality and Social Psychology Bulletin* 15: 543–58.

Echeverri-Gent, Elisavinda. 1992. 'Workers: British West Indians and the Early Days of the Banana Industry in Costa Rica and Honduras', in *Journal of Latin American Studies*, 24.2: 275–308.

Edison, Thomas Wayne. 2002. 'The Afro-Caribbean Novels of Resistance of Alejandro Carpentier, Quince Duncan, Carlos Guillermo Wilson, and Manuel Zapata Olivella', PhD thesis, University of Kentucky.

Editorial Costa Rica. 2015. *Editorial Costa Rica* website <https://www.editorialcostarica.com/main.cfm> [accessed 3 June 2015].

Espinosa, Julio García. 1976. *Por un cine imperfecto* (La Habana, Cuba: Castellote).

Fábrega, Paz. 2011. *Agua fría de mar* (Costa Rica: Temporal).

—. 2015. Personal Interview, 7 July (San José, Costa Rica).

Falicov, Tamara. 2008. 'Hollywood in Latin America: How Mexico and Argentina Cope and Cooperate with the Behemoth of the North', in *The Contemporary Hollywood Film Industry*, ed. by Paul McDonald and Janet Wasko (Oxford: Blackwell), pp. 264–76.

Falicov, Tamara and Jeffrey Midents. 2012. 'Voices from the Small Cinemas: Beyond "The Remaining Countries"', in *Studies in Spanish and Latin American Cinemas*, 9.2: 1–6.

Fanon, Frantz. 1963. *The Wretched of the Earth*, trans. by Constance Farrington (Harmondsworth: Penguin).

—. 1986. *Black Skin, White Masks*, trans. by Charles Lam Markmann, 2nd edn (London: Pluto).

—. 1994. 'On National Culture', in *Colonial Discourse and Post-Colonial Theory*, ed. by Laura Chrisman and Patrick Williams (Harlow: Pearson Education), pp. 36–52.

Felski, Rita. 2011. 'Doing Time: Feminist Theory and Postmodernist Culture', in *Feminist Literary Theory: A Reader*, ed. by Mary Eagleton, 3rd edn (Oxford: Wiley-Blackwell), pp. 37–40.

Finn, Julio. 1988a. *Black Literature and Humanism in Latin America* (Athens: University of Georgia Press).

—. 1988b. *Voices of Négritude* (London: Quartet Books).

Fletcher, Angus. 2012. *Allegory: The Theory of a Symbolic Mode* (Princeton, NJ: Princeton University Press).

Flórez-Estrada, María. 2007. *Economía del género: el valor simbólico y económico de las mujeres* (San José, Costa Rica: Editorial Costa Rica).

Fonseca, Elizabeth. 1986. *Costa Rica colonial: la tierra y el hombre* (San José, Costa Rica: Editorial Universitaria Centroamericana).

Foster, David William. 1997. *Sexual Textualities: Essays on Queer/ing Latin American Writing* (Austin: University of Texas Press).

—. 2002. 'Latin American Literature', in *The Gay and Lesbian Literary Heritage: A Reader's Companion to the Writers and their Works from Antiquity to the Present*, ed. by Claude Summers (Oxford: Routledge), pp. 425–31.

Freud, Sigmund. 1919. 'The "Uncanny"', trans. by Alix Strachey (*Imago*, 5: 297–324) <http://web.mit.edu/allanmc/www/freud1.pdf> [accessed 15 August 2018].

Furlong, William L. 1987. 'Costa Rica: Caught between Two Worlds', *Journal of Interamerican Studies and World Affairs*, 29.2: 119–54.

Gane-McCalla, Casey. 2011. 'Athletic Blacks vs Smart Whites: Why Sports Stereotypes are Wrong', in *HuffPost* <https://www.huffingtonpost.com/casey-ganemccalla/athletic-blacks-vs-smart_b_187386.html> [accessed 17 August 2017].

García Canclini, Nestor. 1995. *Hybrid Cultures* (Minneapolis: University of Minnesota Press).

Gates, Henry Louis. 1988. *The Signifying Monkey: A Theory of Afro-American Literary Criticism* (New York: Oxford University Press).

—. 2006. 'Writing Race', in *The Post-Colonial Studies Reader*, ed. by Bill Ashcroft, Gareth Griffiths, and Helen Tiffin (London: Routledge), pp. 216–18.

—. 2010. *Tradition and the Black Atlantic: Critical Theory in the African Diaspora* (New York: Basic Civitas).

Gateward, Frances K. and Murray Pomerance. 2002. *Sugar, Spice, and Everything Nice: Cinemas of Girlhood* (Detroit, MI: Wayne State University Press).

Gente 10. 2012. 'Gente 10 Edición 104', *Gente 10* website <https://issuu.com/revistagente10/docs/edicion__104> [accessed 3 June 2015].

Gordon, Donald K. 1988. 'The Sociopolitical Thought and Literary Style of Quince Duncan', in *Afro-Hispanic Review*, 7.3: 27–31.

—. 1989. *Lo jamaicano y lo universal en la obra del costarricense Quince Duncan* (San José, Costa Rica: Editorial Costa Rica).

Graves, John L. 1962. 'The Social Ideas of Marcus Garvey', in *Journal of Negro Education*, 30.1: 65–74.

Griffiths, Gareth. 2006. 'The Myth of Authenticity', in *The Post-Colonial Studies Reader*, ed. by Bill Ashcroft, Gareth Griffiths, and Helen Tiffin (London: Routledge, 2006), pp. 165–8.

Grinberg Pla, Valeria. 2006. '¿Complejo de un negro?: Ensayo sobre El negro en Costa Rica, de Quince Duncan y Carlos Meléndez', in *Istmo*, 12.

Guha, Ranajit. 1997. *A Subaltern Studies Reader, 1986–1995* (Minneapolis: University of Minnesota Press).

Guha, Ranajit and Gayatri Chakravorty Spivak. 1988. *Selected Subaltern Studies* (Oxford: Oxford University Press).

Gutiérrez, Tatiana. 2012. 'Multitud caminó en Marcha de los Invisibles y "limpió" el Congreso', in *La Nación* <https://www.nacion.com/archivo/multitud-camino-en-marcha-de-los-invisibles-y-limpio-el-congreso/DP3PYKIGEJCZ7BZT DAO7ZJK5BU/story/> [accessed 3 June 2015].

Gutiérrez Alea, Tomás. 1982. *Dialéctica del espectador* (Havana, Cuba: Unión de Escritores y Artistas de Cuba).

Halberstam, J. 2005. *In a Queer Time and Place: Transgender Bodies, Subcultural Lives* (New York: NYU Press).

Hall, Stuart. 1986. 'Gramsci's Relevance for the Study of Race and Ethnicity', in *Journal of Communication Inquiry*, 10.5: 5–27.

—. 1993. 'Minimal Selves', *Studying Culture: An Introductory Reader*, ed. by Ann Gray and Jim McGuigan (London: Routledge), pp. 134–8.

—. 1994. 'Cultural Identity and Diaspora', in *Colonial Discourse and Post-Colonial Theory*, ed. by Laura Chrisman and Patrick Williams (Harlow: Pearson Education), pp. 392–403.

—. 1996. 'New Ethnicities', in *Critical Dialogues in Cultural Studies*, ed. by David Morley and Kuan-Hging Chen (New York: Routledge), pp. 441–9.

Hall, Stuart and Mark Sealy. 2001. *Different: A Historical Context, Contemporary Photographers and Black Identity* (London and New York: Phaidon).

Hampton, Janet Jones. 1985. 'The Image of the Black Woman in the Spanish-American Novel: A Study of Characterization in Selected Spanish-American Novels', PhD thesis, Catholic University of America, Washington, DC.

Happy Planet Index. 2015. *Happy Planet Index* website <www.happyplanetindex.org> [accessed 15 June 2015].

Hardt, Michael and Antonio Negri. 2000. *Empire* (Cambridge, MA: Harvard University Press).

Harpelle, Ronald. 1993. 'The Social and Political Integration of West Indians in Costa Rica: 1930–50', in *Journal of Latin American Studies*, 25.1: 103–20.

—. 2000. 'Racism and Nationalism in the Creation of Costa Rica's Pacific Coast Banana Enclave', in *The Americas*, 56.3: 29–51.

—. 2002. *The West Indians of Costa Rica: Race, Class and the Integration of an Ethnic Minority* (London: McGill–Queen's University Press).

—. 2003. 'Cross Currents in the Western Caribbean: Marcus Garvey and the UNIA in Central America', in *Caribbean Studies*, 31.1: 35–73.

Hart, Stephen. 1995. 'Is Women's Writing in Spanish America Gender Specific?', in *Modern Language Notes*, 110.2: 335–52.

—. 2004. *A Companion to Latin American Film* (London: Tamesis, 2004).

—. 2008. 'Art in the Gerund in the Work of Luisa Valenzuela', in *Journal of Iberian and Latin America Studies*, 14.2–3: 87–92.

—. 2015. *Latin American Cinema* (London: Reaktion).

Harvey, Liz. 2017. 'Rendering the Invisible Visible: Reflections on the Costa Rican Film Industry in the Twenty-First Century', in *A Companion to Latin American Cinema*, ed. by Maria Delgado, Stephen Hart, and Randal Johnson (Oxford: Wiley-Blackwell), pp. 325–39.

Harvey-Kattou, Liz. 2015. *Retratico*. Documentary, University College London.

—. 2018. 'Performing for Hollywood: Coloniality and the Tourist Image in Esteban Ramírez's *Caribe* (2004)', in *Studies in Spanish and Latin American Cinemas*, 15.2: 249–66.

Helmuth, Chalene and Carmen Naranjo. 1996. 'Carmen Naranjo', in *Hispamérica*, 25.74: 47–56.

Hernández Adrián, Francisco-J. 2015. 'Excess and Playfulness in Latin American Film: The Seascape Scene from *Y tu mamá también* to *Post tenebras lux*', at UCL Research Seminar, London, 11 March.

Hernández Cruz, Omar. 1998. 'Culturas y dinámica regional en el Caribe costarricense', in *Anuario de Estudios Centroamericanos*, 24.1–2: 129–62.

Herra Monge, Mayra. 2011. 'La presencia de la Africanía en la poesía de dos escritoras Afro-costarricense', in *Ponencia*, 10.

Hidalgo, Roxana. 2004. 'Historias de las mujeres en el espacio público en Costa Rica ante el cambio del siglo XX al XXI', in *Cuaderno de Ciencias Sociales*, 132: 1–73.

Hjort, Mette and Duncan Petrie. 2007. *The Cinema of Small Nations* (Edinburgh: Edinburgh University Press).

Hoare, Quintin and Geoffrey Nowell Smith. 1971. *Selections from the Prison Notebooks of Antonio Gramsci* (London: Lawrence & Wishart).

Hodge, Bob and Vijay Mishra. 1994. 'What is Post(-)colonialism?', in *Colonial Discourse and Post-Colonial Theory*, ed. by Laura Chrisman and Patrick Williams (Harlow: Pearson Education), pp. 276–90.

hooks, bell. 2000. *Feminist Theory: From Margin to Center: From Margin to Centre* (London: Pluto Press).

Hopewell, John. 2016. 'IFF Panama: Jurgen Ureña's "Abrazame Como Antes", a Humanist Vision of Prostitution', in *Variety* <https://variety.com/2016/film/festivals/iff-panama-jurgen-urenas-abrazame-como-antes-prostitution-1201752403/> [accessed 16 August 2017].

Hughey, Matthew W. 2014. *The White Savior Film: Content, Critics, and Consumption* (Philadelphia: Temple University Press).

Huhn, Sebastian. 2012. *Criminalidad y discurso en Costa Rica: Reflexiones críticas sobre un problema social* (San José, Costa Rica: FLACSO).

Instituto Costarricense de Turismo (ICT). 2015. *ICT* website <https://www.visitcostarica.com/en> [accessed 5 June 2015].

Jackson, Richard. 1976. *The Black Image in Latin American Literature* (Albuquerque: University of New Mexico Press).

—. 1979. *Black Writers in Latin America* (Albuquerque: University of New Mexico Press).

—. 1988. *Black Literature and Humanism in Latin America* (Athens: University of Georgia Press).

—. 1989. 'Afro-Hispanic Literature: The New Frontier of Avant-Garde Criticism', in *Callaloo*, 38: 255–60.

—. 1997. *Black Writers and the Hispanic Canon* (New York: Twayne).

—. 1998. *Black Writers and Latin America: Cross-Cultural Affinities* (Washington, DC: Howard University Press).

Jackson, Shirley. 1985. 'The Gift of Literature', in *Monographic Review*, 83–9.

Janmohamed, Abdul R. 2006. 'The Economy of Manichean Allegory', in *The Post-Colonial Studies Reader*, ed. by Bill Ashcroft, Gareth Griffiths, and Helen Tiffin (London: Routledge), pp. 19–23.

Jaramillo Levi, Enrique. 1991. *When New Flowers Bloomed: Short Stories by Women Writers from Costa Rica and Panama* (Pittsburgh, PA: Latin American Literary Review Press).

Jehenson, Myriam Yvonne. 1995. *Latin-American Women Writers: Class, Race, and Gender* (Albany: State University of New York Press).

Jiménez Arguedas, Verónica. 2014. 'Costa Rica empieza a construir un mapa de estadísticas culturales', in *Red Cultura* <http://redcultura.com/php/Articulos1331.htm> [accessed 20 February 2015].

Johnson, Roberta. 1980. 'The Paradigmatic Story Mode of Carmen Naranjo, Eunice Odio, Yolanda Oreamuno, Victoria Urbano, and Rima Valbona', in *Letras Femeninas*, 6.1: 14–24.

Koch, Charles W. 1977. 'Jamaican Blacks and their Descendants in Costa Rica', in *Social and Economic Studies*, 26.3: 339–61.

Lacan, Jacques. 1977. *Écrits: A Selection*, trans. by Alan Sheridan (London: Tavistock Publications).

Lamming, George. 2006. 'The Occasion for Speaking', in *The Post-Colonial Studies Reader*, ed. by Bill Ashcroft, Gareth Griffiths, and Helen Tiffin (London: Routledge), pp. 14–18.

Landry, Donna and Gerald Maclean. 1996. *The Spivak Reader* (London: Routledge).

Láscaris, Constantino. 1975. *El costarricense* (San José, Costa Rica: Editorial Universitaria Centroamericana).

Lauretis, Teresa de. 1987. *Technologies of Gender* (Bloomington: Indiana University Press).

Leach, MacEdward. 1961. 'Jamaican Duppy Lore', in *Journal of American Folklore*, 74: 207–15.

Leal, Luis. 1966. *Historia del Cuento Hispanoamericano* (Mexico City: Ediciones de Andrea).

Leitinger, Ilse Abshagen. 1997. *The Costa Rican Women's Movement: A Reader* (Pittsburgh, PA: University of Pittsburgh Press).

Lim, Song Hwee. 2007. 'Is the Trans- in Transnational the Tras- in Transgender?', in *New Cinemas: Journal of Contemporary Film*, 5.1: 39–52.

López, Melissa. 2012. 'Alfonso Chase, una leyenda de la literatura costarricense', in *Cultura Costa Rica* <https://web.archive.org/web/20150709031457/http://www.culturacr.net/12/c3/Alfonso_Chase_una_leyenda_de_la_literatura_costarricense.html> [accessed 13 January 2019].

Love, Tim. 2011. 'Child Narrators in Adult Fiction', in *Litrefs Blog* <http://litrefs articles.blogspot.co.uk/2011/01/child-narrators-in-adult-fiction.html> [accessed 5 September 2014].

Luis, William. 1984. *Voices from Under: Black Narrative in Latin America and the Caribbean* (Westport, CT: Greenwood Press).

Lukács, Georg. 1971 *History and Class Consciousness*, trans. by Rodney Livingstone (Cambridge, MA: MIT Press).

Lutsch, Stacy Elaine. 2007. 'A Cinematic Dialogue between Nicaragua and Costa Rica: Shaping a Transnational Cinema through Filmic Exchanges', Master's thesis, University of Kansas.

Lykke, Nina. 2010. *Feminist Studies: A Guide to Intersectional Theory, Methodology and Writing* (London: Routledge).

Magnarelli, Sharon. 1988. *Reflections/Refractions: Reading Luisa Valenzuela* (New York: Peter Lang).

Magro, Estefanía. 2015. 'Patricia Velásquez habla de "Dos aguas", su sorprendente ópera prima', in *Programa Ibermedia* <http://www.programaibermedia.com/nuestras-cronicas/patricia-velasquez-habla-de-dos-aguas-su-sorprendente-opera-prima/> [accessed 16 August 2017].

Maloof, Judy. 2000. 'Recovering and Discovering Another Perspective: Recent Books on Latin American Women Writers', in *Latin American Research Review*, 35.1: 243–55.

Martin, Deborah. 2011. 'Wholly Ambivalent Demon-Girl: Horror, the Uncanny and the Representation of Feminine Adolescence in Lucrecia Martel's *La niña santa*', in *Journal of Iberian and Latin American Studies*, 17.1: 59–76.

Martin-Ogunsola, Dellita. 1987. 'Invisibility, Double Consciousness and the Crisis of Identity in *Los cuatro espejos*', in *Afro-Hispanic Review*, 6.2: 9–15.

—. 1991. 'Translation as a Poetic Experience/Experiment: The Short Fiction of Quince Duncan', in *Afro-Hispanic Review*, 10.3: 42–50.

—. 2004. *The Eve/Hagar Paradigm in the Fiction of Quince Duncan* (Columbia: University of Missouri Press).

Martínez, Luz Ivette. 1987. *Carmen Naranjo y la narrativa femenina en Costa Rica* (Costa Rica: Editorial Universitaria Centroamericana).

Marting, Diane. 2001. *The Sexual Woman in Latin American Literature: Dangerous Desires* (Gainesville: University Press of Florida).

Masís Iverson, Daniel. 1999. 'Poder político y sociedad', in *Costa Rica contemporánea: raíces del estado de la nación*, ed. by Juan Rafael Quesada Camacho (San José, Costa Rica: Editorial de la Universidad de Costa Rica), pp. 45–96.

Meza Márquez, Consuelo. 2010. 'La diáspora afrocaribeña en Centroamérica: Identidad y Literatura de Mujeres', Ponencia presentada en el X Congreso Centroamericano de Historia <http://www.hcentroamerica.fcs.ucr.ac.cr/Contenidos/hca/cong/mesas/x_congreso/genero/diaspora-mujeres.pdf> [accessed 16 June 2015; no longer available].

Meza Ocampo, Tobías Alberto. 1999. 'Ecología y población', in *Costa Rica contemporánea: raíces del estado de la nación*, ed. by Juan Rafael Quesada Camacho (San José, Costa Rica: Editorial de la Universidad de Costa Rica), pp. 197–240.

Mignolo, Walter. 2009. *The Idea of Latin America* (Oxford: Wiley-Blackwell).

Ministerio de Cultura y Juventud (MCJ). 2015. *MCJ* website <www.mcj.go.cr> [accessed 5 September 2014].

Ministerio de Educación Pública de Costa Rica (MEP). 2015. *MEP* website <https://www.mep.go.cr/> [accessed 3 June 2015].

Miranda Hevia, Alicia. 1981. 'Introducción a la obra novelesca de Carmen Naranjo', in *Cahiers du monde hispanique et luso-brésilien*, 36: 121–9.

Mitchell, Meg Tyler and Scott Pentzer. 2008. *Costa Rica: A Global Studies Handbook* (Oxford: ABC-CLIO).

Molina, Iván and Steven Palmer (eds.). 2004. *The Costa Rica Reader: History, Culture, Politics* (Durham, NC: Duke University Press).

Molloy, Sylvia and Robert McKee Irwin (eds.). 1998. *Hispanisms and Homosexualities* (Durham, NC: Duke University Press).

Moreiras, Alberto. 2001. *The Exhaustion of Difference: The Politics of Latin American Cultural Studies* (Durham, NC: Duke University Press).

—. 2012. '¿Puedo madrugarme a un narco? Posiciones críticas en la Asociación de Estudios Latincamericanos', in *Fronterad* <http://www.fronterad.com/?q=puedo-madrugarme-a-narco-posiciones-criticas-en-asociacion-estudios-latinoamer-icanos> [accessed 3 June 2015].

Morgan, Thais E. 1994. *Men Writing the Feminine: Literature, Theory, and the Question of Genders* (Albany: State University of New York Press).

Mosby, Dorothy E. 2003. *Place, Language and Identity in Afro-Costa Rican Literature* (Columbia: University of Missouri Press).

Muecke, D. C. 1970. *Irony* (London: Meuthen & Co.).

Mulvey, Laura. 1935. 'Visual Pleasure and Narrative Cinema', in *Film Theory and Criticism*, ed. by Marshal Cohen and Gerald Mast (New York: Oxford University Press), pp. 803–16.

—. 1999. 'Afterthoughts on "Visual Pleasure and Narrative Cinema" Inspired by King Vidor's *Duel In The Sun* (1946)', in *Feminist Film Theory*, ed. by Sue Thornham (New York: NYU Press), pp. 31–40.

—. 2006. *Death 24x a Second* (London: Reaktion).

Muñoz, Willy. 2000. 'El lenguaje y la devaluación del cuerpo preñado en "Simbiosis del encuentro" de Carmen Naranjo', in *Letras Femeninas*, 26.1-2: 99–110.

Murillo, Álvaro. 2014. 'Costa Rica concede el primer seguro familiar a una pareja homosexual', in *El País de Costa Rica* <https://elpais.com/internacional/2014/11/21/actualidad/1416600219_003975.html> [accessed 3 June 2015].

Murillo, Carmen. 1991. *Identidades de humo y hierro: La construcción del ferrocarril al Atlántico, 1870-1890* (San José, Costa Rica: Editorial Universidad de Costa Rica).

Museo de Juan Santamaría. 2015. *MJS* website <http://www.museojuansantamaria.go.cr/> [accessed 17 August 2015].

Namaste, Ki. 1996. '"Tragic Misreadings": Queer Theory's Erasure of Transgender Subjectivity', in *Queer Studies: A Lesbian, Gay, Bisexual, and Transgender Anthology*, ed. by Brett Beemyn and Michele Eliason (New York: NYU Press), pp. 183–203.

Naranjo, Carmen. 1981. 'Mitos de la mujer: El mito de la maternidad', in *Letras Femeninas*, 7.2: 3.

—. 1983. *Ondina* (San José, Costa Rica: Editorial Universitaria Centroamericana).

—. 1984. *Nunca hubo alguna vez* (San José, Costa Rica: Editorial Universidad Estatal a Distancia).

—. 1989. *Mujer y Cultura* (San José: Editorial Universitaria Centroamericana).

Noble, Andrea. 2005. *Mexican National Cinema* (London: Routledge).

Nwankwo, I. K. 2009. 'Introduction: Making Sense, Making Selves: Afro-Latin Americans of British Caribbean Descent', in *Latin American and Caribbean Ethnic Studies*, 4.3: 221–30.

O'Donnell, Daniel. 2012. *Derecho Internacional de los Derechos Humanos: Normativa, jurisprudencia y doctrina de los Sistemas Universal e Interamericano* (Mexico: Tribunal Superior de Justicia del Distrito Federal).

O'Neal Coto, Katzy. 2010. 'ALCOA en perspectiva histórica', *Noticias UCR* wesbite <https://www.ucr.ac.cr/noticias/2010/04/19/alcoa-en-perspectiva-historica.html> [accessed 24 August 2015].

Obando, Alexánder. 2008. *La gruta y el arcoiris: Antología de narrativa gay/lésbica costarricense* (San José, Costa Rica: Editorial Costa Rica).

Ovares, Flora and Margarita Rojas. 2005. '"Los relojes" de Alfonso Chase', in *Ensenanza de la literatura* (Costa Rica: Editorial UNA).

Oxford English Dictionary Online (OED). 2015. *OED* website <www.oed.com>.

Padva, Gilad. 2004. 'Edge of Seventeen: Melodramatic Coming-out in New Queer Adolescence Films', in *Communication and Critical/Cultural Studies*, 1.4: 355–72.

Palmer, Paula. 1994. *Wa'apin Man* (San José, Costa Rica: Editorial Universidad de Costa Rica).

——. 2004. 'West Indian Limón', in *The Costa Rica Reader: History, Culture, Politics*, ed. by Iván Molina and Steven Palmer (Durham, NC: Duke University Press), pp. 237–42.

Parker, Robert Dale. 2012. *Critical Theory: A Reader for Literary and Cultural Studies* (Oxford: Oxford University Press).

Parry, Benita. 2006. 'Problems in Current Theories of Colonial Discourse', in *The Post-Colonial Studies Reader*, ed. by Bill Ashcroft, Gareth Griffiths, and Helen Tiffin (London: Routledge), pp. 44–50.

Paul-Ureña, Jeana. 2007. 'Voces sublevadas: Escritoras costarricenses develan la historia y vislumbran el futuro de su país', in *Hispania*, 90.3: 423–30.

Pauwels, Anne. 1999. 'Feminist Language Planning: Has It Been Worthwhile?', in *Linguistik Online*, 2.1 <https://bop.unibe.ch/linguistik-online/article/view/1043/1707> [accessed 19 October 2015].

Peden, Margaret Sayers (ed.). 1983. *The Latin American Short Story: A Critical History* (Boston: Twayne).

Pérez, Karol. 2014. 'Costa Rica lidera la penetración de internet en Centroamérica', in *Revista Summa* <http://www.revistasumma.com/49866/> [accessed 5 September 2015].

Perry, Franklin and Kathleen Sawyers Royal. 1995. *No Longer Invisible: Afro-Latin Americans Today* (London: Minority Rights Group Publications).

Pessoa, Carlos. 2003. 'Debate: On Hegemony, Post-Ideology and Subalternity', in *Bulletin of Latin American Research*, 22.4: 484–90.

Picado, Clodomiro. 2004. 'Our Blood is Blackening', in *The Costa Rica Reader: History, Culture, Politics*, ed. by Iván Molina and Steven Palmer (Durham, NC: Duke University Press), pp. 243–4.

Picon Garfield, Evelyn. 1987. 'La luminosa ceguera de sus días: Los cuentos 'humanos' de Carmen Naranjo', in *Revista Iberoamericana*, 3.138–9: 287–301.

Piedra, José. 1987. 'Literary Whiteness and the Afro-Hispanic Difference', in *New Literary History*, 18.2: 303–32.

Podalsky, Laura. 2011. *The Politics of Affect in and Emotion in Contemporary Latin American Cinema: Argentina, Brazil, Cuba, and Mexico* (New York: Palgrave Macmillan).

Poe Lang, Karen. 2017. 'Abrázame como antes o el discreto encanto de lo trans', in *Semanario Universidad* <https://semanariouniversidad.com/suplementos/abrazame-discreto-encanto-lo-trans/> [accessed 25 January 2017].

Portugés de Bolaños, Elizabeth. 1964. *El cuento en Costa Rica* (San José, Costa Rica: Imprenta Lehmann).

Pozuelo. 2015. *Pozuelo* website <www.pozuelo.com> [accessed 13 June 2015].

Prada Ortiz, Grace. 2005. *Mujeres forjadores del pensamiento costarricense: ensayos femeninos y feministas* (Heredia, Costa Rica: Editorial Universidad Nacional).

Prescott, Laurence E. 1980. 'Afro-Hispanic Writers', in *Callaloo*, 8.10: 211–16.

——. 1996. 'Afro-Hispanic and Caribbean Literatures in Recent Theory and Criticism: Affirmations and Implications', in *Latin American Research Review*, 31.1: 148–61.

Purcell, Trevor W. 1985. 'Dependency and Responsibility: A View from West Indians in Costa Rica', in *Caribbean Quarterly*, 31.4: 1–15.

—. 1987. 'Transformation and Social Inequality in a Plural Society: The Case of Limón, Costa Rica', in *Caribbean Quarterly*, 33.1–2: 20–43.

Putnam, Lara E. 2000. 'La población Afrocostarricense según los datos del censo de 2000', in *Costa Rica a la Luz del Censo 2000* <https://ccp.ucr.ac.cr/> [accessed 20 October 2012].

Puwar, Nirmal. 2004. *Space Invaders: Race, Gender and Bodies Out of Place* (Oxford: Berg).

Quesada, Armando. 2017. 'Jurgen Ureña: "El cine es más que sólo el relato"', in *Delefoco* <http://revista.delefoco.com/9968-jurgen-urea-el-cine-es-ms-que-slo-el-relato.aspx> [accessed 2 February 2017].

Quesada Pacheco, Miguel Ángel. 2007. *Nuevo Diccionario de Costariqueñismos*, 5th edn (San José, Costa Rica: Editorial Tecnológica de Costa Rica).

Quesada Soto, Álvaro. 2008. *Breve historia de la literatura costarricense* (San José, Costa Rica: Editorial Costa Rica).

Ramírez, Esteban. 2009. *Gestación* (feature film; Costa Rica: Cinetel).

—. 2014. Personal Interview. Costa Rica: 2 September 2013.

Ramsay, Paulette. 1994. 'The African Religious Heritage in Selected Works of Quince Duncan: An Expression of Cultural and Literary Marronage', in *Caribbean Quarterly*, 40.1: 13–26.

—. 1998. 'Quince Duncan's Literary Representation of the Ethno-Racial Dynamics between Latinos and Afro-Costa Ricans of West Indian Descent', in *Afro-Hispanic Review*, 17.2: 52–60.

—. 1999. 'From Object to Subject: The Affirmation of Female Subjectivity in Quince Duncan's *La Paz del pueblo* (1978) and *Kimbo* (1989)', in *Caribbean Quarterly*, 45.1: 17–26.

Real Academia Española (RAE). 2017. *RAE website* <www.rae.es> [accessed 3 June 2015].

Recuerdos TV Cuba. 2011. 'A los payasos todos los quieren', *YouTube* <https://www.youtube.com/watch?v=MJJcJ-vxB24?> [accessed 18 June 2015].

Restall, Matthew. 2000. 'Black Conquistadors: Armed Africans in Early Spanish America', in *The Americas*, 57.2: 171–205.

Richards, Keith John. 2011. *Themes in Latin American Cinema: A Critical Survey* (Jefferson, NC: MacFarland and Co.).

Rigby, S. H. 1987. *Marxism and History: A Critical Introduction* (Manchester: Manchester University Press).

Rigney, Melissa. 2008. 'Brandon Goes to Hollywood: *Boys Don't Cry* and the Transgender Body in Film', in *Queer Youth Cultures*, ed. by Susan Driver (New York: SUNY Press), pp. 181–98.

Rodríguez Vega, Eugenio. 2003. *Biografía de Costa Rica* (San José, Costa Rica: Editorial Costa Rica).

Rovinski, Samuel. 1985. 'El teatro y el cine contemporáneos en Costa Rica', in *Confluencia*, 1.1: 56–64.

Said, Edward W. 1995. *Orientalism: Western Conceptions of the Orient* (Harmondsworth: Penguin Books).

Salas, José. 2015. 'Estreno de la película Dos aguas', in *Yo amo Chepe* <http://www.yoamochepe.com/estreno-de-la-pelicula-dos-aguas/> [accessed 16 August 2017].

Salas Murillo, Bértold. 2011. 'De Elvira a Gestación: amor e identidad, mujer y sociedad', *Revista Comunicación*, 20.2: 44–51.

Salas Víquez, Diana Lucía. 2013. 'Costa Rica lidera 4G y consumo de datos en Centroamérica', in *El financiero* <https://web.archive.org/web/20150923235556/http://www.elfinancierocr.com/tecnologia/Telefonia_movil-consumo_de_datos-Internet-Centroamerica_0_427157310.html> [accessed 3 June 2015].

Salas Zamora, Edwin. 1987. 'La identidad cultural del negro en las novelas de Quince Duncan. Aspectos temáticos y técnicos', in *Revista Iberoamericana*, 3.138–9: 377–90.

Sanabria, Carolina. 2011a. 'La fascinación paisajística en los cortometrajes El mar de Maricarmen Merino y Temporal de Paz Fábrega', in *Revista Comunicación*, 20.2: 60–73.

—. 2011b. 'La referencialidad a la Nación en la cinematografía costarricense del siglo XXI. Apreciaciones críticas', in *Revista Comunicación*, 20.2: 18–31.

Sánchez, Alexander. 2013. 'Esteban Ramírez, preso en su próxima película', in *La Nación* <https://www.nacion.com/viva/cine/esteban-ramirez-preso-en-su-proxima-pelicula/GUFSJEONVZFSBDWJCKMMIX4TX4/story/> [accessed 3 June 2015].

—. 2015. 'Nuevo fondo audiovisual repartirá 250 millones de colones', in *La Nación* <https://www.nacion.com/viva/cine/nuevo-fondo-audiovisual-repartira-c-250-millones/2WOF7FMKSJA53OKT7PBU65WLCU/story/> [accessed 3 June 2015].

Sánchez Carballo, Susana. 2011. 'Uno de los crímenes más horribles: A propósito del documental Bajo el límpido azul de tu cielo', in *Revista Comunicación*, 20.2: 83–7.

Sandoval García, Carlos. 2000. 'The Role of the Nicaraguan "Other" In the Formation of National Identities in Costa Rica', PhD thesis, University of Birmingham.

Santí, Enrico. 1992. 'Latin Americanism and Restitution', in *Latin American Literary Review*, 20.40: 88–96.

Schroeder Rodríguez, Paul. 2012. 'After New Latin American Cinema', in *Cinema Journal*, 51.2: 87–112.

Schwarz, Roberto. 1995. 'Nation by Imitation', in *The Postmodernism Debate in Latin America*, ed. by Michael Aronna, John Beverley, and José Oviedo (Durham, NC: Duke University Press).

Sedgwick, Eve Kosofsky. 2008. *Epistemology of the Closet* (Berkeley: University of California Press).

Seibel, Alexandra and Timothy Shary. 2007. *Youth Culture in Global Cinema* (Austin: University of Texas Press).

Senghor, Léopold Sédar. 1995. 'Négritude and the Civilisation of the Universal', in *African Presence in the Americas*, ed. by Carlos Moore (Trenton, NJ: World Press), pp. 21–32.

Senior Angulo, Diana. 2007. *La incorporación social en Costa Rica de la población Afrocostarricense durante el siglo XX, 1927–1963* (San José, Costa Rica: Universidad de Costa Rica).

Sequeira, Aarón. 2014. 'Diputados establecen que Costa Rica es un Estado multiétnico y pluricultural', in *La Nación* <https://www.nacion.com/el-pais/diputados-establecen-que-costa-rica-es-un-estado-multietnico-y-pluricultural/GIDEMIWXQVATVI3FIQT6WVI6S4/story/> [accessed 3 June 2015].

—. 2018. 'Primera acción de Fabricio Alvarado sería cambiar decreto contra discriminación a personas LGBTI', in *La Nación* <https://www.nacion.com/el-pais/politica/primera-accion-de-fabricio-alvarado-seria-cambiar/3PMH7IZVVVEIFJT VLU6CJRUHOE/story/> [accessed 15 August 2015].

Seraphinoff, Michael. 2007. 'Through a Child's Eyes: A Special Role of the Child as Narrator in Macedonian Literature', Ohio State University, Occasional Papers in Slavic Studies <www.makedonika.org/whatsnew/Michael%20Seraphinoff/ Through%20a%20Child's%20Eyes.pdf> [accessed 9 January 2019].

Sharman, Russell Leigh. 2006. 'Re/Making La Negrita: Culture as an Aesthetic System in Costa Rica', in *American Anthropologist*, 108.4: 842–53.

—. 2011. 'The Caribbean Carretera: Race, Space and Social Liminality in Costa Rica', in *Bulletin of Latin American Research*, 20.1: 46–62.

Shaw, Deborah. 2003. *Contemporary Cinema of Latin America: Ten Key Films* (London: A&C Black).

— (ed.). 2007. *Contemporary Latin American Cinema: Breaking into the Global Market* (Lanham, MD: Rowman & Littlefield).

—. 2013. 'Theories of "Transnational Cinema"', in *Contemporary Hispanic Cinema: Interrogating the Transnational in Spanish and Latin American Film*, ed. by Stephanie Dennison (Woodbridge: Tamesis), pp. 47–66.

Shea, Maureen. 1993. *Women as Outsiders: Undercurrents of Oppression in Latin American Women's Novels* (London: Austin & Winfield).

Showalter, Elaine. 2011. 'A Literature of Their Own: British Women Novelists from Brontë to Lessing', in *Feminist Literary Theory: A Reader*, ed. by Mary Eagleton, 3rd edn (Oxford: Wiley-Blackwell, 2011), pp. 11–14.

Slemon, Stephen. 2006. 'Unsettling the Empire: Resistance Theory for the Second World', in *The Post-Colonial Studies Reader*, ed. by Bill Ashcroft, Gareth Griffiths, and Helen Tiffin (London: Routledge), pp. 102–6.

Smart, Ian. 1984. *Central American Writers of West Indian Origin: A New Hispanic Literature* (Washington, DC: Three Continents Press).

—. 1985. 'The Literary World of Quince Duncan: An Interview', in *College Language Association Journal*, 28: 281–98.

—. 1987. 'Eulalia Bernard: A Caribbean Woman Writer and the Dynamics of Liberation', in *Letras Femeninas*, 13.1–2: 79–85.

Snodgrass, Mary Ellen. 2013. *Isabel Allende: A Literary Companion* (Jefferson, NC: McFarland).

Solano Gómez, Sofía. 2011. 'Cine tico crece a pasos agigantados', in *deleFOCO* <http://www.delefoco.com/Default.aspx?action=article-view&id=57> [accessed 3 June 2015].

Soliño, María Elena. 2008. 'Revealing Beauty/Revealing History in *El sueño de Venecia*', in *Hispanic Review*, 76.4: 335–59.

Solís, José. 2010. 'Cold Water of the Sea', in *Movies Kick Ass Blog* <http://movies kickassblog.blogspot.co.uk/2010/04/cold-water-of-sea-12.html> [accessed 3 June 2015].

Sollors, Werner. 2006. 'Who is Ethnic?', in *The Post-Colonial Studies Reader*, ed. by Bill Ashcroft, Gareth Griffiths, and Helen Tiffin (London: Routledge), pp. 191–3.

Sommer, Doris. 1991. *Foundational Fictions: The National Romances of Latin America* (Berkeley: University of California Press).

Sotela, Rogelio. 1920. *Valores literarios de Costa Rica* (Buenos Aires: Imprenta Alsina).

—. 1923. *Escritores y Poetas de Costa Rica* (San José, Costa Rica: Imprenta Lehmann).

—. 1927. *Literatura costarricense: Antología y bibliografías* (San José, Costa Rica: Imprenta Lehmann).

—. 1942. *Escritores de Costa Rica* (San José, Costa Rica: Imprenta Lehmann).

Spivak, Gayatri Chakravorty. 1999. *A Critique of Postcolonial Reason: Toward a History of the Vanishing Present* (Cambridge, MA: Harvard University Press).

—. 2006. 'Can the Subaltern Speak?', in *The Post-Colonial Studies Reader*, ed. by Bill Ashcroft, Gareth Griffiths, and Helen Tiffin (London: Routledge), pp. 28–37.

—. 2010. *Nationalism and the Imagination* (London: Seagull).

—. 2011. *An Aesthetic Education in the Era of Globalization* (Cambridge, MA: Harvard University Press).

Stam, Robert. 2000. *Film Theory: An Introduction* (New York: Blackwell).

Stevens Rojas, Daisy. 2009. 'Between Tradition and Modernity: Changing Gender Roles among the Bribri and Boruca Women of Costa Rica', in *Cuadernos de Antropología*, 19: 113–22.

Subero, Gustavo. 2008. 'Fear of the Trannies: On Filmic Phobia of Transvestism in the New Latin American Cinema', in *Latin American Research Review*, 43.2: 159–79.

Summers, Claude J. (ed.). 2002. *The Gay and Lesbian Literary Heritage: A Reader's Companion to the Writers and their Works from Antiquity to the Present* (London: Taylor & Francis).

Swanson, Philip. 2005. *Latin American Fiction: A Short Introduction* (Oxford: Blackwell).

Tabernero, Santiago. 2011. 'Interview with Paz Fábrega', *YouTube* <https://www.youtube.com/watch?v=ERCAJM-lqxg> [accessed 3 June 2015].

Tatum, Charles. 1973. 'The Child Point of View in Donoso's Fiction', in *Journal of Spanish Studies: Twentieth Century*, 1.3: 187–96.

Tillis, Antonio D. (ed.). 2012. *Critical Perspectives on Afro-Latin American Literature* (New York: Routledge).

Tinney, Oscar B. 1988. 'Social Criticism in the Novels of Quince Duncan', PhD thesis, University of North Carolina.

Tisnado, Carmen. 2005. 'El cuerpo femenino y el concepto de belleza en dos cuentos de Carmen Naranjo', in *Filología y Lingüística*, 31: 23–33.

Todorov, Tzvetan. 2006. 'Race and Racism', in *The Post-Colonial Studies Reader*, ed. by Bill Ashcroft, Gareth Griffiths, and Helen Tiffin (London: Routledge), pp. 213–15.

Ulloa, David. 2011. 'Alfonso Chase: La rebeldía que nunca muere', in *Cultura Costa Rica* <https://web.archive.org/web/20111030060304/http://culturacr.net/entrevistas/alfonso_chase.html> [accessed 3 June 2015].

Ureña, Jurgen. 2016. *Abrázame como antes* (feature film; Costa Rica: Mina Films).

Vallbona, Rima de. 1987. '*La ruta de su evasión*, de Yolanda Oreamuno: Escritura Proustiana Suplementada', in *Revista Iberoamericana*, 53.138–9: 193–217.

Valverde Alfaro, Elena. 2007. '*Los cuatro espejos* de Quince Duncan y la representación del sujeto subalterno Afro-caribeño', in *Revista Pensamiento Actual*, 7.8–9: 55–63.

Vandegrift, Darcie. 2007. 'Global Tourism and Racialized Citizenship Claims: Citizen-Subjects and the State in Costa Rica', in *Race/Ethnicity: Multidisciplinary Global Contexts*, 1.1: 121–43.

Vargas, Carlos Alonso. 1974. 'El use de los pronombres "vos" y "usted" en Costa Rica', in *Revista de Ciencias Sociales de la Universidad de Costa Rica*, 8: 7–30.

Velásquez, Patricia. 2014. *Dos aguas* (feature film; Costa Rica: Tiempo Líquido).

Venegas, William. 2014. '"Muñecas rusas": la paradoja de Jürgen Ureña: ser o no ser', in *La huella del ojo* <http://lahuelladelojo.blogspot.co.uk/2014/11/munecas-rusas-la-paradoja-de-jurgen.html> [accessed 16 August 2017].

—. 2015. 'Crítica de cine: Dos aguas', in *La Nación* <https://www.nacion.com/viva/cine/critica-de-cine-dos-aguas/7CVLPWNJ4ZFYXEZYTIO633CEEY/story/> [accessed 16 August 2017].

Villazana, Libia. 2008. 'Latin American Co-Production Cinema: Economics and Hegemony Since 1980', PhD thesis, University of the West of England.

—. 2013. 'Redefining Transnational Cinemas: A Transdisciplinary Perspective', in *Contemporary Hispanic Cinema: Interrogating the Transnational in Spanish and Latin American Film*, ed. by Stephanie Dennison (Woodbridge: Tamesis), pp. 25–46.

Wade, Peter. 1988. 'The Cultural Dynamics of Blackness in Colombia: Black Migrants to a "White" City', in *Afro-Hispanic Review*, 7.1–3: 53–9.

—. 2006. 'Afro-Latin Studies: Reflections on the Field', in *Latin American and Caribbean Ethnic Studies*, 1.1: 105–24.

Woodward, Ralph Lee. 1985. *Central America: A Nation Divided* (New York: Oxford University Press).

—. 1987. 'La historiografía centroamericana moderna desde 1960', in *Anuario de Estudios Centroamericanos*, 13.1: 43–65.

Zeledón, José María. 1903. 'National Anthem', *Costa Rica* website <https://www.costarica.com/culture/national-anthem/> [accessed 17 August 2015].

Zimmer, Tanja. 2007. 'El español hablado por los afrocostarricenses: Estudio lingüístico y sociolingüístico', thesis, University of Cologne; published by Kassel University Press, 2011.

Index